BEST of the BEST
from
WISCONSIN
COOKBOOK

Selected Recipes from Wisconsin's
FAVORITE COOKBOOKS

Boat tours are a great way to see the glacially-sculpted cliffs which rise 100 feet above the beautiful seven-mile stretch of the Wisconsin River known as the Wisconsin Dells.

BEST of the BEST from
WISCONSIN
COOKBOOK

Selected Recipes from Wisconsin's
FAVORITE COOKBOOKS

Edited by
GWEN MCKEE
and
BARBARA MOSELEY

Illustrated by Tupper England

QUAIL RIDGE PRESS
Preserving America's Food Heritage

Recipe Collection ©1997 Quail Ridge Press, Inc.

Reprinted with permission and all rights reserved under the name of the cookbooks, organizations or individuals listed below.

All in Good Taste © 1979 Service League Inc.; *All in Good Taste II* © 1989 Service League Inc.; *Apples, Brie & Chocolate* © 1996 Nell Stehr; *Cooks Extraordianries* © 1993 Service League of Green Bay, Inc.; *Create Share Enjoy!* © 1991 St. Joseph's Christian Women; *Drink Your Beer & Eat It Too!* © 1995 Joanie Steckart; *Encore Wisconsin* © 1992 Palmer Publications, Inc.; *Favorite Recipes from the Old Rittenhouse Inn* © 1992 Innside Press; *Favorite Recipes of Pommern Cooks* © 1992 Favorite Recipes of Pommern Cooks; *50 Years of Regal Recipes* © 1995 Regal Ware, Inc.; *Four Seasons At Hawks Inn* © Hawks Inn Historical Society, Inc.; *Foxy Ladies* © 1981 Ellen Kort; *Fresh Market Wisconsin* © 1993 Terese Allen; *Grandma's Home Kitchen* © 1994 Wanda Peterson Mango; *Grandmothers of Greenbush* © 1996 Greenbush...remembered; *Green Thumbs in the Kitchen* © 1996 Green Thumb, Inc.; *Growing & Using Herbs* © 1996 Rosemary Divock; *Have Breakfast with Us...Again* © 1995 Amherst Press; *Have Breakfast with Us II* © 1993 Wisconsin Bed and Breakfast Homes and Historic Inns Assn.; *License to Cook Wisconsin Style* © 1996 Penfield Press; *Luscious—Low Calorie Recipes* © 1975 Maxine Toler Vaneven; *The Madison Herb Society Cookbook* © 1995 The Madison Herb Society; *The American Club* © 1993 Kohler Co.; *Our Best Cookbook 2* © 1995 Wisconsin Restaurant Assn. Education Foundation; *Our Favorite Recipes* © 1987 St. John's Guild; *The Ovens of Brittany* © 1991 Terese Allen; *Picnics on the Square* © 1994 Wisconsin Chamber Orchestra, Inc.; *Seasons of a Farm Family* © 1996 JDK Productions; *Spice of Life Cookbook* © 1995 Spice of Life™; *The Sunday Cook Collection* © 1993 Grace Howaniec; *Vegetarian International Cuisine* © 1996 The Cheese Factory Cookbook, LLC; *The White Gull Inn* © 1990 Andy and Jan Coulson; *The Wild Food Cookbook* © 1989 Frances Hamerstrom; *Wisconsin Cooks with Wisconsin Public Television* © 1996 Friends of WHA-TV, Inc.

Library of Congress Cataloging-in-Publication Data

Best of the best from Wisconsin: selected recipes from Wisconsin's favorite cookbooks / edited by Gwen McKee and Barbara Moseley; illustrated by Tupper England.
    p. cm.
    Includes index
    ISBN 0-937552-80-1
    1. Cookery, American.   2. Cookery—Wisconsin.
    I. McKee, Gwen. II. Moseley, Barbara.
    TX715.B485653 1997
    641.59774–dc21   97-16073
                                       CIP

Copyright ©1997 Quail Ridge Press, Inc.
ISBN-13: 978-0-937552-80-3 • ISBN-10: 0-937552-80-1
Printed by Tara TPS in South Korea

First printing, November 1997 • Second, October 1999 • Third, March 2001
Fourth, January 2004 • Fifth, May 2008 • Sixth, September 2009

Photos courtesy of: Circus World Museum, Wisconsin Tourism Development, Stevens Point Area Convention & Visitors Bureau, Door County Chamber of Commerce, Carol Christensen, Wisconsin Dells Convention & Visitors Bureau, Larson's Famous Clydesdales, Rutley, Greater Milwaukee Convention & Visitors Bureau, and Cave of the Mounds

QUAIL RIDGE PRESS
P.O. Box 123 • Brandon, MS 39043 • 1-800-343-1583
info@quailridge.com • www.quailridge.com

CONTENTS

The Mississippi Bluffs along the incredibly scenic Great River Road.

PREFACE

"All you can imagine begins in Wisconsin," we were told, and after researching our way through the state in search of cookbooks, we found that to be amazingly true! Wisconsin has so much natural beauty, so much well-preserved history and plenty of regional pride, with a variety of activities to go along with everything! And where there are good times and good friends . . . there is good food! Welcome to wonderful Wisconsin!

Gathered here are favorite recipes from ninety-three of the leading cookbooks from all over the state. Many of the people who wrote and compiled these contributing cookbooks are from a variety of ethnic backgrounds and have brought their culinary heritage to life here. (Norwegian, Danish, Swedish, Cornish, German, Czechoslovakian, and Belgian recipes are the most prevalent.) We are pleased to present these popular recipes chosen as "the best" from each contributing cookbook.

It stands to reason that recipes are created because of what the cook has on hand. In Wisconsin there is an abundance of cranberries, cherries, snap beans, sweet corn, potatoes, wild rice, so many varieties of fish, lot of white tail deer, and of course, dairy products. Wisconsin is the dairy state, known for its cheeses the world over. Also known for its breweries, Wisconsin has some tasty dishes made with cheese and beer! We are delighted to present favorite recipes for Danish Kringle, Wild Rice Casserole, Wisconsin Beer Cheese Soup, and Norwegian Sour Cream Waffles, to name only a sampling.

Also included in the book for those who like to read cookbooks are interesting facts about the state. Did you know that Door County has more shoreline (250 miles!) than any other county in the US?; or that the town of Seymour is the official "Home of the Hamburger?" The innovative idea of taking a meatball and flattening it into patties and serving them in between bread to make them more portable was first conceived here. You'll find out why Wisconsin is called "The Badger State," some interesting beer and cheese facts, and a mention or two of those incredible Green Bay Packers.

Along with a dedicated staff, we have put together what we feel is one of the most complete collections of recipes related to Wisconsin cuisine to be found. Sheila and Annette helped locate photographs, information, and those hard-to-reach, busy people who are essential to the completion of such a project. Our thanks also to the many tourist bureaus and visitor center personnel who helped in so many ways. The search for just the right photographs was no easy task, and our hats are off to all who contributed. As always, Tupper England, our talented illustrator, has put her pen to work to create just the right touch to enhance the recipe pages.

Chatting with all our contributors and working with so many friendly people gave us a warm and happy feeling toward Wisconsin. We have surely enjoyed the process of testing the recipes and getting a chance to sample the marvelous cooking of Wisconsin. Contributing cookbooks came from junior leagues, churches, schools, restaurants, bed and breakfasts, families, and individuals, and represent the tremendous diversity of cooking found in the Badger State. To find out more about these ninety-five cookbooks, see the catalog of contributing cookbooks section that begins on page 251.

If you're not lucky enough to live in or visit Wisconsin, we invite you to partake of a culinary journey through the state via the delicious recipes in this book you're going to love it! I know we have . . . again, and again, and again.

Gwen McKee and Barbara Moseley

Contributing Cookbooks

A-Peeling Apple Recipes
All in Good Taste I
All in Good Taste II
Apples, Brie & Chocolate
The Best Cranberry Recipes
Blessed Be the Cook
Camp Hope Cookbook
Cardinal Country Cooking
Celebrating 150 Years of Faith and Food
Celebration of Grace
Centennial Cookbook
Cherry Berries on a Cloud and More
A Collection of Recipes
Cooking at Thimbleberry Inn
Cooking in West Denmark
Cooking with Grace
Cooking with Pride
Cooking with the Lioness Club
Cooks Extraordinaires
Country Cupboard
Country Heart Cooking
Create Share Enjoy!
The Crooked Lake Volunteer Fire Department Cookbook
Dr. Martin Luther Church 100th Anniversary Cookbook
Drink Your Beer & Eat It Too!
Encore Wisconsin
Every 1 A Winner! Blue Ribbon Recipes
Family Fare
Favorite Recipes from the Old Rittenhouse Inn
Favorite Recipes of Pommern Cooks
Favorite Recipes of the Wisconsin NFO
Fifth Avenue Food Fare
50 Years of Regal Recipes
Flavors of Washington County
Four Seasons at Hawks Inn
Foxy Ladies
Fresh Market Wisconsin
Good Cooking, Good Curling
Grandma's Home Kitchen
Grandmothers of Greenbush
Green Thumbs in the Kitchen
Growing & Using Herbs
Have Breakfast with Us . . . Again
Have Breakfast with Us II
Here's to your Heart: Cooking Smart
License to Cook Wisconsin Style
Look What's Cookin' at Wal-Mart

Contributing Cookbooks

Look What's Cooking at C.A.M.D.E.N
Luscious Low-Calorie Recipes
The Madison Herb Society Cookbook
Marketplace Recipes Volume I
Marketplace Recipes Volume II
Marquette University High School Mother's Guild Cookbook
Masterpiece Recipes of The American Club
Mt. Carmel's "Cooking with the Oldies"
The Octagon House Cookbook
Old World Swiss Family Recipes
Our Best Cookbook 2
Our Favorite Recipes
The Ovens of Brittany Cookbook
The Palmyra Heritage Cookbook
Pelican Lake Women's Civic Club
Peterson Pantry Plus Lore
Picnics on the Square
Sacred Heart Centennial Cookbook
Seasoned with Love
Seasons of a Farm Family
Sharing Our Best
Sparks from the Kitchen
Spice of Life Cookbook
St. Charles Parish Cookbook
St. Frederick Parish Centennial Recipe Collection
St. John Evangelical Lutheran Church
St. Mark's Lutheran Church Cookbook
St. Mary's Family Cookbook
The Sunday Cook Collection
Sunflowers & Samovars
Taste and See
A Taste of Christ Lutheran
A Taste of Home
Thank Heaven for Home Made Cooks
Trinity Lutheran Church of Norden Anniversary Cookbook
Unbearably Good! Sharing Our Best
Vegetarian International Cuisine
What's Cook'n?
What's Cooking in St. Francis
What's on the Agenda?
The White Gull Inn, Door County
The Wild Food Cookbook
Winning Recipes from Wisconsin with Love
Wisconsin Cooks with Wisconsin Public Television
Wisconsin Pure Maple Syrup Cookbook
Wisconsin's Best

Appetizers and
Beverages

Balancing Rock. Stockton Island.

Minty Grape Cooler

1 cup sugar	1 cup lemon juice
1½ cups water	2 cups grape juice
1 cup mint leaves, bruised	1 (12-ounce) bottle ginger ale

Cook combined sugar and water for 5 minutes. Cool slightly and pour over the mint leaves. Add lemon juice, cover and steep for one hour. Strain; add grape juice. Just before serving add chilled ginger ale. Garnish with mint sprigs. Serve over ice. Makes 2 quarts.

The Madison Herb Society Cookbook

Cherry Bounce

1 cup Cherry De-Lites (dried cherries)	1 tablespoon whole cloves
	1 stick cinnamon
1 cup sugar or honey	1 quart whiskey or brandy
1 tablespoon allspice	

Fill a large-mouth jar or wine jug with Cherry De-Lites, sugar, and spices. Add whiskey or brandy. Cork and let stand in a dark place for 2 months or more. The longer it ages, the better it is. Strain before serving as a liqueur. (Use the Cherry De-Lites for hors d'oeuvres.)

License to Cook Wisconsin Style

Slush

Make Slush two days in advance so it has time to freeze.

1½ quarts cran-raspberry juice
1 (12-ounce) can frozen lemonade concentrate
1 (12-ounce) frozen orange juice concentrate
4 cups 7-Up
2 cups vodka

Mix these ingredients and freeze. To serve, fill glass ⅔ full with slush and ⅓ 7-Up.

Marketplace Recipes Volume I

Citrus Slush

2½ cups sugar
3 cups water
1 (12-ounce) can frozen orange juice concentrate
1 (12-ounce) can frozen lemonade concentrate
1 (46-ounce) can pineapple juice
3 cups cold water
4 quarts lemon-lime soda or ginger ale, chilled
Lime slices

In 6-quart Dutch oven over high heat, bring sugar and 3 cups water to a boil, stirring until sugar dissolves; remove from heat. Stir in frozen orange juice and lemonade concentrates until melted. Stir in pineapple juice and 3 cups cold water until well blended.

Pour into 2 (13x9x2-inch) baking pans. Cover and freeze overnight until juice mixture is firm. Cut each panful of frozen juice mixture into 24 squares. Place squares in 2-gallon punch bowl or Thermos jug. Slowly pour chilled soda over squares; stir until punch is slushy. Ladle into glasses. Garnish each glass with a lime slice. Makes about 2 gallons or 32 (1-cup) servings.

Thank Heaven for Home Made Cooks

Racine is the birthplace of the malted milkshake. In 1883 William Horlick made the first malted.

Sugar-Free Party Punch

1 small envelope un-
   sweetened Kool-Aid
   (any flavor)
1 (2-liter) bottle diet 7-Up
1 (1-liter) bottle sugar-free
   ginger ale (can substitute
   sugar-free Fresca or
   Sprite)

1 (12-ounce) can 100%
   pineapple juice concentrate
12 ounces water
1 quart rainbow sherbet

Freeze Kool-Aid with water (any amount under 2 liters). Mix in order given in punch bowl: 7-Up, ginger ale, juice, water, and sherbet. Put frozen Kool-Aid in bowl; mix and serve. Excellent, even those who hate sugar-free will love it, guaranteed!

Look What's Cooking at C.A.M.D.E.N

Strawberry Frost

1 pint ripe strawberries
½ cup sugar
2 cups cold milk
¼ cup cream

2 tablespoons lemon juice
1 teaspoon vanilla
⅛ teaspoon salt
Vanilla ice cream

Crush strawberries; add sugar and one cup milk. Beat until creamy. Gradually add remaining ingredients except ice cream. Beat well. Put 1 or 2 scoops ice cream into chilled glass. Fill with strawberry mixture. Makes about 5½ cups.

Taste and See

Irish Cream

Irish Cream is an ideal after-dinner drink complimenting good cuisine. This recipe is one of our favorites.

3 eggs
1 can sweetened condensed
   milk
1 cup brandy

½ pint whipping cream
1½ tablespoons chocolate
   syrup
¼ teaspoon coconut extract

Blend in blender. Put in bottle. Keeps one month in refrigerator.

Sparks from the Kitchen

Bulk Spiced Coffee

12 ounces Folger's Instant
Coffee Crystals
4 cups sugar
6 cups powdered non-dairy
creamer

¾ teaspoon cloves
4 teaspoons cinnamon
¾ teaspoon allspice
¾ teaspoon nutmeg

Mix all ingredients together well. Store in tightly covered container. To serve: Use 4 heaping teaspoons to 8 ounces boiling water.

Note: Decaffeinated coffee may be used without affecting flavor.

A Collection of Recipes

Hot Spiced Cider

1 cup packed dark brown
sugar
1 cinnamon stick
1 tablespoon whole cloves
2 cups water
1½ quarts cranberry
cocktail juice

1½ quarts apple cider or
juice
⅓ cup lemon juice
4 cups orange juice
1 thin sliced lemon
1 thin sliced orange

Combine sugar, spices, and water in saucepan and heat to boiling, stirring until sugar dissolves. Reduce heat and simmer 10 minutes. Strain and discard spices. Pour syrup into large kettle and add cider, lemon juice, and orange juice. Heat just to simmer point and serve with fruit slices. May also be served cold.

Pelican Lake Women's Civic Club

Broccoli-Cheese Appetizer

1 (10-ounce) package
   frozen chopped broccoli
   (thawed and drained)
1 cup mayonnaise or salad
   dressing
⅔ cup Mozzarella and
   Parmesan cheese, grated

½ cup fresh chives, chopped
½ cup fresh parsley, chopped
1 tablespoon dried basil
1 tablespoon lemon juice
½ teaspoon chili powder

Combine all ingredients in lightly greased 1-quart baking dish.
Bake, uncovered, at 350° for 20 minutes or until done. Serve
with crackers and turnip or other vegetable sticks.

Note: For extra color, when serving, place the vegetable sticks
in a halved, seeded sweet red pepper.

Fifth Avenue Food Fare

Broccoli or Spinach Cheese Roll-Ups

1 (10-ounce) package
   frozen chopped broccoli
   or spinach, thawed
   and drained
½ pound Velveeta cheese,
   cubed

¼ cup bread crumbs
3 slices bacon, cooked and
   crumbled
2 (8-ounce) tubes crescent
   rolls

Combine vegetable, cheese, bread crumbs, and bacon in
1½-quart saucepan. Cook over low heat until cheese is melted.
Unroll crescent rolls. Separate into 16 triangles; cut each in
half lengthwise forming 32 triangles. Spread each with approximately one teaspoon of mixture. Roll up, starting with wide
end. Place on greased cookie sheet and bake at 375° for 10-12
minutes, or until golden brown.

Taste and See

Denver Crescent Roll Squares

1 (8-ounce) package
Pillsbury Crescent Rolls
2 tablespoons soft
margarine
1 teaspoon prepared
yellow mustard

1 cup (½ pound) diced ham
¼ cup chopped green pepper
¼ cup chopped green onions
1 cup shredded Cheddar
cheese

Spread dough out onto a cookie sheet into a rectangle, being sure to press perforations together. Combine margarine and mustard and spread on dough. Sprinkle remaining ingredients over margarine mixture in order listed. Bake at 375° for 20-25 minutes until lightly browned and set. Cut into squares. May be reheated.

Create Share Enjoy!

Mexican Snack Squares

2 (8-ounce) cans crescent
dinner rolls
1 (16-ounce) can spicy
refried beans (with
green chilies)
1 cup sour cream
2 tablespoons taco
seasoning
6 ounces (1½ cups) shredded
Cheddar cheese

½ cup chopped green onions
½ cup chopped green bell
pepper
1 cup chopped, seeded
tomatoes
½ cup sliced ripe olives
Salsa, if desired

Heat oven to 375°. Unroll dough into 4 rectangles. Place crosswise in ungreased 15x10x1-inch pan. Press over bottom and 1-inch up sides to form crust. Firmly press perforations to seal. Bake at 375° for 14-19 minutes or until golden brown. Cool completely. Spread beans over crust. Combine sour cream and taco seasoning mix. Spread over beans. Cut into small squares. Sprinkle onions, green pepper, tomatoes, olives, and cheese over sour cream. Cover, refrigerate. Serve with salsa.

Centennial Cookbook

Rolled Tortillas

16 ounces softened
cream cheese
1 package Hidden Valley
Ranch Dressing Mix
2 green onions, minced

½ cup diced red peppers
½ cup diced celery
1 cup black olives, chopped
4 (12-inch) flour tortillas

Mix together cream cheese and dressing mix. Add remaining ingredients except tortillas together and spread on tortillas. Roll tightly and wrap in plastic wrap. Chill at least 2 hours. Cut in 1-inch slices and serve.

Seasoned with Love

Creamy Horseradish Ham Roll-Ups

This appetizer looks great when served with deviled eggs.

1 (8-ounce) package cream
cheese, softened
2 tablespoons prepared
horseradish
2 tablespoons mayonnaise

1 teaspoon Worcestershire
sauce
⅛ teaspoon salt
⅛ teaspoon pepper
1 pound baked deli ham

Blend all ingredients except ham. Spread on ham slices and roll up lengthwise. Refrigerate until time of serving. Slice into 1-inch pieces. Serve on lettuce leaves.

Wisconsin's Best

Stuffed Mushrooms

1-2 boxes fresh mushrooms
1 small bottle soy sauce
1 pound ground chuck
½ cup chopped green pepper

4 tablespoons bread crumbs
2 egg yolks
2 tablespoons minced onion

Remove stems from mushrooms and chop; set aside. Soak caps in soy sauce for one hour.

Drain caps; save soy sauce. Mix remaining ingredients with chopped stems. Stuff and mound meat mixture into caps. Brush with soy sauce. Bake at 350° for 20-25 minutes, or broil for 8-10 minutes.

The Crooked Lake Volunteer Fire Department Cookbook

Mushroom Liver Pate

¼ pound mushrooms, chopped fine
1 tablespoon butter
1 tablespoon chopped green onion
½ teaspoon sharp mustard

½ pound braunschweiger, room temperature
Dash cayenne pepper
½ cup sour cream
2 tablespoons brandy
Parsley
Pimento

In skillet, sauté mushrooms in butter until very dark brown. Mix well with next 6 ingredients. Pour in well-greased 2-cup mold. Chill. To serve, unmold and garnish with parsley and pimento.

A Collection of Recipes

Beer & Cheese Spread

Since the 1960s when it was brought to Kavanaughs', Madison, by a member of the staff, this spread has been featured at the restaurant and is a favorite of our guests.

2 cups shredded, sharp Wisconsin Cheddar cheese
2 cups shredded Wisconsin Swiss cheese
1 teaspoon Worcestershire sauce

½ teaspoon dry mustard
1 small clove garlic, minced
½ - ⅔ cup beer

Combine cheese, Worcestershire sauce, mustard, and garlic. Beat in enough beer to make spreading consistency. Serve on assorted crackers or rye bread. Yields 2 cups.

Our Best Cookbook 2

Beer Facts from *Drink Your Beer & Eat It Too!*: One of the first recorded references to beer appears on an Assyrian tablet, which names it as a supply aboard Noah's Ark.

When someone lifts a glass to toast your good health, they are reviving a very old custom, which was to place a piece of toasted bread in a wine cup to add nutritive value.

Before cash registers, beer sales in taverns were recorded on a board by the barmaids—P's for pints and Q's for quarts. Tavern owners would remind the barmaids to "Mind your P's and Q's."

Crab Cake Appetizers

These crab cakes are simple to prepare and are very tasty. They work well as a first course to a meal or are great with cocktails.

2 ounces uncooked angel
  hair pasta
6 ounces crabmeat, well
  drained
2 tablespoons minced celery
2 tablespoons minced
  green onion
1 tablespoon minced
  green pepper

1 teaspoon Worcestershire
  sauce
½ cup bread crumbs
2 tablespoons Miracle Whip
1 egg
Vegetable oil for frying
2 lemons, garnish

Break uncooked pasta into 1 - 1½-inch lengths. Cook, drain well, and cool. Combine next 7 ingredients in medium-size bowl. Beat egg well and add to mixture. Add cooled pasta, mix well, and refrigerate 2 hours or overnight.

Pour oil in deep fryer or place ¾-inch oil in heavy skillet; heat oil to 350°. Form mixture into small mounds and flatten to ¾-inch-thick cakes or form into small balls. Deep-fry 3-4 minutes or until golden brown and crisp. Keep warm in 200° oven until serving. Cut lemons into wedges and use as garnish. Yields 12-14 appetizer servings.
Recipe by Polecat & Lace, Minocqua.

Our Best Cookbook 2

Crab Spread

2 (3-ounce) packages
  cream cheese (room
  temperature)
2 tablespoons mayonnaise
1 teaspoon minced parsley
½ small onion, grated

1-2 dashes Tabasco sauce
1-2 dashes Worcestershire
  sauce
1 (8-12 ounce) package sea
  legs, cut in small chunks

Cream all ingredients together (except sea legs) until smooth. Add sea legs to creamed mixture. Mix until shredded. Chill overnight.

Centennial Cookbook

Crab-N-Cream Cheese Won Tons

2 (8-ounce) packages
  cream cheese
1 package mock crabmeat
3 tablespoons minced garlic
1 package won ton skins
Cooking oil for wok/fryer/
  frying pan (preferably
  peanut oil for flavor)

Mix cream cheese, crab, and garlic. Place spoonful of mixture in the middle of won ton skin. Dip finger in bowl of water and wet adjacent 2 sides of won ton skin. Fold opposite side of skin over to meet corner to corner, making a triangle. Press sides down firmly together. Drop into fryer/wok/frying pan of hot oil. Flip when browned. Remove. Drain on paper towel or rack. Serve with hot mustard and sweet-n-sour sauce.

Mt. Carmel's "Cooking with the Oldies"

Shrimp in Mustard Sauce

¼ cup tarragon vinegar
¼ cup red wine vinegar
1 teaspoon ground black
  pepper
¼ cup dry mustard
2 teaspoons hot red
  pepper flakes
2 teaspoons salt
½ cup vegetable oil
¼ cup minced fresh parsley
  leaves
6 green onions, chopped
2½ pounds uncooked shrimp,
  peeled and deveined
1 (3-ounce) package crab/
  shrimp boil
Cucumber slices
Crackers

In 3-quart bowl, whisk vinegars, pepper, mustard, pepper flakes, and salt. While whisking, add oil until slightly thickened. Stir in parsley and onion. Set aside.

To cook shrimp add shrimp boil to pot of water and boil for 3-4 minutes. Add shrimp and cook until pink, 2-3 minutes, or one minute after second boil. Drain shrimp and run under cold water. Add shrimp to sauce and refrigerate overnight or up to 2 days. To serve, place shrimp in bowl and surround with cucumbers and crackers and toothpicks. Serves 8-10.

Marquette University High School
Mother's Guild Cookbook

Sauerkraut Balls

These taste great!

8 ounces bulk pork
  sausage
¼ cup finely chopped
  onion
1 (14-ounce) can sauerkraut,
  well drained and
  snipped
2 tablespoons bread crumbs
1 (3-ounce) package
  cream cheese

Garlic salt to taste
Celery salt to taste
Pepper to taste
2 tablespoons parsley flakes
1 teaspoon prepared mustard
Flour for coating
¼ cup milk
2 eggs, beaten
Cracker crumbs
Barbecue sauce

In skillet cook sausage and onion until meat is browned; drain. Add sauerkraut and bread crumbs. Combine cream cheese, garlic salt, celery salt, pepper, parsley flakes, and mustard and stir into sauerkraut mixture. Chill. Shape into 1-inch balls.

Coat with flour, dip into milk and eggs, mixed. Roll in crushed cracker crumbs. Deep-fry in hot oil until golden brown. Serve with barbecue sauce for dipping.

What's Cook'n?

Tuna Puff Appetizer

PUFFS:

1 cup water

½ cup margarine

½ teaspoon salt

1 cup sifted flour

4 eggs

Bring water, margarine, and salt to a full boil in a 4-quart sauce-pan. Add flour all at once and beat rapidly over low heat until mixture leaves sides of pan and forms a smooth compact ball. Remove from heat. Add eggs, one at a time, beating well after each. Drop by teaspoonful onto ungreased baking sheet. Bake at 400° for 30 minutes or until golden brown. Cool. Slice back tops and fill with a teaspoon of tuna filling.

FILLING:

1 (12½-ounce) can tuna

1 small onion, finely chopped

1 (4-ounce) package finely shredded Swiss cheese

1 (6-ounce) can ripe olives, chopped

1 (5-ounce) can water chestnuts, chopped

About 4 tablespoons Miracle Whip

2 tablespoons sour cream

Makes about 36 puffs.

The Octagon House Cookbook

Franks in Cransauce

2 frankfurters, cut in ½-inch pieces

CRANSAUCE:

2 tablespoons catsup

2 tablespoons cranberry juice

Slight dash marjoram

Slight dash onion salt

Mix catsup, cranberry juice, marjoram, and onion salt together and bring to a boil. Remove from heat to a warming or chafing dish. Add frankfurters and heat thoroughly before serving. Have colored toothpicks on a side dish to serve franks. Serves 20. Calories per serving: 16.

Luscious Low-Calorie Recipes

Corned Beef in Round Rye

2 tablespoons minced
  onion
1 teaspoon dill weed
1¼ cups sour cream
1¼ cups mayonnaise

3 packages corned beef,
  snipped into small pieces
1 teaspoon Beau Monde
  seasoning
1 small round rye loaf

Mix and refrigerate all ingredients, except rye loaf, for 24 hours. Scoop out small round rye loaf and cut center into serving-size bites for the dip. Fill center of loaf with dip just before serving.

Picnics on the Square

Mini Reubens

Rye bread (party rye or
  small slices)
Mayonnaise or sour cream

Corned beef
Sauerkraut
Swiss cheese

Spread bread with mayonnaise or sour cream. Arrange on a flat pan—broiler pan or cookie sheet. Then layer remaining ingredients in order given. Bake in a 400° oven for about 10 minutes or until cheese melts. Serve hot. Can be prepared several hours ahead and popped in oven just before serving.

The Palmyra Heritage Cookbook

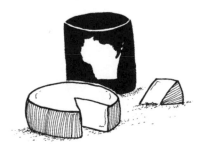

Glazed Chicken Wings
(Microwave)

2 pounds chicken wings
¼ cup currant jelly

¼ cup catsup
½ teaspoon salt

Separate wing sections at joint. Set aside tips. (Boil the tips in water to make a good soup stock.) Arrange wing pieces in a 9-inch round microwave pan with the small ends to the center. Cover loosely with Saran Wrap. Cook at FULL POWER 5-7 minutes, or until no longer pink. Drain and cool.

Combine jelly, catsup, and salt. Place wings in 12x8-inch dish. Pour the sauce over the wings. Cover loosely with Saran Wrap. Heat on HIGH until glazed, about 7 minutes.

Four Seasons at Hawks Inn

Baked Cheese Wings

½ cup butter
1 cup grated Parmesan cheese
1 tablespoon oregano
1 teaspoon salt

2 tablespoons chopped parsley
2 teaspoons paprika
½ teaspoon pepper
4 pounds chicken wings, cut apart

Melt butter. Mix remaining ingredients except chicken wings. Using only the "big" part of the wing, dip in butter, then in cheese mixture. Arrange in shallow baking dish on foil. Drizzle with the rest of the butter, if any, and bake at 350° for 45 minutes to one hour or until done. This may be prepared the day before and reheated. You can also freeze them and reheat when thawed.

What's on the Agenda?

Smoked Eggs with Citrus Herb Sauce

This is a "must try" dish for the adventuresome palate. It is simply, uniquely delicious. Easy to prepare in advance; it's a show-stopper!

MARINADE:

1 cup soy sauce
¼ cup liquid smoke
¼ cup sugar
1 tablespoon salt

8 large hard boiled eggs, peeled
½ cup thinly sliced scallions

In a small bowl, combine soy sauce, liquid smoke, sugar, and salt. Place eggs in marinade for 2 hours, swishing eggs around every 30 minutes. Remove eggs and refrigerate. Freeze marinade for later use.

On a small appetizer dish, make a pool of Citrus Herb Sauce (about 2 tablespoons), sprinkle with 1-2 teaspoons scallions, cut egg in half lengthwise and place cut-side-down on top of the sauce. Garnish with sprig of fresh parsley or mint. Yield: 8 eggs.

CITRUS HERB SAUCE:

½ cup mayonnaise
½ cup sour cream
1 tablespoon Dijon mustard
1 tablespoon Worcestershire sauce
Juice of ½ lemon (2 tablespoons)

Zest of 1 lemon (2 teaspoons)
2 tablespoons chopped fresh dill, packed, or 2 teaspoons dried dill, crumbled
2 tablespoons chopped fresh Italian parsley (do not use dried parsley)

In a small bowl, combine all ingredients. Whisk until well blended. Yield: 1½ cups.

Vegetarian International Cuisine

Bugle Dip

3 cups sour cream
1 package Original
  Hidden Valley Ranch
  dry dressing
⅓ cup mayonnaise
½ cup powdered Cheddar
  cheese

Mix all ingredients and refrigerate for several hours. Serve with Bugles for dip.

Cardinal Country Cooking

Caramel Apple Dip

1 (8-ounce) package cream
  cheese
1 cup brown sugar, packed
½ cup chopped dry roasted
  peanuts (optional)
1 teaspoon vanilla

Cream all together. Serve with crisp apple slices (Granny Smiths do especially well).

Cooking with Grace

BLT Dip

1 cup chopped tomatoes
1 cup chopped lettuce
1 cup sour cream
1 cup Miracle Whip
1 cup bacon bits

Mix together and serve with crunchy snack bread or bagels.

Dr. Martin Luther Church 100th Anniversary Cookbook

Smoked Salmon Dip

1 (6-ounce) can salmon
1 (6-ounce) package cream
  cheese, softened
¼ cup milk
2 teaspoons lemon juice
Several drops liquid smoke, to
  taste
⅛ teaspoon pepper
Dill weed, to taste
Assorted crackers or fresh
  vegetables

Finely chop salmon. Stir together with salmon, cream cheese, milk, lemon juice, liquid smoke, and pepper. Add dill and serve. Makes 1½ cups.

Seasoned with Love

My Fruit Dip

1 jar marshmallow cream
1 (8-ounce) package cream
  cheese, softened
½ cup shredded Cheddar
  cheese or cheese spread

Combine all ingredients. Serve with fresh fruit slices or chunks.

Country Heart Cooking

Tijuana Tidbits

4 cups tortilla chips, broken
3 cups Crispix cereal
1 bag microwave popcorn,
  popped
1 (12-ounce) can mixed nuts
½ cup light corn syrup
½ cup butter or margarine
½ cup brown sugar
1 tablespoon chili powder
⅛ teaspoon cinnamon
⅛ - ¼ teaspoon ground
  red pepper

Combine first 4 ingredients in large pan. Combine syrup, butter, sugar, and seasonings in small saucepan. Heat to boiling. Pour over cereal mixture in pan, stirring. Spread on jellyroll pan sprayed with Pam. Bake at 250° for one hour, stirring every 20 minutes. Remove from oven and turn onto waxed paper to cool. Store in airtight container up to 2 weeks. Makes 18 cups.

St. Charles Parish Cookbook

Laura Ingalls Wilder, the renowned author of the immensely popular "Little House" books, was born on a farm near Pepin in 1867.

Bread and Breakfast

The Little House Wayside marks the birthplace of Laura Ingalls Wilder. This is a replica of the log cabin described in her childhood memories of the Pepin area.

Curlers Bread

¾ cup chopped olives
¼ cup oil
3 tablespoons vinegar

1 loaf French bread (cut lengthwise)
Grated Parmesan cheese
Paprika

TOPPING:
2 (3-ounce) packages cream cheese
2 tablespoons mayonnaise
1 stick margarine
¼ teaspoon salt (optional)
¼ teaspoon oregano

½ cup fresh parsley or 3 tablespoons dried
1-2 small cloves garlic (crushed) or ¼ teaspoon garlic powder

Marinate olives overnight in oil and vinegar. Mix topping ingredients. Spread topping on bread. Top with olive marinade (press into cheese mixture.) Sprinkle with grated Parmesan cheese and paprika. Bake 15-20 minutes uncovered in 400° oven. Let set a few minutes. Cut into 1-inch slices.

Good Cooking, Good Curling

Herb Bread Sticks

3 cups all-purpose flour
1 envelope rapid-rise dry
  yeast
1 tablespoon salt
¼ cup chopped fresh
  parsley
1 bunch fresh chives,
  chopped
2 tablespoons chopped fresh
  dill
7 tablespoons olive oil
6 tablespoons very warm
  water (130°)
Cornmeal

In a large bowl, mix flour, yeast, salt, and herbs. Add olive oil and water, and mix until a dough is formed. On a floured surface, knead dough until smooth and elastic, about 5 minutes. Place dough in an oiled bowl, cover with a towel, and set in a warm place to rise. When dough has doubled in size, about 30 minutes, punch it down and divide it into 16 pieces. Roll each piece into a 12-inch "snake."

Sprinkle 2 sheet pans with cornmeal. Transfer bread sticks to the sheet pans, cover with dish towels, and leave in a warm place to rise for about 20 minutes. Preheat oven to 400°. Bake until lightly browned, 15-20 minutes. Makes 16 bread sticks.

Growing & Using Herbs

Cheddar Jalapeño Corn Bread

1 cup yellow cornmeal
½ cup flour
1½ teaspoons baking
  powder
¾ teaspoon baking soda
¾ teaspoon salt
2 eggs, lightly beaten
1 cup buttermilk
¼ cup melted butter
½ - 1 cup grated Cheddar
  cheese
1-2 jalapeño peppers, seeded
  and chopped

Combine cornmeal, flour, baking powder, baking soda, and salt. Add eggs, buttermilk, and butter. Stir until moistened. Fold in cheese and pepper. Pour into a greased 8x8-inch baking dish. Bake at 350° for 25-30 minutes, or until toothpick tests clean.

Marquette University High School
Mother's Guild Cookbook

Bacon Cheddar Biscuits

Chef Amy Crowns adds a bit of downhome taste to her uptown biscuits. Jim and Ellen Jensen, owners of The Vintage, Wisconsin Rapids, recommend these as a fine brunch or supper fare.

2 cups flour	¼ cup minced onion
4 teaspoons baking powder	½ cup crisply fried bacon bits
½ teaspoon salt	(8 strips)
¼ teaspoon black pepper	½ cup shredded sharp
½ cup shortening	Cheddar cheese
⅔ cup milk, room	
temperature	

In a medium mixing bowl, whisk together flour, baking powder, salt and pepper. Cut in shortening with pastry blender until mixture resembles cornmeal. Add milk, stir in onion, bacon, and cheese until dough just clings together. Do not overmix. Drop rounded tablespoons of dough on greased cookie sheet, 2 inches apart. Bake in preheated 450° oven for about 10 minutes or until golden brown. Makes 12 biscuits.

Encore Wisconsin

Cheese Drop Biscuits

2 cups flour	1 cup grated cheese
2 teaspoons baking powder	1 cup milk
4 tablespoons butter	

Sift flour and baking powder; cut in remaining ingredients. Mix and drop by teaspoonfuls on greased baking sheet. Bake at 450° for 12-15 minutes.

Look What's Cooking at C.A.M.D.E.N

Horicon Marsh (31,653 acres) is locally known as "The Everglades of the North." In spring and fall, thousands of migrating geese stop here for food and rest. It is Wisconsin's most popular place to watch animals.

Orange Raisin Scones with Orange Butter

Scones are a great alternative to muffins for breakfast. These are particularly popular, and the orange butter enhances the flavor of the scones.

1¾ cups flour
3 tablespoons sugar
2½ teaspoons baking powder
2 teaspoons grated orange peel

⅓ cup butter
½ cup golden raisins
2 eggs
4-6 tablespoons half-and-half

ORANGE BUTTER:
½ cup butter, softened

2 tablespoons orange marmalade

Preheat oven to 400°. In medium bowl, combine flour, sugar, baking powder, and orange peel. Cut in butter until crumbly. Stir in raisins, one egg, lightly beaten, and enough half-and-half to just moisten mixture.

Turn dough onto lightly floured surface; knead lightly 10 times. Roll into 9-inch circle. Cut into 8-12 wedges. Place on cookie sheet one inch apart. Brush with remaining egg, beaten. Bake 10-12 minutes or until golden brown. Immediately remove from cookie sheet.

Make Orange Butter by mixing together butter and marmalade until combined. Serve with warm scones. Makes 8-12 scones.

Recipe from Courthouse Square Bed & Breakfast, Crandon, WI.

Have Breakfast with Us . . . Again

Almond Kringle

1 cup flour	1 (12-ounce) can almond
¼ teaspoon salt	pastry filling
¼ cup butter	1 egg white
½ cup sour cream	3 tablespoons sugar
¼ teaspoon almond extract	3 tablespoons pecans,
	chopped

Sift flour and salt together. Cut in butter with pastry blender until it resembles coarse meal. Stir in the sour cream with a fork and add the almond extract. Shape into a ball, place in bowl, cover and refrigerate for at least 2 hours or overnight.

Turn dough out onto floured board. Divide into two parts. Roll each to 9x13-inch rectangle. Spread half the almond filling down the center of the dough in a 3-inch strip. Fold one side of the dough over the filling, then fold the other side over that. Pinch the ends to seal. Repeat with other half of dough. Place both on a buttered cookie sheet. Beat the egg white slightly and brush onto each pastry. Combine the sugar and nuts and sprinkle over the top of each. Bake at 350° for 30-35 minutes or until golden brown. Cool and cut into 1-inch slices. Makes 6 servings.

Winning Recipes from Wisconsin with Love

Easy Caramel Rolls

2 loaves frozen bread	1 (3-ounce) box vanilla
Pecans (1 cup or more)	pudding, not instant
Cinnamon	1 cup brown sugar
½ cup butter	2 tablespoon milk

Butter a 13x9-inch pan. Cut bread in 6 slices each. Put pecans in pan and place slices of bread on top. Sprinkle cinnamon on top of bread. Heat butter, pudding, brown sugar, and milk until butter is melted. Pour sauce over bread. Let rise until double. Bake at 350° for 30 minutes.

St. Charles Parish Cookbook

Aunt Mary Ellen's Swedish Kringle

BASE:

½ cup butter   2 tablespoon water
1 cup flour

Cut butter into flour. Add water and mix well with a fork. Divide in half and shape into balls. On a cookie sheet, shape dough into two strips 3 inches wide and 15 inches long.

FILLING:

1 cup water   3 eggs
½ cup butter   ½ teaspoon vanilla extract
1 cup flour   ½ teaspoon almond extract
1 teaspoon sugar

FROSTING:

1 cup powdered sugar   ¼ teaspoon vanilla extract
1 tablespoon cream   Chopped almonds or pecans
¼ teaspoon almond extract

Bring butter and water to a rolling boil. Add flour and sugar all at once. Stir vigorously until mixture forms a ball that does not separate. Remove from heat and cool slightly. Add eggs, one at a time, with extracts. Beat vigorously after each addition. Spread evenly over pastry. Bake at 350° for 60 minutes. While still warm, drizzle with frosting made by combining sugar with cream and extracts. Sprinkle with chopped nuts. Yield: 2 kringles.

All in Good Taste I

Danish Coffee Strips

4 cups flour
4 tablespoons sugar
½ teaspoon salt
1½ cups margarine
2 packages dry yeast

⅓ cup warm water
4 eggs, separated
⅔ cup evaporated milk
Brown sugar

Mix flour, sugar, salt, and margarine as for pie crust. Soften yeast in water. Combine beaten yolks and milk. Add to flour mixture. Add yeast which has been dissolved in warm water. Beat well. Refrigerate overnight. Divide dough into 6 portions. Roll out thin. Spread with beaten egg whites and brown sugar. Put fruit filling or almond filling down the center of strip. Fold in sides. Spread top with beaten egg whites. Sprinkle with sugar. Top with slivered almonds. Let rise 1-2 hours. Bake at 350° for 20 minutes.

ALMOND FLAVORED FILLING:
2-3 tablespoons butter
⅔ cup sugar
1 tablespoon milk

1 tablespoon almond
flavoring
2 tablespoons quick oatmeal

Mix softened butter with other ingredients. Spread on coffee strips. Beaten egg white may be spread on strips first, then the filling.

Cooking in West Denmark

Candlewick Strawberry Bread

1 cup sugar
1½ cups flour
1½ teaspoons cinnamon
½ teaspoon baking soda
¼ teaspoon salt

⅔ cup sliced almonds
2 eggs
½ cup cooking oil
10 ounces strawberries, sliced

Preheat oven to 350°. Grease and flour a 5x9-inch loaf pan. Mix together first 6 ingredients. Add eggs and oil and blend together. Fold in berries. Put mixture in prepared pan and bake at 350° from 1 hour to 1 hour and 10 minutes. Remove from pan and cool on wire rack.

Have Breakfast with Us II

Almond Tea Cakes

Not too sweet, yet these tender little almond-stuffed cakes are just the right thing to serve with tea or coffee when you want something fancier than a muffin or scone. Our thanks to Executive Chef James Simmers, Carvers on the Lake, Green Lake, for sharing his recipe.

2½ cups flour	½ cup white wine
½ teaspoon salt	½ cup apple juice
2 teaspoons baking powder	1 teaspoon almond extract
2 cups sugar	1 teaspoon vanilla extract
4 large eggs	½ cup sliced almonds
1 cup vegetable oil	Sliced almonds—garnish

Sift flour, salt, and baking powder together; set aside. In a large mixing bowl with electric mixer, combine sugar and eggs. Beat at medium speed for one minute. Add vegetable oil, wine, juice, almond and vanilla extracts and continue beating at medium speed for one minute more. Fold in flour mixture and almonds, taking care not to overmix batter.

Spoon batter into greased miniature muffin tins, ¾ full. Top lightly with additional sliced almonds. Bake in preheated 375° oven for 17-20 minutes or until golden brown. Cool in tins on wire rack. Remove from tins; store in covered container. Makes 36 mini-tea cakes.

Encore Wisconsin

Cran-Apple Bread

1 cup sugar	1 teaspoon salt
4 tablespoons oil	1 teaspoon vanilla
1 egg	1 cup milk
3 cups flour	1 cup cranberries, chopped
3 teaspoons baking powder	1 cup apples, chopped
1 teaspoon baking soda	½ cup nuts, chopped

Cream sugar, oil, and egg. Add rest of ingredients, folding cranberries, apples, and nuts last. Put into greased and lightly floured loaf pan, 9x5 inches. Bake at 350° for about one hour. Cool and remove from pan. Great when spread with cream cheese.

A-Peeling Apple Recipes

Glazed Cranberry Orange Nut Bread

1 cup sugar
2 cups plus 2 tablespoons
  flour
1 teaspoon salt
2 teaspoons baking powder
½ teaspoon soda

1 cup orange juice and
  grated peel from 1 orange
¼ cup melted shortening
1 cup chopped cranberries
½ cup chopped nuts
1 egg, beaten

Sift dry ingredients together. In separate bowl, combine remaining ingredients. Lightly mix all the ingredients together. Bake in a lightly greased loaf pan for 40-50 minutes at 375°. Toothpick should come out clean when it is done. Before loaf cools, pour glaze (cooked a few minutes) over the top.

GLAZE:
¼ cup sugar
2 tablespoons orange juice

2 tablespoons coarsely
  chopped cranberries

The Best Cranberry Recipes

Orange Prune Bread

1 cup pitted prunes
Water to cover prunes
2 eggs
3 tablespoons vegetable oil
1 cup sugar
1 tablespoon grated orange
  peel

1 teaspoon orange extract
½ cup orange juice
2¼ cups flour
1½ teaspoons baking powder
¼ teaspoon cinnamon
¾ teaspoon salt
¾ cup chopped nuts

Cover prunes with water and cook until tender. Drain and reserve ½ cup prune water. Cool prunes, then dice. In a bowl, beat eggs slightly with fork and add oil, sugar, orange peel, extract, reserved prune water, and orange juice. Mix in flour, baking powder, cinnamon, and salt. Add nuts and diced prunes. Stir only enough to moisten. Grease and flour (or coat with spray shortening) a 9x5x3-inch loaf pan. Pour batter in pan and bake in 350° oven for 55-60 minutes or until it tests done when wooden pick inserted in center comes out clean. Cool 10 minutes. Remove from pan and cool completely before slicing. Makes one loaf.

Every 1 A Winner! Blue Ribbon Recipes

Blueberry Lemon Bread

⅓ cup butter
1 cup sugar
3 tablespoons lemon juice
2 tablespoons lemon rind
2 eggs
1½ cups flour

1 teaspoon baking powder
1 teaspoon salt
½ cup milk
1 cup blueberries, coated with flour
½ cup walnuts or almonds, chopped

Mix butter, sugar, lemon juice, and rind. Beat in eggs. In separate bowl mix flour, baking powder, and salt. Alternately add flour mixture and milk. Fold in blueberries and nuts. Pour into 2 (9x5x3-inch) loaf pans and bake at 350° for 60 minutes.

Cooks Extraordinaires

Carrot-Pineapple Bread

2 eggs
2 cups sugar
1 cup oil
4 teaspoons vanilla
3 cups flour
1 teaspoon salt

1 teaspoon soda
1 teaspoon cinnamon
2 cups grated raw carrots
1 (8½-ounce) can crushed pineapple with juice
1 cup chopped nuts

Beat eggs and sugar; add oil and vanilla. Add all dry ingredients and finally, carrots, pineapple and nuts. Bake at 325° for 50-60 minutes. Makes 4 small loaves.

The Palmyra Heritage Cookbook

Poppy Seed Bread

3 cups flour
2½ cups sugar
1½ teaspoons baking powder
⅓ cup poppy seed
1½ teaspoons salt
3 eggs

1½ cups milk
1½ cups oil
1½ teaspoons vanilla extract
1½ teaspoons almond extract
1½ teaspoons butter flavoring
Yellow food coloring

Mix and beat 2 minutes. Bake 1 - 1½ hours in 350° oven in 2 greased loaf pans.

GLAZE:

¼ cup orange juice
¾ cup sugar

½ teaspoon each vanilla and almond extract and butter flavoring

Heat in saucepan orange juice, sugar, extracts and butter flavoring. Brush over hot loaves.

Dr. Martin Luther Church 100th Anniversary Cookbook

Artichoke Bread

¼ cup butter or margarine
2-3 cloves garlic, pressed
2 teaspoons sesame seeds
1 (14-ounce) can artichoke hearts, drained and chopped
1 cup grated Parmesan cheese

½ cup sour cream
1 cup (4 ounces) shredded Monterey Jack cheese
1 (16-ounce) loaf unsliced French bread
½ cup (2 ounces) shredded Cheddar cheese

Melt butter in a large skillet over medium-high heat. Add garlic and sesame seeds; cook, stirring constantly, until lightly browned. Remove from heat. Stir in artichoke hearts and next 3 ingredients. Cover mixture and refrigerate, if desired. If refrigerated, let stand at room temperature 10 minutes before assembling.

Cut bread in half lengthwise; scoop out center of each half, leaving 1-inch shell. Set aside. Crumble removed pieces and stir into artichoke mixture. Spoon evenly into shells. Sprinkle with Cheddar cheese. Place on baking sheet. Cover with aluminum foil. Bake at 350° for 25 minutes. Uncover. Bake 5 minutes. Cut in slices. Yield: 12 servings.

Mt. Carmel's "Cooking with the Oldies"

Banana Split Banana Bread

1 cup sugar	2 cups flour
1 large egg	1 teaspoon baking powder
½ cup butter, softened	½ teaspoon baking soda
1 cup mashed ripe banana	1 cup semi-sweet chocolate
(about 2 large bananas)	chips
3 tablespoons milk	½ cup chopped pecans

In large mixing bowl, cream sugar, egg, and butter with electric mixer until mixture is fluffy, about 3 minutes; set aside. In small bowl, mix bananas and milk; set aside.

Sift together flour, baking powder, and baking soda onto paper plate. Add dry ingredients to creamed butter mixture alternately with banana mixture, stirring together with rubber spatula until dry ingredients are blended, about one minute. Stir in chocolate chips and pecans.

Spoon batter into a greased and floured loaf pan. Drop pan twice, from height of 6 inches to counter, to remove any air bubbles. Bake in preheated 350° oven one hour, or until wooden toothpick inserted in center of crack comes out clean. Cool in pan on wire rack 10 minutes. Remove bread to wire rack to complete cooling. Makes one loaf.

Cherry Berries on a Cloud and More

Chocolate Almond Zucchini Bread

3 eggs	3 cups flour
2 cups sugar	1 teaspoon cinnamon
1 cup oil	1 teaspoon salt
2 ounces melted chocolate	¼ teaspoon baking powder
(Choco Bake works well)	1 teaspoon baking soda
1 teaspoon vanilla	1 cup toasted almonds
2 cups zucchini, shredded	

Beat eggs until lemon colored; add sugar and oil. Mix. Add chocolate, vanilla, and zucchini; mix. Add dry ingredients; mix. Mix in almonds. Bake at 350° in 2 greased or Pam-sprayed loaf pans for 50 minutes.

Fifth Avenue Food Fare

Mushroom Bread

1 (1-pound) loaf unsliced
Vienna bread
8 ounces fresh mushrooms,
chopped or sliced
4 ounces Swiss cheese,
grated
4 ounces Mozzarella cheese,
grated

2 tablespoons chopped onion
2 sticks butter
2 tablespoons poppy seeds
1 teaspoon salt
½ teaspoon lemon juice
1 tablespoon dry mustard

Make 1½-inch diagonal cuts in crust almost to bottom. (Electric knife works great.) Turn bread and slice other way in criss-cross. Mix mushrooms, cheeses, and onion and put into sliced bread. First one direction, then the other. (Will look overstuffed.) Melt butter. Add remaining ingredients and pour over bread and into bread sections. Wrap lightly in foil and place on cookie sheet. Bake at 350° for 50-60 minutes.

Sunflowers & Samovars

Quick & Moist Beer Bread

5 cups unsifted self-rising
flour
5 tablespoons sugar
1½ cups sour cream

1 (12-ounce) can beer, room
temperature
Melted butter to coat bread

In large bowl, combine flour and sugar. Add sour cream and beer alternately; mix well. Pour batter into greased 2-quart round baking dish. Bake 45 minutes at 350°. Remove from oven and brush top of bread with butter. Return to oven and bake for 15-20 minutes or until done. Cool slightly. Serve warm. Can toast. Makes one loaf.

Cooking with Grace

 In early Europe people referred to beer as "liquid bread" because the basic ingredients and processes are very similar.

Pub Bread

3 cups self-rising flour
1 (12-ounce) can beer,
room temperature

4 tablespoons butter, melted
2 tablespoons sugar

Mix all ingredients except melted butter. Pour into well-greased pan. Bake at 350° for 45 minutes. Remove from oven, pour melted butter over the bread, and return to oven for an additional 10 minutes. Makes one loaf.

Drink Your Beer & Eat It Too

English Muffin Bread

2 tablespoons active dry
yeast
½ cup warm water (115°)
1 tablespoon honey
3 cups all-purpose white
flour

1 cup whole wheat flour
½ cup cornmeal
1 tablespoon salt
2 cups warm milk
¼ cup warm honey
¾ - 1¼ cups flour to finish

Proof yeast in water with one tablespoon honey in small bowl. Combine flours, cornmeal and salt in large bowl. Add milk, honey, and yeast mixture to dry ingredients and beat for 5-10 minutes, or until a sticky batter is formed. Beating slowly, add enough flour to mixture to develop a soft dough.

Turn into a medium-sized, greased bowl. Let rise until double in size and punch down. Preheat oven to 325° and grease pans. Form into 2 loaves or 18 rolls. Put into pans. Let rise until double in size. Bake until golden brown (30-35 minutes for loaves or 12-15 minutes for rolls).

Favorite Recipes from the Old Rittenhouse Inn

Apple Bran Cinnamon Muffins

A smash hit at Friend's Booth at the Retzer Apple Harvest Festival.

1 egg
1 cup milk
3 tablespoons vegetable oil
1 large apple, shredded
1½ cups bran cereal

1 cup flour
2½ teaspoons baking powder
1 teaspoon cinnamon
¾ teaspoon salt
½ cup light brown sugar

Beat together egg, milk, oil, apple; stir in bran cereal. Let stand 5 minutes. Mix together flour, baking powder, cinnamon, salt. Blend in sugar, and bran mixture, stirring till just combined. Fill greased pans ⅔ full. Makes 12 muffins. Bake at 400° for 18-20 minutes.

A-Peeling Apple Recipes

Apple-Cranberry Muffins

1 cup all-purpose flour
½ cup quick oats
1 teaspoon baking powder
1 teaspoon cinnamon
¼ teaspoon salt
1 large egg
¾ cup packed dark brown sugar

¼ cup oleo
1 teaspoon vanilla
¾ cup diced, unpeeled tart apple
¾ cup fresh or frozen cranberries
¼ cup raisins

Heat oven to 350°. Grease muffin cups or use foil cups. Mix flour, oats, baking powder, cinnamon, and salt in large bowl. Break egg into another bowl. Add sugar and whisk until smooth. Whisk in oleo and vanilla. Stir in apple, cranberries, and raisins. Pour over dry ingredients. Fold in just until dry ingredients are moistened. Pour batter into muffin cups. Bake 20-25 minutes until firm to the touch. Store in plastic bag. Do not freeze.

Wisconsin's Best

Cherry Muffins

4 cups flour
1 cup sugar
2 tablespoons baking powder
1 teaspoon cinnamon
3 cups tart cherries, rinsed and drained
1 cup butter or margarine, melted
1 cup milk
4 eggs
1 teaspoon vanilla

In a large bowl, sift together flour, sugar, baking powder, and cinnamon. Put cherries in another bowl; add one tablespoon of flour mixture and toss into cherries. In another bowl, mix together butter, milk, eggs, and vanilla; stir this into dry ingredients and fold in cherries. Spoon into greased muffin tins to ¾ full.

TOPPING:
1 cup flour
½ cup sugar
½ teaspoon cinnamon
⅓ cup butter, softened

To make topping, mix together flour, sugar, and cinnamon in a small bowl. Cut in butter with a pastry blender or fork until uniformly crumbly. Sprinkle topping over muffins. Bake at 425° for 15-20 minutes. Makes 2 dozen.

Seasons of a Farm Family

Raisin Bran Muffins

1 quart buttermilk
5 teaspoons baking soda
4 eggs, slightly beaten
1 cup vegetable oil
1 (15-ounce) box of raisin bran
5 cups flour
3 cups sugar

Stir together buttermilk and baking soda until soda is dissolved. Mix in remaining ingredients. Put in large container (like Rubbermaid) and let sit overnight. Spoon into muffin cups and bake at 400° for 15-20 minutes. Batter is good for 6 weeks in refrigerator.

Camp Hope Cookbook

Blueberry Pumpkin Muffins

1⅔ cups flour
1 teaspoon baking soda
½ teaspoon baking powder
½ teaspoon salt
1 teaspoon cinnamon
½ teaspoon allspice
1 cup pumpkin

¼ cup evaporated milk
⅓ cup shortening
1 cup firmly packed brown
  sugar
1 egg
1 cup blueberries
1 tablespoon flour

Combine first 6 ingredients. Combine pumpkin and evaporated milk until blended. Cream shortening and sugar in large mixer bowl. Add egg; beat until mixture is fluffy. Add flour mixture alternately with pumpkin mixture, beating well after each addition. Combine blueberries and flour. Gently stir into batter. Fill paper-lined muffin tins ¾ full. Sprinkle Streusel over top of muffins. Bake in 350° oven for 40 minutes or until toothpick inserted in center comes out clean. Makes 1½ dozen.

STREUSEL:
2 tablespoons flour
2 tablespoons sugar

¼ teaspoon cinnamon
1 tablespoon butter

Combine flour, sugar and cinnamon. Cut in butter until mixture is crumbly.

St. Mark's Lutheran Church Cookbook

Sharon's Blueberry Muffins

These outstanding muffins boast a fair helping of fiber. You can use pure bran, or Kelloggs All-Bran Cereal, Nabisco 100% Bran Cereal, or any kind of bran. These muffins also freeze beautifully.

2 eggs	½ cup bran
1 cup milk	4 teaspoons baking powder
½ cup salad oil	1 teaspoon salt
1 cup sugar	1 teaspoon orange rind
1 cup white flour	½ cup chopped nuts
1 cup whole wheat flour	2 cups blueberries
½ cup wheat germ	

In large bowl mix together well the eggs, milk, and salad oil. Add combined remaining ingredients and mix until just blended. Do not overmix. Place batter evenly in two dozen regular-size muffin cups in tins (greased well or use paper liners) and bake at 400° for 18-20 minutes.

Note: Save fresh berries by rinsing, quick-freezing on a cookie sheet for several hours, then bagging 2 cups in each freezer bag.

Marketplace Recipes Volume I

Waffle Cheese Bake

1 (10-ounce) package frozen jumbo waffles	1½ cups milk
6 slices bacon, fried and crumbled	4 eggs, beaten
1 cup (4 ounces) shredded Cheddar cheese	½ teaspoon salt

Place 4 waffles onto bottom of greased 8-inch baking dish. Sprinkle with bacon and cheese. Cut remaining waffles in half diagonally. Arrange over cheese in 2 rows, overlapping slightly. Combine milk, eggs, and salt. Pour over waffles. Refrigerate at least an hour or overnight. Microwave on HIGH for 16 minutes or until knife inserted into center comes out clean, turning every 4 minutes. Let stand for 5-10 minutes and serve with warm maple syrup. Serves 9.

Note: This recipe may also be prepared with bread, instead of waffles and baked at 350° for about 40 minutes.

Wisconsin Pure Maple Syrup Cookbook

Baked Apple Pancake

Baked Apple Pancake is one of my guests' favorite breakfasts. Nothing could be simpler than putting all of the ingredients except the apples and butter in a blender. The combination of crisp apples and custard, sprinkled with brown sugar, not only tastes scrumptious but will bring oh's and ah's from your guests as you bring this puffy creation from the oven to the table.

6 large eggs	½ teaspoon salt
1½ cups milk	¼ teaspoon cinnamon (more
1 cup flour	if desired, up to 1 teaspoon)
3 tablespoons granulated	½ cup butter or margarine
sugar	2 large Granny Smith apples
1 teaspoon vanilla extract	3 tablespoons brown sugar

Place eggs, milk, flour, granulated sugar, vanilla, salt, and cinnamon in blender. Set aside. Put butter or margarine in a 9x13-inch glass baking dish. Place in 425° oven to melt. (Don't let it burn.) Remove from oven when melted.

Peel apples, slice thinly, and arrange in bottom of dish over melted butter. Put in oven until butter sizzles. Remove. Blend ingredients in blender until smooth. Pour slowly over apples. Sprinkle with brown sugar.

Bake in 425° oven for 20 minutes. Test for doneness by inserting a knife in center. If it comes out clean, it is done. Cut in serving portions and serve immediately. Pass the maple syrup, if desired. Serves 10.

Have Breakfast with Us . . . Again

Skier's French Toast

2 tablespoons corn syrup	5 eggs
½ cup margarine or butter	1½ cups milk
1 cup brown sugar, packed	1 teaspoon vanilla
1 loaf white bread (unsliced)	¼ teaspoon salt (optional)

In small saucepan, combine corn syrup, butter, and brown sugar; simmer until syrupy. Pour into 9x13-inch casserole or 10x15 jelly roll pan. Remove crust from bread; slice into 12-16 pieces. Place in casserole over brown sugar mixture. Beat eggs, milk, vanilla, and salt with whisk; pour over bread. Cover and refrigerate overnight. Uncover pan and bake at 350° for 45 minutes. Can be reheated.

Sunflowers & Samovars

Norwegian Sour Cream Waffles with Apple Pecan Topping

2 cups sour cream
2 fresh eggs
1 cup unbleached flour
1 teaspoon baking powder
½ teaspoon baking soda

½ teaspoon salt
2 tablespoons sugar
½ teaspoon ground cardamon
3 tablespoons water

In large bowl beat sour cream until fluffy. In separate bowl beat eggs until light; combine with sour cream and beat again. Sift dry ingredients; fold into sour cream/egg mixture; add water. Bake according to wafflemaker directions. Serve with maple syrup and Apple Pecan Topping.

APPLE PECAN TOPPING:

2 tablespoons butter
¼ cup brown sugar
2 large apples, cored and sliced

½ teaspoon cinnamon
¼ cup chopped pecans

In skillet melt butter and brown sugar. Add apples, cinnamon, and pecans. Cook until apples are tender; about 3-4 minutes. Keep warm. Serves 4.

From The Mustard Seed Bed and Breakfast.

Have Breakfast with Us II

Peach French Toast Supreme

A favorite served at the Historic Bennett House.

SAUCE:

3 tablespoons cornstarch
¼ cup white sugar
½ teaspoon cinnamon
1 small can apricot nectar

Juice from 1 (29-ounce) can
   peach slices, reserve peaches
¼ teaspoon almond extract
1 tablespoon brandy
   (optional)

Mix cornstarch with sugar and cinnamon. Whisk into juices, almond extract, and brandy. Heat and stir until thickened. Serve over hot French Toast.

FRENCH TOAST:

5 eggs
1½ cups milk
1 teaspoon vanilla
1 stick (½ cup) butter

1 cup dark brown sugar
2 tablespoons water
12 slices of French bread

Mix together the eggs, milk, and vanilla in a bowl. Set aside. In a saucepan mix the butter, brown sugar, and water. Heat until mixture bubbles; stir (mixture looks foamy). Pour into 9x13-inch pan. Place drained peaches on top of brown sugar mixture. Cover fruit with slices of bread. Pour milk mixture over. Cover and refrigerate overnight.

Next day, uncover, and bake at 350° for 40 minutes. For each serving, pour hot sauce over and top with dollop of sour cream. Serve with your favorite breakfast sausage. Serves 6-8.

Have Breakfast with Us II

Wisconsin French Toast

4 eggs
⅔ cup orange juice
⅓ cup milk
¼ cup sugar
¼ teaspoon nutmeg
½ teaspoon vanilla extract

½ loaf Italian bread (cut in
    1-inch slices)
⅓ cup butter, melted
Ground orange peel to taste
¾ cup pecan pieces

Using a wire whisk, beat together eggs, juice, milk, sugar, nutmeg, and vanilla in a large bowl. Place bread, edges touching, in a single layer in a large baking dish. Pour milk mixture over bread; cover and refrigerate overnight, turning once. When ready to cook, preheat oven to 400°. Pour melted butter on a jellyroll pan, spreading evenly. Arrange soaked bread slices in a single layer on pan. Sprinkle evenly with orange peel and pecans. Bake until golden, 20-25 minutes. Check slices during last 5 minutes to avoid burning. Serve with maple syrup and butter. Yield: 4 servings.

Green Thumbs in the Kitchen

Freezer French Toast

4 eggs
1 cup milk
2 tablespoons sugar
1 teaspoon vanilla

¼ teaspoon ground nutmeg
8 slices day-old French bread,
    cut ¾-inch thick
Butter or margarine, melted

In a medium-sized bowl, beat together first 5 ingredients. Place bread slices on a rimmed baking sheet. Pour egg mixture over bread and let stand until all the egg mixture is absorbed (turning slices every few minutes). Freeze uncovered until firm, then package airtight and return to freezer.

To serve, place desired number of frozen slices on a lightly-greased baking sheet. Brush each slice with melted butter. Bake at 500° for 8 minutes. Turn slices over, brush with butter. Bake an additional 10 minutes or until nicely browned. Serve topped with powdered sugar, honey, or syrup.

What's on the Agenda?

Cherry Stuffed French Toast

1 loaf unsliced egg bread
1 (8-ounce) package cream
  cheese, at room
  temperature
⅓ cup heavy cream

1 cup red tart Door County
  cherries, drained
6 eggs, well beaten
Cinnamon

Slice the egg bread into 1½-inch slices. Cut each slice down ¾ of its length so that you have almost formed two slices of bread, but the bottom ¼ still holds the entire piece together. Set aside.

Beat cream cheese, heavy cream, and cherries together on medium speed until well combined. Spread approximately ¼ cup of the mixture into the pocket of each slice, and press the slice together very gently, distributing the filling evenly.

Dip each slice of the stuffed egg bread lightly into the beaten eggs to coat all sides. Place immediately onto a lightly oiled griddle. Sprinkle lightly with cinnamon and turn when golden brown. After frying the second side until golden, remove each slice to a cutting board, and very gently slice each piece in half diagonally. To garnish, sprinkle with powdered sugar. Arrange the triangles on plates and serve immediately with Door County maple syrup. Yield: 4 servings.

The White Gull Inn, Door County

Norwegian Lefse

5 pounds potatoes
1 tablespoon salt
½ cup cream

¼ cup (½ stick) butter
1½ cups flour

Peel and cook potatoes. Drain, mash, and rice potatoes. Measure potatoes; there should be 8 cups. Add salt, cream, and butter. Mix well. Cool overnight or for several hours. Add flour and mix well. Form dough into small balls the size of an egg. Roll very thin on a floured pastry cloth with a lefse rolling pin. Fry on a hot lefse grill or ungreased frying pan or griddle until brown spots appear; about one minute. Flip and cook the other side for about one minute. Cool between sheets of wax paper. Serve buttered and rolled up. You may sprinkle brown sugar on them. Makes about 20 lefse.

Seasons of a Farm Family

Milwaukee Breakfast

1 small potato	1 small piece onion, diced
2 eggs	2 button mushrooms, diced
1 small tomato, diced	1-2 pats butter
1 small piece green pepper, diced	

Cook potato in microwave on HIGH for 3-4 minutes, until you can get a fork in easily. Peel and dice potato into ¼-inch pieces. Beat eggs until smooth. Combine all ingredients and add to scrambled eggs. Cook on HIGH for one minute, stir, cook for one more minute, stir. If eggs are a little wet, let sit for about 10 seconds and then stir again. Do not overcook unless you like it dry.

Taste and See

"South of the Border" Eggs

3 corn tortillas, cut into 2-inch strips	1 cup julienne cooked ham
3 tablespoons margarine	½ cup green pepper, diced
½ cup diced onion	6 eggs, beaten
1 (14½-ounce) can stewed tomatoes	¾ cup shredded Monterey Jack cheese

Cook tortillas in margarine. Remove and set aside. Add onion; cook until tender. Drain tomatoes, reserving liquid. Add liquid to skillet; cover and heat over high heat for 3 minutes, stirring frequently. Stir in tomatoes, meat and green pepper; heat through. Reduce heat to low, add tortillas and eggs. Cover and cook 4-6 minutes or until eggs are set. Sprinkle with cheese; cover one minute until cheese melts.

Sparks from the Kitchen

Elegant Egg Puff

⅔ cup chopped ham
(turkey ham is
very good)
⅔ cup grated yellow or
white cheese
2 teaspoons Dijon mustard
3 teaspoons lite salad
dressing

1 teaspoon horseradish
2 teaspoons onion, finely
chopped
Tabasco sauce
4 slices white or wheat bread
2 eggs
1⅓ cups milk
Paprika

Grease 4 ovenproof dishes (ramakins). In a medium bowl, combine the ham, cheese, mustard, salad dressing, horseradish, and onion, plus a few shakes of Tabasco sauce. Makes 2 sandwiches. Cut each diagonally into 4 pieces. Place 2 pieces of sandwich in each of the prepared dishes, arranging so the points are on top.

In a small bowl combine the eggs and milk. Whisk well. Pour over the sandwich pieces. Sprinkle with paprika. Refrigerate overnight. Bake in a 325°-350° oven for 30-35 minutes. This recipe can be doubled very easily. Serves 2-4.

From the Kraemer House Bed and Breakfast.

Have Breakfast with Us II

Lucia's Mt. Carmel Brunch Casserole

4 cups cubed French bread
2 cups shredded Cheddar
cheese
10 eggs, lightly beaten
4 cups milk
1 teaspoon salt
Dash of pepper

1 teaspoon dry mustard
¼ teaspoon onion powder
8-10 slices cooked bacon,
crumbled
½ cup chopped tomatoes
½ cup mushrooms, sliced

Butter 9x13-inch pan. Layer bread cubes. Sprinkle cheese. Beat next 6 ingredients. Pour in and sprinkle bacon, tomatoes, and mushrooms. Chill, covered, overnight. Bake at 325°, uncovered, for about one hour. Tent with foil if overbrowning. Serves 12.

Mt. Carmel's "Cooking with the Oldies"

A Door County Style Brunch

1 pound bulk lean pork
 sausage or turkey sausage,
 crumbled into small
 pieces
1 (6-ounce) box onion-
 garlic flavored croutons
 (3 cups)
2 cups shredded sharp
 Cheddar cheese, divided
4 eggs

2¾ cups milk, divided
¾ teaspoon dry mustard
½ teaspoon salt
1 (10¾-ounce) can mush-
 room soup
2 cups frozen country-style
 hash brown potatoes
 (shredded)
1 teaspoon paprika

Brown sausage in skillet, stirring frequently, drain sausage on paper towel. Spread croutons evenly over bottom of 9x13-inch ungreased baking dish. Sprinkle evenly with drained sausage and 1½ cups of the cheese. Set aside. In blender or mixing bowl, whip eggs, 2¼ cups of the milk, mustard, and salt until well-blended. Pour over sausage mixture, cover and refrigerate overnight.

In small bowl, whisk together soup and remaining ½ cup milk until smooth. Pour over casserole. Sprinkle lightly with frozen hash browns. Top with remaining ½ cup cheese. Bake, covered with aluminum foil at 350° for one hour. Uncover, bake 30 minutes more or until center is set. Remove from oven and sprinkle with paprika. Let stand 5 minutes before cutting into serving pieces. Makes 8 servings.

Fifth Avenue Food Fare

Spinach Strata

Wonderful for brunch or Sunday supper served with spiced peaches.

1 package (4 cups) seasoned croutons, crushed
½ cup margarine, melted
½ cup Parmesan cheese
2 (10-ounce) packages spinach, chopped, thawed and drained

2 cups cottage cheese
8 ounces Monterey Jack cheese, cubed
6 eggs
½ cup onion, chopped
2 cloves garlic
4 tablespoons sour cream

Put crouton crumbs in 9x13-inch pan; pour melted margaine over croutons. Mix remaining ingredients together and pour over croutons. Bake 35 minutes at 350°. Let stand 5 minutes before serving. Serves 6-8.

Cooks Extraordinaires

Breakfast Pizza

1 roll pork sausage
1 package refrigerator crescent rolls
1 cup frozen hash browns, loose-pack, thawed
1 cup shredded Cheddar cheese

5 eggs
¼ cup milk
½ teaspoon salt
2 tablespoons Parmesan cheese, optional

Cook sausage until brown; drain. Separate rolls; place on round 12-inch pan (points to center). Press up sides and press seams together to form crust. Sprinkle with potatoes, sausage, and cheese. Mix together eggs, milk, salt and pepper; pour over all. Sprinkle with Parmesan cheese. Bake at 350° for 25-30 minutes.

Sacred Heart Centennial Cookbook

 Known as America's Dairyland, Wisconsin is the largest producer of milk, butter, and cheese in the nation. Monroe is called the "Swiss Cheese Capital of the World." Area factories produce more than 55 million pounds of cheese each year.

Baked Swiss on Rye

10 slices rye bread	5 apple slices (rings)
Butter	5 slices Swiss cheese
Russian dressing	Sauerkraut, drained
5 thick slices corned beef	

Butter bread; spread lightly with Russian dressing. On 5 slices of bread place corned beef, apple slice, cheese slice, kraut, and top with other slice of bread. Arrange slices to form a loaf, wrap in foil and bake at 350° until heated through, about 45 minutes. Open and serve immediately.

A-Peeling Apple Recipes

Duesseldorfer Sandwich

12 slices rye bread	24 dill pickle slices
¾ cup tartar sauce	12 (2-ounce) slices liverwurst
2 cups shredded lettuce	6 (1-ounce) slices Swiss cheese
6 hard cooked eggs, sliced	Butter, softened

Spread each slice of bread with 1 tablespoon tartar sauce. On each of six slices, layer ⅓ cup shredded lettuce, sliced egg, 4 pickle slices, 2 liverwurst slices, and one cheese slice. Close sandwiches with remaining bread slices. Butter sandwiches on both sides and grill until golden brown on both sides.

Flavors of Washington County

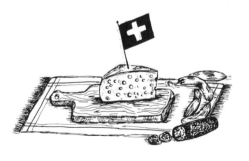

Egg Salad Sandwiches

2 (8-ounce) cartons
  Egg Beaters
2 tablespoons Dijon
  mustard
½ cup Kraft fat-free
  mayonnaise

¼ cup chopped celery
¼ cup chopped red pepper
2 tablespoons chopped
  scallions
12 slices whole wheat bread
6 lettuce leaves

In a large non-stick skillet, pour Egg Beaters in and cover tightly, cooking over a very low heat for 10 minutes or until just set. Remove from skillet and cool completely. Chop into fine pieces.

In a bowl, combine hard-cooked Egg Beaters that have been chopped, Dijon mustard, mayonnaise, celery, red peppers, and scallions. Divide and spread on 6 bread slices. Top with lettuce and remaining bread. Serve immediately. Serves 6.

Per Serving: Cal 233 (9.1% from fat); Fat 3.4g (SAT 0.6g); Chol 1.7mg; Fiber 5.4g; Sod 897mg. Diabetic Exchange: 2½ starch + 1 lean meat.

Here's To Your Heart: Cooking Smart

 Wisconsin is home to 280 caves, although only a handful are open to the general public. Crystal Cave in Spring Valley is the only three-level cave in this part of the country.

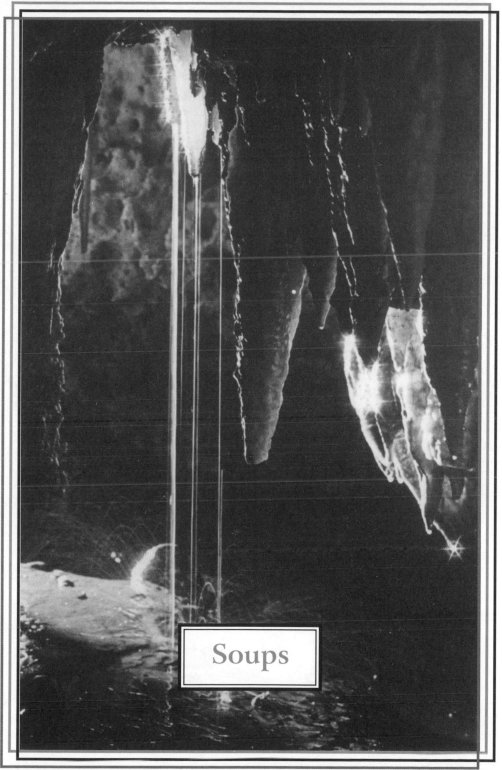

Soups

Cave of the Mounds is a miracle of nature formed far beneath the ground millions of years ago and still forming. West of Madison.

Tomato Dill Soup

This is such a pretty soup, with a vivid red color and flecks of green herbs. We make it often because it seems to go with everything (and our customers are always asking for it). The rich taste and texture make it perfect as a first course to an important dinner. Don't worry about leftovers; it tastes even better the second day and freezes well.

7½ tablespoons butter, divided
½ cup flour
1 cup diced onions
1 large clove garlic, minced
4 cups chicken stock
1 (29-ounce) can tomato purée, or 2 (15-ounce) cans
1 (16-ounce) can whole peeled tomatoes, chopped, juices reserved

3 tablespoons honey
1 tablespoon dill weed
1 teaspoon basil
½ teaspoon ground black pepper
½ teaspoon chili powder
⅛ teaspoon ground red (cayenne) pepper
3 dashes hot pepper sauce
Salt and pepper to taste

To make roux, melt 4½ tablespoons butter in small saucepan. Stir in flour until well blended. Cook over low heat, stirring often, for 3-5 minutes. Remove from heat and set aside. Melt remaining 3 tablespoons of butter in large, heavy pot. Add onions; cook gently 5 minutes. Add garlic, cook 2 minutes more. Add chicken stock, bring to a boil, and reduce to a simmer. Whisk in roux until stock is thickened and smooth. Add remaining ingredients, including juice from canned tomatoes. Simmer 30-45 minutes, stirring often to prevent scorching. This is a thick soup, but you may adjust to your taste by adding more chicken stock. Add salt and pepper to taste. Serves 8-10.

The Ovens of Brittany Cookbook

Harvest Tomato Soup

3 tablespoons chopped shallots
½ cup grated, peeled carrot
½ cup chopped green pepper
1 cup thin bias-cut celery
4 tablespoons butter or margarine
1 (49.5-ounce) can chicken broth, divided
4 cups fresh tomatoes, peeled, seeded and diced into ¼-inch cubes
½ teaspoon salt
¼ teaspoon pepper
1 tablespoon sugar
4 tablespoons flour
Croutons (optional)

In 10-inch skillet, sauté shallots, carrots, pepper, and celery in butter until vegetables are tender. Stir in 4 cups broth, tomatoes, salt, pepper, and sugar. Bring mixture to boil. Reduce heat and simmer. Cook about 20 minutes.

In medium bowl, whisk together flour and remaining broth. Slowly whisk into tomato mixture. Cook, stirring until mixture thickens, 2-3 minutes. Top bowls of soup with croutons. This is a good way to use tomatoes and your kitchen smells wonderful while cooking. I use red or yellow tomatoes and sometimes have used 2 cups of each.

Celebration of Grace

Onion Soup in the Microwave

1 cup thinly sliced onions
2 tablespoons margarine
1 can condensed beef broth
1 slice toasted French bread
½ cup Swiss cheese, shredded
2 tablespoons Parmesan cheese, grated

In 1-quart glass dish, combine onions and margarine. Cook 2-3 minutes until onions are soft. Stir. Add beef broth and cook on HIGH for 2-3 minutes. Stir. Pour into large soup bowl. Cover mixture with bread slice and sprinkle with cheeses. Cook, uncovered, for 45 seconds on HIGH until cheese is melted. Serves 1.

Thank Heaven for Home Made Cooks

Chicken and Wild Rice Soup

1 chicken or chicken pieces
2 (13-ounce) cans chicken
  broth
Celery (small inside stalks)
Onion (your preference to
  how much)
Salt and pepper

1 package Uncle Ben's
  Long Grain & Wild Rice
1 can mushrooms, drained
1 tablespoon butter
1 cup milk
1 tablespoon flour

Boil the chicken in the chicken broth with celery, onion, and seasoning. Simmer until chicken is done. Remove chicken and celery. Prepare rice according to package directions. When rice is cooked, add to broth, along with mushrooms. Debone and cut up chicken; add to soup. Make a white sauce out of the butter, milk, and flour. Add to soup; add water to soup if it becomes too thick.

Look What's Cookin' at Wal-Mart

Chicken Booyah

3 stewing chickens
1 tablespoon salt
1 bunch celery, chopped
1 head cabbage, chopped
3 potatoes, peeled, chopped
1 can corn
¼ pound butter or oleo

1 bunch carrots, peeled,
  chopped
3 onions, chopped
1 can peas
1 (6-ounce) can tomato paste
¼ cup salt
1 tablespoon pepper

Cook chickens with salt and enough water to cover chickens. Cook until bones can easily be removed. Remove chickens and add remaining ingredients to broth. Cook slowly until everything is cooked well. May be 4-5 hours. If too thick, add more water. Remove bones from chickens and put meat back into broth. Serve with oyster crackers. Serves 18-20.

What's on the Agenda?

 Many of the foods of Wisconsin reflect the heritage of its ancestors: German bratwurst, sauerbraten and beer; Norwegian boiled codfish (Torsk, Lutefisk); Danish kringle; Cornish pasty; French Brie and Camembert cheese; Swiss cheese; Italian Provolone and Parmesan cheese; Czechoslovakian kolaches; and Belgian chicken booyah.

Parsley, Sage, Rosemary and Thyme Chicken Soup

2 large leeks, thinly sliced
¾ - 1 pound boneless
  chicken, cubed
1 tablespoon olive oil
2 cups sliced fresh
  mushrooms
1 (14-ounce) can chopped
  tomatoes with juice
1 (15-ounce) can black
  beans, drained
  and rinsed
1 (15-ounce) can cannellini
  beans, undrained
1 (8-ounce) can whole
  kernel corn, drained
3½ cups red potatoes
  (with skins on)
  cut in ¼-inch cubes

1 cup thinly sliced carrots
1 cup fresh green beans,
  cut in ½-inch lengths
1 (49½-ounce) can chicken
  broth
3 tablespoons fresh parsley,
  finely minced
2 tablespoons dry sage,
  finely minced
2 tablespoons fresh
  rosemary, finely minced
1 tablespoon dry thyme,
  finely minced
3 bay leaves
½ teaspoon fresh ground
  black pepper
Salt to taste

Sauté leeks and chicken in olive oil until chicken is cooked. Add mushrooms and sauté until mushrooms are cooked. Add tomatoes with juice, black beans, cannellini beans, and corn. Set aside.

Boil potatoes, carrots, and green beans until all are cooked soft. Add to above. Add chicken broth, parsley, sage, rosemary, thyme, bay leaves, and black pepper. Mix well; simmer about 12 hours. I always refrigerate this soup overnight after this step to blend flavors, then reheat and taste for salt.

The Madison Herb Society Cookbook

Turkey Soup Continental

A hearty soup . . . a good main dish for a meal.

½ cup butter or oleo
1½ cups cooked turkey,
 cut up
3 tablespoons finely
 chopped onion
3 cups diced raw potatoes
1½ cups diced celery
3 cups turkey broth
1 (17-ounce) can cream-
 style corn

1½ (13-ounce) cans
 evaporated milk
3 tablespoons chopped
 parsley
1½ teaspoons salt
½ teaspoon ginger
½ teaspoon paprika
¼ teaspoon pepper or less

Melt butter over low heat. Add turkey and onion. Cook until onion is transparent. Add potatoes, celery, and broth. Stir and cook until mixture is well blended and slightly thick. Simmer until vegetables are done. Add corn, milk, and seasonings. Heat thoroughly, stirring occasionally. Serve hot. Garnish with parsley and serve with crackers, hard rolls, or toast.

Celebrating 150 Years of Faith and Food

Ham and Vegetable Soup

¼ cup butter
2 cups cabbage,
 shredded
1 onion, chopped
¼ cup flour
1 teaspoon salt
½ teaspoon paprika
½ teaspoon dry mustard

⅛ teaspoon black pepper
1 (10-ounce) can chicken
 broth
2½ cups milk
2 cups cauliflower, chopped
1 cup broccoli, chopped
1 cup carrots, thinly sliced
1½ cups ham, diced

Melt butter in a 3-quart saucepan. Add cabbage and onion; sauté until tender. Stir in flour and seasonings. Blend until smooth. Gradually stir in chicken broth and milk. Bring to a boil, stirring constantly. Precook the vegetables, then add to the soup. Add ham. This recipe freezes well.

Blessed Be The Cook

Bavarian Liver Dumpling Soup

Soups with dumplings are very special to the Germans—almost required at most meals. And "liver dumpling soup is as good a soup as can be made."

2 slices calf or beef liver (about ¼ pound)
½ teaspoon salt
1 egg, slightly beaten
1 tablespoon soft butter or margarine

1 teaspoon finely minced parsley
1-2 teaspoons finely minced onion
2 slices dry bread
½ cup flour, approximately
Meat stock

Place liver on a chopping board and scrape to separate connective tissue. Combine with salt, egg, softened butter, chopped parsley, onion, and bread which has been softened in hot water and squeezed dry. Beat well to blend. Add flour to make a medium-stiff dough. Drop from a teaspoon into gently boiling meat stock. Cook, covered, for 20-25 minutes, depending on size of dumplings. Serve at once. Makes 14-16 dumplings.

Note: Avoid having mixture too thick. Test by dropping one dumpling into hot stock. If it does not hold together, add a little more flour. Serve liver dumplings in clear beef broth.

Recipe from Mader's German Restaurant, Milwaukee. Owner Vic Mader.

Wisconsin Cooks with Wisconsin Public Television

Autumn Soup

1½ pounds ground beef
1 cup chopped onion
4 cups water
1 cup carrots, cut up
1 cup celery, diced
1 cup potatoes, cubed

1 teaspoon seasoning salt
½ teaspoon Beau Monde
  seasoning
¼ teaspoon lemon pepper
½ teaspoon salt
6 fresh tomatoes, chopped

Cook and stir meat until brown. Cook and stir onion with meat until tender. Stir in remaining ingredients except fresh tomatoes. Heat to boiling, reduce heat, cook and simmer for 20 minutes. Add tomatoes. Cover and simmer for 10 minutes or until vegetables are tender. Serve. This soup can be frozen nicely.

Note: A 28-ounce can of tomatoes can be substituted for the 6 fresh tomatoes; use liquid and cut water to 3 cups.

The Crooked Lake Volunteer Fire Department Cookbook,

Hearty Potato Soup

8 potatoes, peeled and diced
2-3 cups water
1 teaspoon salt
⅔ teaspoon black pepper
1 teaspoon celery salt

½ cup chopped onion
1 tablespoon chopped parsley
6 slices bacon
2 tablespoons flour
2 cups skim milk

Cover potatoes with water; cook until soft. Mash well. Add salt, pepper, celery salt, onion, and parsley. Cook until tender. Fry bacon and reserve 6 tablespoons drippings. Add flour to hot reserved drippings in pan and allow to bubble for 2 minutes. Add milk and stir until thick. Add to potatoes. Crumble bacon and add to soup. Heat through.

Optional: Can add ¼ cup instant mashed potatoes to thicken more and make a creamier texture.

Pelican Lake Women's Civic Club

Unbearably Good!
(Cream of Broccoli Soup)

1 small head broccoli	¼ cup flour
1 medium onion	2 teaspoons salt
½ teaspoon thyme	½ teaspoon pepper
1 quart chicken broth	4 cups milk
4 tablespoons butter	1 cup cheese

Cook together broccoli, onion, thyme, and chicken broth until tender. In other pan, melt butter; stir in flour, salt and pepper. Put in milk and cook until bubbly. Mix with broccoli. Stir in cheese until it melts.

Unbearably Good! Sharing Our Best

Cheese Soup

1 cup finely chopped carrots	¼ cup flour
¼ cup finely chopped celery	Dash of paprika
¼ cup chopped onion	1 cup shredded American or
1¾ cups chicken broth	Cheddar cheese
2 cups milk	

In medium saucepan, combine carrots, celery, and onion. Add chicken broth; heat to boiling. Reduce heat; cover and simmer for 15 minutes. In a medium bowl, combine milk, flour and paprika. Stir into broth mixture. Cook and stir until thickened and bubbly. Add cheese, stirring, until melted.

A Taste of Christ Lutheran

Vegetable Soup
(Tomato/Beef/Macaroni)

2 pounds ground chuck	4 cups hot water
½ teaspoon salt	1 (15-ounce) can tomato soup
¼ teaspoon oregano	1 tablespoon soy sauce
¼ teaspoon basil	1 large can tomatoes
½ teaspoon garlic salt	1 cup celery leaves
1 package dried onion soup	1 cup elbow macaroni

Brown meat. Remove excess fat. Add remaining ingredients, except macaroni. Let simmer for awhile. Add macaroni and continue to simmer til macaroni is done.

Wisconsin's Best

Wisconsin Beer Cheese Soup

An admirable rendition of one of Wisconsin's famous tourist attractions readily converts to a zesty cheese sauce. Reduce the water by one and a half cups and pour the sauce over baked potatoes, broccoli or cauliflower. Serve as a topping on crêpes, pasta or as a dip for chips and pretzels.

¾ cup butter (1½ sticks)
1 cup finely chopped onions
1 tablespoon minced garlic
½ cup finely chopped celery
½ cup finely chopped carrots
½ cup flour
¼ cup vegetarian chicken-flavored powder
3 cups hot water
½ cup Old Milwaukee Beer

2 teaspoons Worcestershire sauce
2 cups whole milk
¼ cup heavy cream
2 tablespoons sugar
2 teaspoons dry mustard
½ teaspoon ground fennel
⅛ teaspoon cayenne pepper
5 cups grated Wisconsin Cheddar cheese

Heat butter in a heavy 5-quart soup pot and add onions and garlic. Sauté until onions are translucent and add celery and carrots. Cook 2-3 minutes and stir in flour. Dissolve vegetarian powder in hot water and add to pot. Bring to a boil over high heat. Add beer, Worcestershire, milk, and cream.

Reduce heat to low, simmer 5 minutes and add sugar, mustard, fennel, and cayenne. Cook one minute longer and add cheeses, stirring constantly until cheese is melted and soup begins to bubble.

If soup seems a little too thick, add additional vegetarian broth or warm milk as desired. Remove from heat and serve garnished with a sprinkle of paprika. Yield: 2½ quarts.

Vegetarian International Cuisine

Wisconsin is known as the "Mother of Circuses" because around 100 circuses have been based in the state, more than any other state in the union. Baraboo is home to Circus World Museum, located at the birthplace of the Ringling Brothers Circus along the banks of the Baraboo River. Delavan, where The Clown Hall of Fame is located, boasts that between 1847 and 1894, no fewer than 26 circuses had their winter quarters there.

Microwave Split Pea Soup

This is a valuable recipe for the summer months, because sometimes it's just too hot to cook, but yet the tummy is asking for something warm and filling. This is one of my favorite recipes.

1 pound split peas (about 2⅓ cups)	1 medium onion, chopped
6 cups water	1½ cups cooked ham, chopped
3 medium carrots, coarsely grated	1 teaspoon salt
	¼ teaspoon pepper

Rinse and drain split peas. In a 3-quart or larger casserole, combine all ingredients; cover. Microwave on HIGH (100% power) 10 minutes. Reduce power to MEDIUM (50% power) and cook 60-90 minutes or until vegetables are tender and soup is thickened. Stir 2 or 3 times during cooking. Makes about 8 cups.

Marketplace Recipes Volume II

Ham and Lima Bean Soup

1 ham bone with meat	2 soup cans water
1 cup dried lima beans	1 bay leaf
2 cans tomato soup	Peppercorns

Simmer ham bone and meat for 1½ hours. Remove bone and excess fat. Add lima beans, tomato soup, and water, along with bay leaf and peppercorns. Cook another hour. Potatoes can be added ½ hour before serving.

St. Frederick Parish Centennial Recipe Collection

St. Nicholas Festival Borscht

2 quarts water
1 medium beef bone
  with meat
2 beets, chopped
2 medium carrots, chopped
1 green pepper, seeded
  (whole)
Salt and pepper to taste
1 small onion, chopped

2 medium potatoes, peeled
  and cubed
½ small head cabbage,
  chopped
1 small can tomatoes,
  chopped or diced
2-3 tablespoons tomato sauce
1 clove garlic, minced
  (optional)

In 3-quart saucepan, bring water with meaty bone to a boil. Skim and simmer 2-3 hours. Remove meat and bone from broth. To liquid, add beets; cook 10 minutes, then add carrots and green pepper. Cook 10 minutes. Add salt, pepper, onion, potatoes, and cabbage. Cook until potatoes and cabbage are tender. Remove green pepper. Add tomatoes, tomato sauce, and garlic if desired. Cook 10-15 minutes. Serves 6.

Note: May add dill weed and parsley. Serve with sour cream and rye bread if desired.

Sunflowers & Samovars

The Capitol in Madison is topped by Daniel Chester French's gilded bronze statue, "Wisconsin." The dome is the only granite dome in the US, and is the largest by volume. The dome is only 17 inches shorter than the national Capitol dome.

Salads

*The wheels of government turn beneath the soaring dome of Wisconsin's beautiful
Capitol in Madison.*

Orange Cottage Cheese Salad

24 ounces small curd
  cottage cheese
12 ounces Cool Whip, or less
2 ounces coconut, optional
1 (3-ounce) package orange
  Jell-O (dry)

1 (20-ounce) can crushed
  pineapple, or less, drained
1 (10-ounce) can mandarin
  oranges, drained

Mix together lightly. Refrigerate 24 hours.

Our Favorite Recipes

De's Salad

2 large cans mandarin
  oranges
1 (40-ounce) can chunk
  pineapple
1 small package vanilla
  pudding (not instant)

3 tablespoons Tang
1 jar maraschino cherries
6 bananas

Drain oranges, pineapple, and save the juice. Make pudding
with 2 cups of juice. Bring to a boil, stirring constantly. Add
Tang. Remove from heat, let cool. Drain cherries. Add bananas,
oranges, pineapple, and cherries. Stir and refrigerate till ready
to serve.

A Collection of Recipes

Cranberry Wine Salad

2 (3-ounce) packages
  raspberry Jell-O
2 cups boiling water
1 (16-ounce) can whole
  cranberry sauce

1 (8-ounce) can crushed
  pineapple, undrained
¾ cup port wine (or sweet
  vermouth)
¼ cup chopped walnuts

Dissolve Jell-O in boiling water; stir in whole cranberry sauce,
crushed pineapple and wine. Chill until partially set. Fold in
chopped walnuts. Pour mixture into 6½-cup mold. Chill until
firm.

Look What's Cooking at C.A.M.D.E.N

Cherry Salad Supreme

1 (3-ounce) package
raspberry gelatin
1 cup boiling water
1 (21-ounce) can tart
cherry pie filling
1 (3-ounce) package
lemon gelatin
1 cup boiling water

4 ounces cream cheese,
softened
⅓ cup mayonnaise
1 (8-ounce) can pineapple
crushed with juice
½ cup heavy cream, whipped
1 cup marshmallows (small)
2 tablespoons nuts, chopped

Dissolve raspberry gelatin in one cup boiling water. Stir in
cherry pie filling. Pour into 13x9-inch pan. Let set. Disolve
lemon gelatin in one cup boiling water. Beat together cream
cheese and mayonnaise. Gradually add lemon gelatin. Stir in
pineapple and juice. Add whipped cream and marshmallows
to gelatin mixture. Spread on top of cherry layer. When set,
sprinkle chopped nuts on top.

Country Cupboard

Wisconsin has some 79,000 farms, which average 90 hectares (222 acres) in
size. Livestock and livestock products account for 70 percent of Wisconsin's
yearly farm production; crops supply the remainder (corn, hay, potatoes, soy-
beans, wheat, barley, tobacco, honey, beets, beans, peas, cucumbers, apples,
cherries, and cranberries).

Raspberry Carousel

1 (3-ounce) package
    raspberry Jell-O
2 cups boiling water
¾ cup cranberry juice
    cocktail
1 cup diced apple
¼ cup sliced celery

¼ cup chopped walnuts
1 (3-ounce) package lemon
    Jell-O
1 (4½-ounce) Cool Whip
    topping
½ cup mayonnaise

Dissolve raspberry Jell-O in one cup boiling water. Add cranberry juice cocktail and chill until thickened, about one hour. Fold in apple, celery, and nuts; spoon into 6-cup ring mold and chill until set, about 15 minutes.

Dissolve lemon Jell-O in remaining boiling water. Chill until slightly thickened, about 45 minutes. Combine whipped topping and mayonnaise; fold into Jell-O. Spoon into mold. Chill until firm, at least 4 hours. Unmold, garnish with crisp salad greens and sliced apples, if desired.

Thank Heaven for Home Made Cooks

Cookie Monster Fruit Salad

1 cup buttermilk
1 (3-ounce) package
    instant vanilla
    pudding
1 (8-ounce) carton
    Cool Whip

1 small can mandarin
    oranges, drained
1 small can crushed
    pineapple, drained
14 chocolate striped
    cookies, crushed

Mix buttermilk and pudding together; fold in Cool Whip. Fold remaining ingredients into pudding mixture. Chill well before serving. Makes 8 servings.

St. Mary's Family Cookbook

Lemon Cream Salad

1 large box lemon Jell-O
⅓ cup sugar
2 cups boiling water

1 (6-ounce) can frozen
lemonade
1 (8-ounce) carton Cool Whip

Mix Jell-O and sugar together. Add the boiling water and stir until all are dissolved. Add the frozen lemonade. Let set in refrigerator until it starts to thicken. Fold in Cool Whip and put in any serving dish. Refrigerate until ready to serve.

Cardinal Country Cooking

Caramel Apple Salad

4-6 frozen Snickers candy
bars
4-6 Granny Smith apples,

1 (8-ounce) carton Cool Whip
1 (3-ounce) package dry
instant vanilla pudding

Smash frozen candy bars with hammer. Mix all ingredients together. You can use other candy bars; Milky Way, KitKat, Twix and others. These are all good, but the peanut flavor in the Snickers makes the salad.

Trinity Lutheran Church of Norden Anniversary Cookbook

Granny Smith Apple Salad

1 small can crushed
pineapple, undrained
1 tablespoon flour
1 egg
½ cup sugar

3 Granny Smith apples,
unpeeled and chopped
1 (8-ounce) carton Cool Whip
1½ cups dry roasted peanuts,
chopped

Cook pineapple, flour, egg, and sugar together until thick, stirring constantly. Cool. Add apples, Cool Whip, and peanuts. Keep some peanuts for topping.

Sparks from the Kitchen

Cranberry-Apple Salad

Karen Maihofer shared this beautiful special occasion salad in one of her popular holiday cooking lessons. It is just one of the many delicious recipes she has shared with students in her Creative Cuisine cooking classes. The lime vinaigrette is especially tasty.

1½ cups fresh or frozen (unthawed) cranberries

4 tablespoons plus 2 teaspoons sugar (divided)

1 teaspoon grated orange zest

2 tablespoons fresh lime juice

2 teaspoons Dijon-style mustard

½ cup olive oil or vegetable oil

2 large Granny Smith apples, cored, coarsely chopped

1 cup coarsely chopped walnuts

¼ cup sliced green onions

½ cup golden raisins

1 head romaine lettuce or green and white kale

Grated lime zest as garnish

Coarsely chop cranberries by hand or in bowl or food processor. In medium-size bowl, combine cranberries, 4 tablespoons of the sugar and orange zest. Cover; chill overnight.

In blender, blend lime juice, mustard, and remaining 2 teaspoons sugar. Add olive oil gradually, blending until mixture is smooth.

In bowl, mix together apples, walnuts, onions, and raisins; pour lime vinaigrette over all, cover and refrigerate 1-4 hours. To serve, line a large platter with romaine. Spoon apple mixture onto platter leaving a 2-inch border of lettuce around edge. Make a well in center of apple salad and spoon in cranberry mixture. Garnish with grated lime zest. Makes 8 servings.

The Sunday Cook Collection

It Ain't The Waldorf But It'll Do Salad

2 cups unpeeled chopped
  apples (2 medium)
2 teaspoons fresh lemon
  juice
¼ cup raisins (or snipped
  pitted dates)
¼ cup seedless grapes

¼ cup chopped celery
¼ cup fat-free whipped
  dressing
¼ cup plain nonfat yogurt
3 tablespoons chopped
  walnuts

In a medium bowl toss apples in lemon juice. If grapes are large, cut in half. Stir in raisins (or dates), grapes and celery. In a small bowl combine mayonnaise and yogurt. Fold dressing into apple mixture. Cover and chill for 2-24 hours. To serve arrange on lettuce leaves on four individual plates and sprinkle with walnuts. Makes four ¾-cup servings.

Nutritional Analysis Per Serving: Total fat 1.976gm; Sat fat 0.203gm; Chol 0.312mg; Cal from fat 22%; Cal 77; Sod 112.9mg; Carb 13.55gm; Sugar 9.765gm; Prot 1.728gm.

Spice of Life Cookbook

Frozen Banana Salad

1 tablespoon lemon juice
1 teaspoon salt
4 tablespoons mayonnaise
2 (8-ounce) packages cream
  cheese
4 tablespoons crushed
  pineapple

½ cup maraschino cherries,
  cut in quarters
½ cup English walnuts,
  chopped
1 cup heavy cream
3 well-ripened bananas, cut
  in cubes

Add lemon juice and salt to mayonnaise and stir into cheese. Mix with pineapple, cherries, and nuts, and fold in cream (whipped until firm). Add bananas and turn into freezer tray; freeze 3 hours or longer. Unmold, cut in slices and serve on bed of lettuce or watercress. Serves 6-8. Garnish with additional cherries.

The Palmyra Heritage Cookbook

Fresh Broccoli Salad

DRESSING:

1 cup mayonnaise
½ cup sugar

2 teaspoons vinegar

Mix dressing ingredients together; let stand 15 minutes.

1 pound fried bacon,
  crumbled
1 bunch fresh broccoli,
  cut in small pieces

½ cup raisins
1 cup cashews
1 medium red onion, diced

Fry bacon until crisp, then crumble. Mix together broccoli, raisins, cashews, onion, and bacon. Stir in dressing. Best to do just before serving.

What's Cook'n?

Raspberry Spinach Salad

1 pound fresh spinach,
  washed and dried
1 pound fresh raspberries
  (or substitute ½ pound
  fresh strawberries
  or mandarin orange slices)

½ cup pecans, slivered (may
  brown pecans in butter
  10 minutes in 350° oven)

DRESSING:

⅓ cup wine vinegar or
  raspberry wine vinegar
1 cup vegetable oil
1 teaspoon salt

½ cup sugar
1 teaspoon dry mustard
1½ tablespoons minced onion
1½ tablespoons poppy seeds

Whip first 6 dressing ingredients in blender (a day ahead). Seal in container and refrigerate after adding poppy seeds. Just before serving, mix spinach with dressing in large bowl. Then add berries and nuts.

Cooking with Grace

Romaine-Spinach Salad

1 bunch Romaine lettuce	4 ounces Swiss cheese
1 (16-ounce) bunch spinach	6-8 ounces whole cashews
2 red apples or 1 pint	
strawberries	

DRESSING:

¾ cup sugar	1 teaspoon dry mustard
1 cup oil, half salad, half	1 teaspoon salt
olive	1½ tablespoons poppy seeds
⅓ cup vinegar (white,	1½ tablespoons grated onion,
red wine, or tarragon)	optional

To make dressing, put sugar, oil, vinegar, mustard, salt, poppy seeds, and onion in a blender for 3 minutes. When ready to serve, toss greens, apples or strawberries, cheese, cashews, and dressing. Great make-ahead buffet salad.

Variation: Seedless green grape halves and 1 (11-ounce) can drained mandarin oranges can be substituted for apples or strawberries. Bacon bits may be added.

Marquette University High School
Mother's Guild Cookbook

Summer Sunrise Melon and Spinach Salad

The bright, sunrise orange of canteloupe and leafy green of spinach make this salad beautiful, while bits of scallions and toasty sesame seeds make it delicious. Serve it in August, when melons are at their market peak. (Or substitute fresh strawberries earlier in the summer.)

1½ pounds fresh spinach
2 tablespoons sesame seeds
⅓ cup red wine vinegar
2 tablespoons minced green onion
1 tablespoon sugar
1 teaspoon paprika
½ teaspoon Worcestershire sauce
⅓ cup vegetable oil
2-3 cups canteloupe chunks (or hulled strawberries)
Freshly ground black pepper

Wash spinach. Tear into bite-size pieces, removing stems. Dry in a salad spinner or clean towel. Chill spinach. Toast sesame seeds in a small, dry skillet over medium heat until golden, about 3-4 minutes. Do not scorch.

Mix vinegar, green onion, sugar, paprika, and Worcestershire sauce in a bowl; whisk in oil in a thin stream. Just before serving, toss spinach, sesame seeds, dressing and fruit in a large glass bowl. Pass the pepper mill. Makes 6-8 large servings.

Fresh Market Wisconsin

Herring Salad

1 (16-ounce) jar herring in wine sauce
2 pared medium potatoes, cooked and finely cubed
1 (16-ounce) can beets, cut up
1 medium apple, pared and finely cubed
1 tablespoon finely chopped onion
2 medium-sized sweet pickles, finely cubed
1 tablespoon sugar
2 tablespoons white vinegar
¼ teaspoon pepper
½ cup whipped cream (optional)

Mix all ingredients together lightly. If using whipped cream, fold in right before serving. Garnish with sieved, hard-cooked egg yolk and finely chopped egg whites.

Favorite Recipes of Pommern Cooks

Warm Pork and Spinach Salad

1 pound boneless pork loin, into thin strips
1 pound fresh spinach leaves, coarsely shredded
3 cup watercress sprigs or other lettuce
1 cup thinly sliced celery
1 cup seedless green grapes
½ cup thinly sliced green onion
1 (8-ounce) can sliced water chestnuts, drained
1 large Golden Delicious cut apple, cored and chopped
1 cup low-calorie Italian salad dressing
2 tablespoons white wine
2 tablespoons Dijon-style mustard
1 tablespoon packed light brown sugar
2 teaspoons sesame seeds

Spray nonstick skillet with Pam and stir-fry pork until cooked, about 4 minutes. Set aside and keep warm. In large serving bowl combine spinach, watercress, celery, grapes, green onion, water chestnuts, and apple. Toss to mix.

In small pan combine salad dressing, wine, mustard, and brown sugar. Heat until sugar dissolves, stirring constantly. Stir cooked pork into hot dressing to coat well. Remove pork, pour half of dressing over greens in bowl and mix. Place pork strips on top of salad. Sprinkle with sesame seed. Pass remaining dressing (or pour on salad). Serves 6.

Thank Heaven for Home Made Cooks

Crunchy Pea Salad

1 (10-ounce) package frozen baby peas
1 cup cauliflower, chopped
1 cup sliced celery
½ cup green onions, chopped
1 cup cashews
½ cup sour cream
1 cup Hidden Valley Ranch bottled salad dressing

Combine vegetables and nuts in large bowl. Mix together sour cream and salad dressing. Pour over vegetable mix. Refrigerate.

Trinity Lutheran Church of Norden Anniversary Cookbook

Green Bean, Walnut & Feta Salad

1½ pounds fresh green
  beans (ends trimmed),
  cut in half cross-wise
¾ cup olive oil
½ cup packed fresh mint
  leaves or parsley
  (or combination)
¼ cup white wine vinegar

¾ teaspoon salt
¼ teaspoon freshly ground
  pepper
½ teaspoon minced garlic
1 cup chopped toasted
  walnuts
1 cup or less diced red onion
1 cup feta cheese, crumbled

Bring 4 quarts salted water to boil in a 6-quart saucepan over medium-high heat. Add beans and cook until crisp and tender, about 4 minutes. Drain well and immediately plunge into ice water. Drain again and pat dry with paper towels (can be made hours ahead). Combine oil, mint/parsley, vinegar, salt, pepper, and garlic in a food processor or blender. Arrange beans in serving bowl. Sprinkle with nuts, onions, and cheese. Just before serving, pour dressing over mixture; toss well. Serves 6.

Note: Take your shopping list to the farmer's market. The secret to this dish is the toasted walnuts. Toast in a 350° oven for 5-8 minutes or until golden brown.

Picnics on the Square

Marinated Cabbage Slaw

1 medium head of cabbage,
  shredded (about 10 cups)
1 green pepper, chopped
1 medium onion, chopped
1 cup sugar

½ teaspoon celery seed
¾ cup white vinegar
¼ cup salad oil
1 teaspoon salt

Add chopped green pepper and onion to shredded cabbage. In a saucepan make marinade of vinegar, salad oil, sugar, salt, and celery seed. Bring to a boil and pour over cabbage mixture. Mix well. Cover and refrigerate overnight. Can be used immediately. Will keep for weeks.

Flavors of Washington County

Simi Salad

2 tablespoons sesame seeds, toasted
½ cup slivered almonds, toasted
1 large head shredded Napa cabbage or ½ gallon regular cabbage (Napa is best)

1 package Ramen noodles from soup mix (uncooked and crumbled)
⅓ cup chopped green onion

Toast sesame seeds and almonds in 475° oven. Spread seeds and almonds on separate cookie sheets. Bake until golden. Watch closely. Seeds will take less than a minute; almonds will take a little more. For a really crunchy salad, add noodles, seeds, and nuts to cabbage and onions just before serving.

DRESSING:

1 seasoning packet from Ramen noodles soup mix, Oriental-flavor
½ cup vegetable oil

3 tablespoons sugar
3 tablespoons seasoned rice vinegar
Pinch salt and pepper

Mix together and toss with salad ingredients.

Good Cooking, Good Curling

Caesar Salad

Most everyone loves a good Caesar salad, but concern over raw egg safety has made some cooks timid about serving this popular classic. Here's a version without the raw egg that my family has loved for years. Purists may blanch at the omission, but I believe your guests will appreciate your thoughtfulness.

2 anchovy fillets
2 medium cloves garlic, minced
1 teaspoon salt or to taste
6 tablespoons vegetable oil
2 tablespoons red wine vinegar
1 tablespoon fresh lemon juice, strained
½ teaspoon Worcestershire sauce
1 teaspoon dry mustard
1 teaspoon freshly ground black pepper
2 large heads romaine lettuce, washed, drained, torn and chilled
1 cup croutons
1 tablespoon freshly grated Parmesan cheese

Drain achovies on paper towel, then put in small bowl and mash fine with fork. Place minced garlic in wooden or glass salad bowl. Add salt. Mash into paste with back of spoon. Add mashed anchovy fillets plus vegetable oil, vinegar, lemon juice, Worcestershire sauce, dry mustard, and black pepper, and mix well.

Just before serving, add lettuce. Toss well to blend with dressing. Garnish with croutons and freshly grated Parmesan cheese. Makes 12 servings.

The Sunday Cook Collection

Chicken Salad

4 chicken breasts, baked,
  cooled and cubed
1 cup salad dressing or
  mayonnaise
12 ounces Cool Whip
1 cup cashews

1 box ring noodles,
  cooked and cooled
2 cups celery, chopped
1 cup green grapes
1 cup red grapes

Mix chicken, salad dressing or mayonnaise, and Cool Whip;
marinate at least 2 hours. Then mix remaining ingredients
and chill.

A Taste of Home

Fruited Chicken Salad

3 tablespoons lemon juice
4 cups cubed, cooked
  chicken
1 cup sliced celery
1 cup cantaloupe balls
1 cup green grapes, halved

⅓ cup finely chopped onion
1 teaspoon salt
½ teaspoon pepper
½ cup mayonnaise or salad
  dressing or vanilla yogurt
¼ cup chopped almonds

Mix lemon juice with chicken. Add remaining ingredients. Toss
until mixed.

What's on the Agenda?

Gizzard Salad Mold

2 envelopes Knox gelatin
3 tablespoons cold water
2 cups stock from cooking
  gizzards (hot)
2 cups cooked gizzards,
  ground
4 eggs, boiled, cooled and
  ground

¾ teaspoon salt
¾ teaspoon Accent (MSG)
½ teaspoon garlic salt
1 teaspoon celery leaves
1 teaspoon parsley flakes
1 tablespoon celery, ground
1 small onion, ground
1½ cups mayonnaise

Dissolve gelatine in cold water. Add hot gizzard stock and
mix all ingredients. Place in greased mold or molds and set in
refrigerator at least 1½ hours.

Sharing Our Best

Crab Salad

Excellent for special salad for luncheons.

1 (6-ounce) can crab (or
  frozen Kemps imitation
  crab)
¼ cup chopped onion
⅓ cup shredded Swiss
  cheese
¼ cup chopped celery

1 hard-cooked egg, chopped
¼ cup green pepper
½ cup mayonnaise
  mixed with ¼ cup
  seafood cocktail sauce
Salt and pepper, to taste

Combine all ingredients and serve on croissants or on greens or
on stuffed tomato. Serves approximately 3-4 people. Increase
amounts as needed.

Peterson Pantry Plus Lore

Salmon Salad

1 small package lemon
  Jell-O
½ cup hot water
2 tablespoons vinegar
1 (6½-ounce) can red
  salmon and juice (skin
  and bones removed)
1 cup celery, chopped fine

1 small jar green stuffed
  olives, finely chopped
4 hard-cooked eggs, chopped
½ cup mayonnaise
  (use part to coat mold;
  preferably a fish mold)
Cucumber slices and sliced
  green olives for garnish

Mix and cool Jell-O, water, and vinegar. Mix in remaining
ingredients and pour into mold. If using fish mold, use sliced
green stuffed olives for eyes and garnish with cucumber slices
for scales. Garnish around fish with endive or greens. Elegant
for luncheon.

Peterson Pantry Plus Lore

American Club Red Bliss Potato Salad

All-American potato salad is one of those quintessential recipes handed down from one generation to the next. This chef's favorite has a few colorful twists that add pizazz and good taste. You may want to pass this one on to your children and grandchildren.

3 pounds red salad
   potatoes
12 slices uncooked apple-
   wood smoked bacon
½ cup red onion, peeled,
   cut ¼-inch dice
½ cup cucumber, peeled,
   cut ¼-inch dice
½ cup finely sliced
   scallions
¼ cup red bell peppers,
   cut ¼-inch dice
¾ cup vegetable oil

2 tablespoons peeled,
   chopped garlic
½ teaspoon stemmed,
   chopped fresh thyme
½ teaspoon stemmed,
   chopped fresh
   rosemary
¼ cup minced chives
¼ cup rice wine vinegar
2 tablespoons apple cider
   vinegar
Salt to taste
Cracked black pepper to taste

Wash the potatoes; place in a one-gallon pot; cover with water. Bring to simmer and cook until they can be easily pierced with a knife. Drain and allow to cool; slice in quarters and place in a large stainless steel bowl.

In a small sauté pan over medium heat, cook bacon until crisp. Drain fat and reserve bacon.

In a large mixing bowl, combine onion, cucumber, scallions, red peppers, oil, garlic, thyme, rosemary, chives, vinegars, and crumbled bacon. Season to taste with salt and pepper. Mix to blend ingredients. Pour over the potatoes and toss gently. Do not overmix. Chill and serve. Yields 4-6 servings.

Masterpiece Recipes of The American Club

Glaciers have formed much of the landscape in Wisconsin, digging out the Great Lakes, smaller lakes, and rivers. Melting glaciers left boulders, kettles, potholes, and all sorts of formations, including the Wisconsin Dells.

Potato Salad

4 cups boiled potatoes, cubed
3 hard boiled eggs, chopped
¼ cup finely chopped onion
¼ cup chopped green pepper, pimento or parsley
1-2 cups diced raw vegetables (celery, cucumber, radish, etc.)
½ cup sweet or sour cream
2 tablespoons vinegar
2 tablespoons sugar
1½ teaspoons salt
⅛ teaspoon black pepper
¼ teaspoon paprika
¼ teaspoon dry mustard
1 cup salad dressing or mayonnaise

Combine potatoes, eggs, and vegetables. Blend remaining ingredients; mix lightly with potato mixture. Chill. Serves 6.

Our Favorite Recipes

Spaghetti Pasta Salad

1 pound extra thin spaghetti
2 green peppers, chopped fine
2 tomatoes, chopped fine
1 onion, chopped fine

DRESSING:
½ bottle McCormick's Salad Supreme Seasoning
8 ounces Seven Seas Viva Italian Salad Dressing
1 pinch garlic powder
1 pinch oregano
1 pinch basil

Cook spaghetti; drain. Add chopped vegetables to spaghetti. Toss with dressing and chill well. Makes a large batch or portion.

Centennial Cookbook

Among the famous folks from Wisconsin: Spencer Tracy, Georgia O'Keefe, Gary Burghoff, Gene Wilder, Tom Wopat, Dan Travanti, Tyne Daly, Frank Lloyd Wright, Gena Rowlands, Frederic March, Jackie Mason, Bunny Berrigan, Glenn Yarborough, Chris Farley, Orson Welles, Laura Ingalls Wilder, Bob Uecker, Pee Wee King, Tom Snyder, Charlotte Rae, Thornton Wilder, Willem Dafoe, Allen Ludden, Don Ameche, Dennis Morgan, Tom Hulce, Al Jarreau, Harry Houdini, Liberace, and US Supreme Court Chief Justice William Rehnquist.

Pasta Salad Italiano

Colorful and delicious. Sure to impress your guests.

1 (8-ounce) bottle Italian dressing (not creamy)
1 cup bite-size broccoli pieces
½ cup cauliflower florets
½ cup sliced fresh mushrooms
1 (8-ounce) can sliced water chestnuts
1 carrot, diced
¼ cup sliced ripe olives
¾ cup cherry tomatoes, halved
4 ounces spaghetti noodles,
¼ cup grated Parmesan cheese
¼ cup real bacon bits

In medium-size bowl, pour dressing over vegetables. Cover and marinate in refrigerator at least 3 hours. Cook spaghetti, drain, and chill.

Drain and reserve marinade from the vegetables. Combine marinade with noodles and cheese. Toss lightly. Place noodles in glass dish, adding vegetables. Sprinkle with more cheese and the bacon. Carry in cooler. Serves 8-10.

Note: If the spaghetti noodles are broken before cooking, it is easier to serve and eat.

Picnics on the Square

Bacon, Lettuce and Tomato Salad

1 (7-ounce) box Creamettes shells, cooked and drained
1½ pounds bacon, diced, fried and drained
½ head lettuce, shredded
2 or 3 tomatoes, seeded and diced
1 tablespoon finely diced onion
Pepper to taste
Mayonnaise or Miracle Whip to coat

In large bowl, mix the first 6 ingredients together. Mix with mayonnaise or Miracle Whip to coat. Refrigerate until ready to serve. Yield: 12 servings.

Hint: The shells, bacon and tomatoes may be prepared the day before and refrigerated.

St. Mary's Family Cookbook

Fruity-Macaroni Salad

Makes a large amount. Good for taking to a potluck.

1 (20-ounce) can crushed
   pineapple, drained
   (save juice)
2 tablespoons flour
½ cup sugar
2 eggs, beaten

3 tablespoons cider vinegar
1 (8-ounce) carton Cool Whip
10-12 ounces macaroni
1 (11-ounce) can mandarin
   orange segments, drained
4 medium-size apples, cored

Prepare dressing using pineapple juice, flour, sugar, eggs, and vinegar. Cook, stirring frequently until thick. Cool completely. Fold in Cool Whip.

Cook macaroni following directions on package. After draining, mix with crushed pineapple (so it doesn't stick together). Cool. Add orange sections. Fold in dressing. Add apples. Put in covered dish and refrigerate.

Note: You may wish to decorate with kiwi fruit before serving. Red or green grapes could be added.

The Octagon House Cookbook

Mandarin Salad

DRESSING:

½ teaspoon salt
Dash pepper
2 tablespoons sugar
2 tablespoons vinegar

¼ cup salad oil
Dash red pepper sauce
1 tablespoon chopped parsley

Shake dressing ingredients in tightly covered jar; refrigerate.

SALAD:

¼ cup sliced almonds
1 tablespoon plus
   1 teaspoon sugar
2 medium heads Boston
   lettuce

1 small head endive
Sliced red onion
1 (11-ounce) can mandarin
   oranges, drained

Cook almonds and sugar over low heat, stirring constantly, until sugar is melted and almonds are coated. Cool and break apart. Store in covered container at room temperature. Combine torn lettuce, endive, onion rings, oranges, and almonds with dressing. Serves 4-6.

All in Good Taste I

Glazed Fruit Salad

A make-ahead salad that keeps well.

1 small package vanilla
   pudding mix (do
   not use instant)
1½ cups pineapple juice
   (add orange juice if
   necessary)
3 tablespoons lemon juice

1 (16-ounce) can mandarin
   oranges, drained
1 (20-ounce) can pineapple
   chunks, drained
1 (16-ounce) can fruit for
   salads, chunky
4 bananas

Cook pudding with juice until thick. Drain canned fruit very
well. Add cooled pudding mixture and blend well. Slice bananas
and fold in just before serving.

Foxy Ladies

Hot Fruit Salad

1 large can pineapple
   chunks, drained
1 large can sliced peaches,
   drained
1 cup raw cranberries
2 tablespoons butter

3 tablespoons tapioca
   granules or minute tapioca
¾ cup orange juice, or juice
   from the above drained
   fruit

Mix the first five ingredients. Place in a buttered 8x11-inch Pyrex
casserole. Put pats of butter on top. Bake at 350° for ½ hour.

Family Fare

Winter Fruit Bowl

4 medium-size pink
   grapefruit
Water
1 cup sugar

½ cup orange marmalade
2 cups (8 ounces) fresh or
   frozen whole cranberries
3 medium bananas

Peel and section grapefruit, reserving any juice. Set grapefruit
sections aside. Add enough water to juice to measure one cup
liquid. In saucepan, combine juice mixture, sugar, and marmalade. Heat to boiling, stirring to dissolve sugar. Add cranberries.
Cook and stir until skins pop, 5-8 minutes. Remove from heat
and cool. Add grapefruit. Cover and chill. Just before serving,
slice bananas and stir into mixture. Makes 10 servings.

Cherry Berries on a Cloud and More

Salad-In-A-Sandwich

A loaf of crusty French bread soaks up all the fresh and exciting flavors in this salad-in-a-sandwich. Serve it with lasagna or Italian spaghetti, as picnic fare, or for a summer lunch.

2 teaspoons minced garlic
½ teaspoon cracked black
  pepper
1 (2-ounce) can anchovy
  fillets, well drained
1 tablespoon balsamic
  or red wine vinegar
2 tablespoons olive oil
⅔ cup coarsely chopped
  stuffed green or Greek
  olives, or a combination
1 long loaf French bread

1 small red onion, thinly
  sliced
1 medium green bell pepper,
  thinly sliced
1 medium red bell pepper,
  thinly sliced
2 medium tomatoes, sliced
Additional vinegar, olive oil,
  and cracked black pepper
2 tablespoons chopped fresh
  basil or pesto (optional)

In a medium bowl, mash garlic and ½ teaspoon cracked black pepper with a fork until a paste is formed. Coarsely chop anchovies and mash them into the garlic paste. Stir in vinegar, olive oil and chopped olives. Slice bread loaf in half horizontally and pull out some of the inside bread from each half. (Bread scraps can be used to make croutons, dried for bread crumbs or donated to the birds.) Place bottom half of loaf on a large sheet of aluminum foil and spread olive mixture evenly over bread surface. Layer onions, peppers, and tomatoes over this. Sprinkle additional vinegar, olive oil and black pepper on the cut surface on the top bread half. Sprinkle with chopped basil or spread with pesto, if available. Place it on the stacked sandwich; press down firmly.

Wrap the loaf securely in the aluminum foil and weight it with whatever heavy articles are available: books, cans, etc. Keep it weighted one hour or longer. Refrigeration isn't necessary unless it won't be served for several hours. To serve, remove foil, insert toothpicks along the length of the loaf, and slice. The sandwich tastes best at room temperature. Makes 3-4 lunch-size servings, twice that as side dish.

Fresh Market Wisconsin

French Dressing

1 cup oil
½ cup vinegar
1½ cups sugar (or more)
2 teaspoons paprika
2 teaspoons salt
1 teaspoon dry mustard

2 small onions, grated
1 teaspoon celery salt
2 cups catsup
1 tablespoon Worcestershire
 sauce

Put ingredients in blender; blend well. Store in refrigerator.

Favorite Recipes of the Wisconsin NFO

Blue Cheese Dressing

1 cup mayonnaise
4 ounces crumbled Blue
 cheese
3 tablespoons milk
2 tablespoons lemon juice

2 teaspoons sugar
1 tablespoon chopped onion
¼ teaspoon Worcestershire
¼ teaspoon dry mustard
¼ teaspoon salt

Combine all ingredients.

Mt. Carmel's "Cooking with the Oldies"

Creamy Garlic Dressing

¼ cup sour cream
¼ cup mayonnaise
¼ cup salad oil
1 teaspoon minced fresh
  garlic

2 teaspoons dried chives or 2
  tablespoons fresh chives
¼ teaspoon white pepper
½ cup buttermilk

Thoroughly mix sour cream and mayonnaise then whisk in oil. Stir in remaining ingredients and refrigerate at least one hour before serving. The garlic flavor will intensify as this dressing ages. Makes 1¼ cups.

The Ovens of Brittany Cookbook

Best in All the World Mustard

4 ounces dry mustard
⅔ cup white or cider
  vinegar

1 cup sugar
¾ teaspoon salt
2 eggs

Cover dry mustard with vinegar and let stand 8 hours or over-night. Place in a double boiler. Add sugar, salt, and eggs. Just beat well, cook until thick and this will keep for months in the fridge.

Cooking with Pride

Pepper-Onion Mayonnaise

2 tablespoons finely
  chopped parsley
3 tablespoons finely
  chopped green pepper
1 tablespoon finely
  chopped red pepper
1 tablespoon finely
  chopped onion

2 tablespoons finely
  chopped pimento
1 cup mayonnaise
⅛ teaspoon paprika
2 teaspoons lemon juice
¼ teaspoon salt
⅛ teaspoon pepper

Combine parsley, green pepper, red pepper, onion, and pimento. Add mayonnaise, paprika, lemon juice, salt and pepper. Mix well. Add to your favorite green salad. Toss. Extra dressing will keep well in refrigerator for several days. Makes 1½ cups.

Apples, Brie & Chocolate

Pasta, Rice, Etc.

There's nothing quite like an Eagle Harbor sunset in Door County.

Wild Rice Casserole

1½ cups wild rice
6-8 slices bacon
1 onion, chopped
4 teaspoons salt
¼ teaspoon pepper
2 beaten egg yolks
1 cup cream
½ cups shredded carrots

Wash wild rice in cold water. Cook in boiling water for 30 minutes or until tender. Fry bacon and onion until brown. Add salt, pepper, egg yolks, cream, and carrots to bacon and onion. Add this mixture to rice and put in greased baking dish. Dot with butter. Cover and bake at 375° for one hour. Yield: 6-8 servings.

A Taste of Home

Chinese-Style Hamburger Casserole

1 pound hamburger
2 medium onions, chopped
1 cup celery, sliced
1 can mushroom soup or
  cream of chicken soup
1 cup warm water
½ cup rice, uncooked
¼ cup soy sauce
¼ teaspoon pepper

Brown hamburger. Add remaining ingredients. Cover and bake for about 1½ hours at 325°. Uncover the last half hour. Shoestring potatoes may be sprinkled on top. Almonds and mushrooms are good additions to this casserole.

Cooking in West Denmark

Rice Pilaf

Delicious with chicken.

¾ cup chopped onion
1 cup chopped celery
1 cup raw rice
¼ cup butter or margarine
1 package dry chicken
  noodle soup mix
2¼ cups water
1 teaspoon salt
¼ teaspoon pepper
¼ teaspoon sage
¼ teaspoon thyme

Sauté onion, celery, and rice in butter until rice is golden brown. Stir in remaining ingredients. Cover. Simmer 15 minutes, or until liquid is absorbed. Remove from heat. Let stand 10 minutes before serving. Serves 4-6.

Country Cupboard

Kenny the Trucker's Casserole

1½ pounds ground beef
Chopped onion
1 can tomato soup

1 can ABC's vegetable soup
1 can water
⅔ cup uncooked rice

Brown ground beef and onion. Add soup and water to ground beef. Bring to boil. Put rice in bottom of greased baking dish. Pour ground beef mixture over rice and stir. Cover pan and bake at 375° for about 45 minutes.

Taste and See

Brown Rice Pilaf with Kiwi Fruit

Even kids will enjoy this high-fiber, low-fat, low-sodium side dish with its hint of sweetness.

1⅓ cups water
1⅓ cups unsweetened
  apple juice
1 cup uncooked long-grain
  brown rice
2 tablespoons currants or
  raisins
¼ teaspoon ground cinnamon

⅔ cup peeled, coarsely
  chopped kiwi fruit (about 2)
¼ cup diced unpeeled red
  apple
¼ teaspoon grated orange
  rind

Combine first 3 ingredients in a large saucepan. Bring to a boil; add currants and cinnamon, stirring well. Reduce heat; cover and cook rice 45 minutes without lifting cover or according to package directions omitting salt. Remove from heat, and add remaining ingredients; toss gently. Yield: 4 cups.

Per Serving: Cal 125 (6.0% from fat); Fat 0.8g (Sat 0.2g); Chol 0mg; Fiber 1.8g; Sod 4mg. Diabetic Exchange: 1 starch + ¼ fruit.

Here's To Your Heart: Cooking Smart

Tuna and Rice

1 cup chopped onion
10 ounces frozen peas
  and carrots
1 can cream of chicken
  soup, reduced sodium,
  reduced fat
1½ cups skim milk
1 (6¼-ounce) can tuna in
  water, drained
1½ cups cooked rice
2 tablespoons fresh parsely or
  2 teaspoons dry

Combine onion, peas and carrots, cream of chicken soup, and skim milk in a 2-quart pan. Bring to a boil and stir in tuna, rice, and parsley. Bake in 350° oven in 2-quart casserole for 20 minutes. Makes 4 servings.

Per Serving: Cal 283 (19.2% from fat); Fat 6g (Sat 1.7g); Chol 19mg; Fiber 4.7g; Sod 240mg. Diabetic Exchange: 2 meat + 1 starch + 1 skim milk.

Here's To Your Heart: Cooking Smart

Tuna Noodle Delight

"Using your noodle" in more ways than one, this tuna dish is enjoyed by everyone who tries it. It makes a large amount.

1 cup sour cream
1 can celery soup
1 (8-ounce) package fine
  noodles, cooked
1 large can chunk tuna
1 (4-ounce) can mushrooms
1 (4-ounce) jar pimientos
2 teaspoons dry onion soup
  mix
2 tablespoons soy sauce
1 cup grated Cheddar cheese

Mix sour cream with soup. Add rest of ingredients and mix. Put in buttered casserole dish. Bake at 325° for 45 minutes.

Sparks from the Kitchen

Kluski Dumplings

1 cup flour
¼ cup milk
¼ teaspoon salt
2 eggs

Mix all ingredients together, like a heavy pancake batter. Drop off tip of teaspoon in boiling salted water. (Use a Spatzle maker for smaller dumplings.) Dumplings come to the top when done. Remove with slotted spoon. Delicious in chicken soup.

Sharing Our Best

Fettuccine Ala Alfredo

1 cup heavy cream
½ cup butter, softened
Salt and pepper, to taste

1 (12-ounce) package
fettuccine noodles, cooked
and drained
1 cup Parmesan cheese, grated

In a heavy saucepan, over medium heat, bring the cream and butter to a bare simmer. Remove from the burner, but keep warm. Heat a large serving bowl for tossing the noodles. Pour in the cream-butter mixture; add the cooked, drained noodles, cheese, salt and pepper. Toss gently until noodles are coated and serve immediately.

Note: Can substitute skim milk for cream and light butter for regular, and my family still loves it.

Fifth Avenue Food Fare

Alpler Macaroni

6 medium potatoes, peeled
and cut into
bite-sized pieces
2 cups macaroni
Chopped onions

1 cup grated Swiss cheese
¼ cup butter
Paprika
½ pint cream

Cook potato pieces in salted water with more water than usual for 8-10 minutes, then add 2 cups of macaroni and cook together until macaroni is done. Pour into colander to drain.

Spray a 13x9-inch baking dish with nonstick spray (or butter it). Add half of potato-macaroni mixture, then ½ cup grated cheese (or as much as you like), then the rest of the potato mixture and another ½ cup cheese. Top with onion (as much as you like) sautéed in butter. Sprinkle with paprika. Pour cream over the top. Cover and bake in 350° oven for 20-30 minutes or until heated through.

Old World Swiss Family Recipes

 The tallest grandfather clock in the world can be seen at Svoboda Industries, Kewaunee, where you can watch artisans work.

Penne Roberto

Penne Roberto is Chef Fedorko's favorite recipe because it is simple, light, fresh and easy to prepare at home.

1 large yellow onion, finely diced	Salt and freshly ground pepper to taste
4 large tablespoons chopped garlic	6 ounces pancetta (Italian bacon) or any good-quality bacon
6 tablespoons extra-virgin olive oil, divided	10 ounces dry Penne pasta
12 Roma tomatoes, peeled and roughly chopped	4 ounces Wisconsin Parmesan cheese, grated
½ cup chopped, fresh basil or 4 tablespoons dry basil, divided	

Sweat onions and garlic in 4 tablespoons oil to flavor oil. When onions are translucent, add tomatoes and a little over ½ of the basil. Cook approximately 20 minutes and season with salt and freshly ground pepper.

Cook bacon until crisp and all fat is rendered; drain. Cook pasta in large amount of boiling, salted water until al dente; chill under cold, running water to stop cooking process.

When you're ready to serve, run pasta under hot water to heat; allow to drain. In large serving bowl, mix remaining oil and basil, toss with pasta, and season with salt and pepper. Top with tomato sauce, bacon, and freshly grated Parmesan cheese. Yields 4 servings.

Recipe from Ristoranté Brissago, Lake Geneva.

Our Best Cookbook 2

Pasta with Broccoli

1 head fresh broccoli
4 tablespoons extra virgin
   olive oil
2 tablespoons minced
   garlic
1 teaspoon hot red pepper
   flakes

1 pound pasta (penne rigatti)
Salt and pepper, to taste
4 cups boiling water
1 cup Asiago or Parmesan
   cheese

Cut flowerettes from broccoli into 2-inch lengths. Peel stems and cut into bite-size pieces about ½-inch thick. Rinse broccoli in cold water. Heat olive oil in large non-stick pot with cover. Add garlic and red pepper flakes. When garlic begins to sizzle (do not burn!), throw in uncooked pasta and stir to coat with oil. Add broccoli, salt and pepper and stir. Add 4 cups boiling water and stir. When water returns to a boil, reduce heat, cover, and cook about 10 minutes or until pasta is done. Stir occasionally to be sure pasta does not stick. Add more water if necessary. Dish should be moist. Serve hot with lots of grated cheese.

Marquette University High School
Mother's Guild Cookbook

Stuffed Shells

1 (12-ounce) package
   jumbo shells
1½ - 2 pounds hamburger
1 (20-ounce) jar Prego
   Spaghetti Sauce with
   Mushrooms

2 eggs, beaten
1 (16-ounce) carton small curd
   cottage cheese
2 cups Mozzarella cheese

Cook shells according to package directions; drain. In a large skillet, cook hamburger; drain. Pour ½ jar sauce into 13x9-inch baking dish. In a large bowl, mix together hamburger, eggs, cottage cheese, and Mozzarella cheese. Fill shells with above mixture and place in baking dish. Pour remaining sauce over shells. Sprinkle with Mozzarella cheese. Bake in a 350° oven for about 30 minutes. Refrigerate leftovers.

Look What's Cookin' at Wal-Mart

Fat-Free Pasta Primavera

1 cup sliced zucchini
½ cup sliced mushrooms
¼ cup sliced onion
½ cup sliced red/green
  pepper
½ cup green beans, cut in
  ½-inch diagonal pieces
1 rounded tablespoon flour
1 (13-ounce) can evaporated
  skimmed milk

½ teaspoon salt
¼ teaspoon pepper
1 tablespoon sliced fresh
  basil
½ cup chicken broth
½ cup white wine
Your favorite pasta
Parmesan cheese

Spary frying pan with Pam. Sauté first 5 ingredients 4-5 minutes and remove from heat. Meanwhile, spread flour in another large skillet. Add can of evaporated skim milk and stir. Do not boil as milk will separate. Add salt, pepper, and fresh basil. When liquid reaches a nice sauce consistency, add chicken broth, wine, and sautéed vegetables, and serve over hot cooked pasta. Sprinkle lightly with Parmesan cheese. Serves 4.

Seasoned with Love

Cavatini

1 pound hamburger
1 large jar Ragu Spaghetti
  Sauce
1½ packages small-size
  macaroni

1½ cups Mozzarella cheese,
  grated
1 small can Parmesan
  cheese

Brown hamburger and drain; add sauce. Cook macaroni; drain and add to hamburger. Stir in ½ cup Mozzarella cheese and all the Parmesan cheese. Pour into baking dish and add remaining Mozzarella as a topping. Brown under broiler until cheese melts.

Cardinal Country Cooking

Carson Park's statue of "Hammerin' Hank" Aaron honors the home run king who first batted for the Eau Claire Bears in 1952.

Spaghetti Pie

You might want to make two pies and freeze one.

6 ounces spaghetti (can use fettucini)
2 tablespoons butter
⅓ cup Parmesan cheese
2 well beaten eggs
1 pound ground beef or bulk Italian sausage
½ cup chopped onion
¼ cup chopped green pepper

1 (8-ounce) can tomatoes, cut up
1 (6-ounce) can tomato paste
1 teaspoon sugar
1 tablespoon dried oregano, crushed
¼ teaspoon salt
1 (8-ounce) carton cottage cheese, drained
½ cup shredded Mozzarella cheese

Cook spaghetti (you should have 3¼ cups). Stir butter into hot spaghetti. Stir in cheese and eggs. Form mixture into a crust in a buttered 10-inch pie dish.

In skillet cook meat, onion, and green pepper until meat is brown and vegetables are tender. Drain off excess fat. Stir in undrained tomatoes, tomato paste, sugar, oregano, and salt.

Spread cottage cheese over bottom of crust. Fill with tomato mixture. Cover with foil and chill 2-24 hours. Bake at 350° covered for 60 minutes. Uncover, sprinkle with Mozzarella cheese. Bake 5 minutes more, until cheese melts.

Thank Heaven for Home Made Cooks

Do-Ahead Dried Beef Casserole

3 tablespoons onion, diced
3 tablespoons green pepper, diced
¼ cup celery, diced
1 (4-ounce) can mushrooms
2 tablespoons butter
1 (10½-ounce) can cream of mushroom soup
1 cup milk
1 cup Cheddar cheese, grated
1 cup uncooked macaroni
1 (5-ounce) package dried beef

Sauté onion, green pepper, celery, and mushrooms in butter. Stir soup until creamy. Add milk, cheese, sautéed vegetables, uncooked macaroni, and dried beef. Pour into greased 2-quart baking dish. Refrigerate for 3-4 hours or overnight. Bake, uncovered at 350° for 45 minutes or until done.

Cardinal Country Cooking

Polish Noodles and Cabbage

¼ cup butter
½ cup peeled and chopped yellow onions
4 cups chopped or thinly sliced cabbage
1 teaspoon caraway seeds
½ teaspoon salt
½ teaspoon ground pepper
1 (8-ounce) package noodles
½ cup sour cream (optional)

Melt butter in large skillet. Add onion; sauté until transparent. Add cabbage and sauté 5 minutes, or until tender, but still crisp. Stir in caraway seeds, salt and pepper. Meanwhile, cook noodles in salted water as directed on package. Do not overcook. Drain well. Stir noodles into cabbage, and add sour cream. Cook 5 minutes longer, stirring frequently. Serves 4-6.

St. Frederick Parish Centennial Recipe Collection

Kenosha's Harmony Hall is the national headquarters for the Society for the Preservation and Encouragement of Barbershop Singing in America.

Cabbage Lasagna

1 large head cabbage	½ teaspoon Italian seasoning
1 pound ground turkey (or beef or veal)	1 (15-ounce) can tomato sauce (1½ cups)
1 medium onion	⅔ cup cottage cheese
½ large green pepper	1 (8-ounce) can mushrooms (optional)
1 teaspoon salt	
½ teaspoon pepper	4 ounces Mozzarella cheese
1 teaspoon garlic powder	2 teaspoons parsley flakes

Boil cabbage until leaves peel apart. Sauté meat with onion, green pepper, salt, pepper, garlic powder, and Italian seasoning. Add tomato sauce. Blend cottage cheese in blender until smooth. Divide sauce in 3 equal parts. Put ⅓ in bottom of 9x13-inch pan sprayed with Pam. Put layer of cabbage (½ head) into pan, then ⅓ of sauce, mushrooms, and cottage cheese mixture. Repeat cabbage and sauce. Sprinkle Mozzarella cheese and parsley flakes over top. Bake at 350° for 35 minutes. Let stand 5 minutes before cutting. Makes 6 servings.

Favorite Recipes of the Wisconsin NFO

Pork-Sauerkraut Casserole

2 pounds pork steak, cubed	1 (4-ounce) can mushrooms
1 package dry onion soup mix	1 (8-ounce) package wide noodles, cooked
1 can mushroom soup	1 can French-fried onion rings (optional)
3 cups water	
1 large can well-drained sauerkraut	

Brown meat. Add onion soup mix, mushroom soup, and water. Simmer 2 hours. Add to meat mixture the sauerkraut, mushrooms, and noodles. Let stand for 3 hours or overnight. Bake one hour at 350°. Top with onion rings during last 10 minutes of baking time. Makes 8 good servings.

Centennial Cookbook

Gisela's Turner Hall Kaesenkuchen
(Cheese Pie)

6 eggs
2 cups cream
1 teaspoon salt
¼ cup grated onion

3 cups grated Swiss cheese
(not too sharp)
1 (9-inch) unbaked pie shell

Preheat oven to 400°. Beat eggs with cream, salt, and onion; fold in cheese and pour into pie shell. Bake at 400° for 10 minutes, then at 350° for 35 minutes. Serve hot, garnished with fresh fruit.

Note: This is a unique and popular entrée available in Monroe at Turner Hall, the home and headquarters of the Monroe Swiss Singers.

Old World Swiss Family Recipes

Three Cheese Enchiladas

1½ cups shredded
  Monterey Jack cheese
1½ cups shredded
  Cheddar cheese
1 (3-ounce) package
  cream cheese, softened
1 cup Picante sauce (mild)

1 medium red pepper, diced
½ cup green onions
1 teaspoon cumin
8 flour tortillas (7-8 inch)
Shredded lettuce
Chopped tomato

Combine one cup of the Monterey Jack, one cup Cheddar, cream cheese, ¼ cup picante sauce, red pepper, onions, and cumin; mix well. Spoon ¼ cup cheese mixture down center of each tortilla; roll and place seam-side-down in greased 9x13-inch baking dish. Spoon remaining picante sauce evenly over enchiladas; cover with remaining cheese. Bake in 350° oven, 20 minutes or until hot. Top with lettuce and tomato and serve with additional picante sauce.

What's Cooking in St. Francis

Carol's Crustless Mexican Quiche

5 eggs, beaten until light
  and lemon colored
½ teaspoon baking powder
¼ cup flour
¼ teaspoon salt
1 cup small curd cottage
  cheese

½ pound combination Mon-
  terey and Cheddar cheese
¼ cup butter, melted
1 can diced green chilies
Tomatoes (optional)
Sour cream and chives
Black olives, sliced
Salsa

Mix first 7 ingredients together. Stir in the green chilies. Spray
an 8- or 9-inch baking dish and pour in quiche. Bake at 350° for
about 45 minutes. Halfway through, you can put tomato slices
on top or cherry tomatoes, cut in half. Top should be lightly
browned and center firm. Garnish with a dollop of sour cream
and chives and sliced black olives. Serve with salsa on the side.
This is great and the chilies do not make it hot.

Cooking at Thimbleberry Inn

Crustless Quiche

4 eggs
½ pint light sour cream
½ pint small curd cottage
  cheese
½ cup grated Parmesan
  cheese

4 tablespoons flour
1 teaspoon onion powder
½ pound shaved ham or crab
2 cups Monterey Jack cheese

Mix together eggs, sour cream, cottage cheese, Parmesan cheese,
flour, and onion powder. Stir in ham or crab and cheese. Pour
into 9- or 10-inch quiche dish. Bake at 350° until center is firm
(approximately 45 minutes). Let set for 5 minutes.

Seasoned with Love

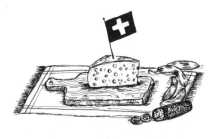

Bubble Up Pizza

Kids love this pizza.

**3 (7.5-ounce) cans
buttermilk biscuits
1½ cups spaghetti sauce,
any flavor
3 cups Mozzarella cheese,
shredded**

**1 clove garlic pressed or
garlic powder
Optional toppings: Onions,
olives, mushrooms, bacon,
ham, peppers, etc.**

Preheat oven to 375°. In large bowl, put in biscuits that have been cut in quarters. Stir in one cup of sauce and 2 cups of cheese. Add garlic. Add any optional toppings desired. Spread in 9x13-inch pan. Pour remaining sauce and cheese on top. Bake for 30 minutes or until sides are golden brown.

A Collection of Recipes

Excellent Pesto

**1½ cups packed fresh
sweet basil leaves
⅓ cup fresh grated
combination Parmesan
and Romano cheese
½ cup extra virgin olive oil**

**¼ teaspoon salt
⅛ teaspoon fresh ground
black pepper
1½ large cloves garlic
¼ - ½ cups chopped pine nuts
or walnuts (optional)**

Place all ingredients except nuts into food processor bowl. Blend with blade attachment till smooth. Stir in nuts. Serve with pasta, as a spread, etc.

Variations: Lemon Basil Pesto—substitute lemon basil leaves. Cinnamon Basil Pesto—substitute cinnamon basil leaves.

The Madison Herb Society Cookbook

Seafood

Sea kayaking. Apostle Islands.

Baked Fillets of Fish

1½ pounds walleye fillets
  (frozen works, but get out
  there and catch 'em
  fresh for best flavor)

½ cup dry white wine
1 cup fresh mushroom slices
1 small onion, sliced
1 tablespoon lemon juice

Defrost fillets if using frozen. Preheat oven to 350°. Place fish fillets in lightly-greased baking dish. Bake 10-15 minutes or until fish flakes easily if you poke at it a little with a fork. Remove fish to serving plate. Put wine in a small skillet, and cook to reduce until you only have half as much as you started with. Add mushroom slices, onion, and lemon juice, and heat. Pour over fish and serve with lemon wedges.

Marketplace Recipes Volume II

Deviled Fish

2-3 haddock or cod fillets
1 (8-ounce) package cream
  cheese
2 tablespoons mayonnaise
2 tablespoons milk

1 tablespoon onion soup mix
1 tablespoon lemon juice
1-2 teaspoons tarragon
1 teaspoon Dijon-style
  mustard

TOPPING:
1½ cups bread crumbs
½ cup Parmesan cheese

1 cup snipped parsley
1½ teaspoons paprika

Prepare fish by cutting large fillets into 3 pieces; set aside. Score fish (as you would a ham) ⅓ of thickness of fillet. Soften cream cheese. Blend in the remaining ingredients. Place fish in shallow baking dish. Coat each piece of fish with cream cheese mixture and bake in 350° oven for 12-15 minutes or until fillets flake. Sprinkle fillets with topping and return to oven until topping is golden brown.

Note: Fish fillet starting size approximately 3x9x1½ inches thick. Also great with orange roughie. Adjust baking times and do not score.

Cooking with the Lioness Club

Beer Batter Fish

1 pound fish fillets
½ cup Mix
⅓ cup lemon juice

⅔ cup beer
1 cup vegetable oil

MIX:

1½ cups unsifted flour
2¼ teaspoons baking
    powder

¾ teaspoon baking soda
1½ teaspoons salt

Place fish on paper towels; pat dry. Coat fish with ½ cup Mix. In large bowl, combine remaining mixture, lemon juice, and beer (this will foam). Stir until consistency of pancake batter. In large skillet, heat oil over medium heat. Dip fish into batter; fry until golden brown on both sides. Drain on paper towels.

Dr. Martin Luther Church
100th Anniversary Cookbook

Seafood Creole Style

3 tablespoons salad oil
¼ cup all-purpose flour
2 large celery stalks, diced
1 medium green pepper, diced
1 medium onion, diced
1 (28-ounce) can tomatoes
⅓ cup minced parsley
2½ teaspoons sugar

2 teaspoons salt
¾ teaspoon chili powder
¼ teaspoon hot pepper sauce
1 pound frozen cod fillets, partially frozen
1 (6-7-ounce) package frozen shelled and deveined shrimp

In 5-quart Dutch oven over medium-high heat, into hot salad oil, gradually stir flour; cook, stirring constantly, until flour is dark brown (mixture will be thick). Add celery, green pepper, and onion; cook 10 minutes or until vegetables are lightly browned, stirring constantly.

Add tomatoes with their liquid, parsley, sugar, salt, chili powder, and hot pepper sauce; heat to boiling. Reduce heat to low; cover and simmer 20 minutes to blend flavors, stirring occasionally.

Meanwhile, with sharp knife, cut fish lengthwise in half, then cut each half crosswise into 6 chunks. Add fish and shrimp to sauce in Dutch oven. Over medium heat, heat to boiling. Reduce heat to low, cover and simmer 12-15 minutes until fish flakes easily when tested with a fork and shrimp turn pink. Makes 6 servings.

Seasoned with Love

Seafood Lasagna

SEAFOOD SAUCE:

1 cup chopped onions
12 ounces sliced mushrooms
⅓ cup butter
¼ cup flour
2 cups whole milk
⅓ cup dry vermouth

16 ounces frozen shrimp
8 ounces crabmeat (imitation)
½ teaspoon salt
¼ teaspoon Lawry's salt
⅓ teaspoon black pepper
Dash cayenne pepper

Sauté onions and mushrooms in butter until just tender. Remove from heat and whisk in flour until smooth. Return to heat and cook several minutes. Gradually add milk, then wine and simmer until flour taste has disappeared. Fold in the shrimp and crabmeat which has had all moisture removed. Season with salts and peppers.

CHEESE SAUCE:

1 (8-ounce) package cream
  cheese
1½ cups cottage cheese
1 beaten egg

1 teaspoon basil
½ teaspoon salt
⅛ teaspoon black pepper
Dash cayenne pepper

With electric mixer or food processor, combine cream and cottage cheese, egg and seasonings until smooth.

9 lasagna noodles, cooked
12 ounces grated Mozzarella
¾ cup grated Parmesan

¾ cup grated Cheddar
Extra shrimp for garnish
¼ cup chopped parsley

Place a small amount of Seafood Sauce in bottom of a deep 9x13-inch greased lasagna pan. Layer in order: noodles, Cheese Sauce, Mozzarella, Seafood Sauce, Parmesan cheese, and Cheddar Cheese. Repeat layers ending with 3rd layer of noodles, Seafood Sauce, Parmesan cheese, and Cheddar Cheese. Arrange extra shrimp for garnish on top. Bake at 350° for 45 minutes. Allow to stand 10 minutes before cutting into squares. Sprinkle with parsley. Serves 12.

All in Good Taste II

 Schlitz coined the slogan "The Beer That Made Milwaukee Famous" in 1872.

Grilled Smoked Salmon
With Fresh Dill Caper Mustard

Do try flavoring this grilled salmon with pre-soaked hardwood chips. Somehow the wood smoke adds heartiness to an otherwise delicate salmon. Chef/owner Jim Jensen (The Vintage, Wisconsin Rapids) suggests that this dish could be used as an entreé as well as an appetizer.

GRILLED SALMON:

**4 salmon steaks or fillets
(4 ounces each)
½ teaspoon salt or to taste
¼ teaspoon freshly ground
black pepper**

**5 or 6 large hardwood chips,
soaked in water for 10
minutes**

Prepare grill to a medium temperature. Place pre-soaked wood chips on top of hot coals in the center of grill. Sprinkle surface of fillets lightly with salt and pepper, if desired and spray surfaces with vegetable oil spray. Place salmon on grill around edge of wood chips. Cover, close vents to avoid flame-ups, and grill without turning until cooked, about 8-9 minutes. Flesh should be opaque throughout.

DILL CAPER MUSTARD:

**½ cup Dijon-style mustard
½ cup olive oil
1 tablespoon capers
2 tablespoons fresh dill,
minced or 1 tablespoon
dried dill weed**

**3 small cloves minced garlic
⅛ teaspoon freshly ground
black pepper
Fresh lemon slices—garnish
Fresh sprigs of dill—garnish**

While salmon cooks, make sauce by whisking mustard in small bowl. Slowly whisk in oil in a thin stream until oil is all absorbed in the emulsion. Mix in capers, dill weed, garlic, and pepper. Arrange salmon on plate, serve with a dollop (2 tablespoons) of Dill Caper Mustard and garnish with lemon slices or fresh sprigs of dill, if desired.

Encore Wisconsin

Jacques Junque

3 tablespoons olive oil
½ cup onion, chopped
½ cup green pepper, chopped
1 cup shrimp, peeled and deveined
1 pound scallops
3 lobster tails, shelled and diced
½ pound grouper or other firm fish
2 cups oysters

2 teaspoons marjoram
1 teaspoon chevil
1 teaspoon celery seed
2 teaspoons salt
5-6 grinds pepper
1 cup clam juice
2 cups Chablis
1 pint light cream
2 teaspoons dry mustard
2 tablespoons arrowroot or cornstarch

Heat oil in large skillet over medium heat. Sauté onion and green pepper. Add seafood and sprinkle with herbs, celery seed, salt, and pepper. Add clam juice, wine and cream. Simmer 5 minutes, stirring occasionally. Put mustard and arrowroot in a cup. Add ½ cup sauce from pan. Blend and return to pan, stirring until thick. Do not boil. Serve over rice. Makes 10 servings.

Seasoned with Love

Shrimp Stroganoff

1 (12-ounce) package fettucini
2 tablespoons butter
2 tablespoons chopped onion
¾ pound fresh shrimp, peeled

1 can cream of shrimp soup
½ cup milk
½ cup sour cream
2 tablespoons chopped fresh parsley
½ teaspoon paprika
Salt and pepper to taste

Cook pasta according to package directions. Meanwhile, in a large skillet, melt butter; add onion and cook until tender. Add shrimp; cook 2-3 minutes, stirring constantly, until shrimp begin to turn pink. Blend in soup and milk; heat thoroughly. Stir in sour cream, parsley, and paprika. Season to taste with salt and pepper. Do not boil. Serve over hot pasta. Makes 2-4 servings.

Sharing Our Best

Shrimp Scampi

3 pounds large shrimp (16-20 per pound)
2 sticks butter
1 cup olive oil
2 tablespoons lemon juice
½ cup shallots or scallions, chopped fine
2 tablespoons finely chopped garlic
2 teaspoons salt
Fresh ground black pepper
½ cup fresh parsley, finely chopped
1 lemon, cut into wedges

Shell the shrimp, being careful not to remove the last segment of shell or tail. With small, sharp knife, slit each shrimp down the back and lift out black or white intestinal vein. Wash shrimp under cold water and pat thoroughly dry with paper towels. Preheat broiler to highest temperature.

In a shallow, flameproof baking dish or pan, just large enough for one layer of shrimp, melt butter over low heat, being careful not to let it brown. Stir in olive oil, lemon juice, shallots, garlic, salt, and a few twists of pepper. Add shrimp and turn them in butter and oil until glistening on all sides. Broil 3-4 minutes. Do not overcook.

Transfer shrimp to heated serving platter. Pour sauce from pan over shrimp and sprinkle with chopped parsley. Garnish with lemon wedges and serve. Serves 8-10.

Wisconsin's Best

Jambogumby

¼ cup butter
1 cup chopped onion
1 cup chopped green or
  red pepper or combination
2 cloves garlic
½ teaspoon thyme
½ teaspoon oregano
1 bay leaf

1 (28-ounce) can stewed
  tomatoes
⅛ teaspoon cayenne
½ teaspoon chili powder
1 (15-ounce) can tomato sauce
1 pound hot sausage (Italian
  or Andouille)
1½ pounds raw shrimp

Melt butter in saucepan and sauté onion and pepper until tender. Add garlic, thyme, oregano, bay leaf, tomatoes, cayenne, chili powder, and tomato sauce. Simmer covered for 15 minutes. Meanwhile sauté sausage until lightly browned and prick to extract the fat from the sausage. Cut into one-inch pieces and add to the pot. Continue to cook for another 15 minutes. Add cleaned raw shrimp and continue cooking for about 5 minutes. Remove bay leaf. Serve over cooked rice. Garnish with fresh-cut onion tops or chives. Makes 6 servings.

Apples, Brie & Chocolate

Macaroni Fish Loaf

1 (8-ounce) package
  macaroni
2 tablespoons chopped
  parsley
1 medium onion, chopped
1 can mushroom soup

1 can tomato sauce
1 teaspoon salt
2 eggs, slightly beaten
2 cups flaked salmon
10 stuffed olives, sliced
½ cup grated cheese

Cook and drain macaroni. Combine parsley, onion, soup, sauce, salt, and eggs. Mix fish and macaroni; pour soup mixture over. Place olive slices in bottom of greased 10x5x3-inch (or loaf) pan. Cover with grated cheese. Carefully put macaroni mixture in pan. Bake at 375° for 50-60 minutes. Serve hot.

Look What's Cooking at C.A.M.D.E.N

Chopstick Tuna

1 can cream of mushroom soup	1 (6-ounce) can tuna
¼ cup water	1 cup sliced celery
1 (3-ounce) can chow mein noodles	½ cup salted toasted cashews
	¼ cup chopped onions
	Dash of pepper

Combine soup and water. Add one cup noodles, tuna, celery, cashews, onions, and pepper. Toss lightly. Place in ungreased 10x6x1½-inch baking dish. Sprinkle remaining noodles over top. Bake 15 minutes at 375°.

Unbearably Good! Sharing Our Best

When the Packers defeated Dallas at Lambeau Field on December 31, 1967 (the temperature was -13 with a wind-chill factor of -48), it earned them a trip to Super Bowl I and they won. With a capacity of 60,790, Lambeau Field has been consistently sold out for home games since 1960. Vince Lombardi, their renowned coach for nine years, led them to many victories.

Vegetables

Summerfest, an 11-day music festival, is one of over fifteen festivals held along Milwaukee's lakefront. Milwaukee has come to be known as the City of Festivals.

Beer Baked Beans

1 (32-ounce) can baked beans
1 cup beer
½ cup brewed coffee
½ cup chopped tomato
¾ cup chopped onion
3 frankfurters, cut in 1-inch diagonal pieces
1 tablespoon horseradish
½ cup ketchup
½ cup molasses

Place all ingredients in oven-proof dish and mix well. Bake at 325° until hot, approximately one hour, stirring occasionally. If beans appear to be drying out, add small amount of additional beer. Serves 6-8.

Drink Your Beer & Eat It Too

Crockpot Beans

1 (16-ounce) can kidney beans, drained
2 (16-ounce) cans pinto beans, drained
1 (15-ounce) can unsalted tomatoes
2 large green peppers, chopped
1 large onion, chopped
1 teaspoon oregano leaves
½ teaspoon ground cumin
1 teaspoon sage
¾ teaspoon pepper
Water to cover beans

Combine ingredients in a slow cooker. Cook on HIGH for 6-8 hours. Serves 4-6.

Per Serving: Cal 192 (4.3% from fat); Fat 0.9g (Sat 0.2g); Chol 0mg; Fiber 11.6g; Sod 702mg. Diabetic Exchange: 2 Starch + 1 vegetable.

Here's To Your Heart: Cooking Smart

Cowboy Beans

4 bacon strips, chopped
1 large onion, chopped
3 tablespoons ketchup
1 teaspoon garlic salt
1 teaspoon chili powder
½ teaspoon ground cumin
¼ teaspoon dried red
** pepper flakes, optional**

1 bay leaf
1 (16-ounce) can whole
** tomatoes with liquid**
** (pureéd in blender)**
3 (15-ounce) cans pinto
** beans, drained**
2 tablespoons brown sugar
1 tablespoon yellow mustard

Lightly brown bacon in a heavy 3-quart saucepan or Dutch oven. Add onion and cook until transparent. Stir in remaining ingredients. Cook over medium-low heat for one hour, covered, stirring often so they do not stick to pan or burn. Add water if too thick.

Fifth Avenue Food Fare

Meatless Chili

2 tablespoons Mazola corn
** oil**
1¼ cups chopped onion
2 cloves garlic
2 tablespoons chili powder
¼ teaspoon dried basil
** leaves**
¼ teaspoon dried oregano
** leaves**

¼ teaspoon ground cumin
2 cups diced zucchini
1 cup diced carrots
2 pounds tomatoes, cut in
** eights**
1 (20-ounce) can chickpeas,
** drained**
1 (16-ounce) can kidney beans
** (undrained)**

In 5-quart saucepan, heat oil over medium heat. Add next 6 ingredients. Cook, stirring, 5 minutes or until onion is tender. Add zucchini and carrots. Cook, stirring, 1-2 minutes. Stir in remaining ingredients. Bring to a boil. Reduce heat and simmer 30-35 minutes. Makes 6 servings.

Pelican Lake Women's Civic Club

The "Father of the Automobile" is Rev. John Carhart of Racine, who built a steam-powered buggy in 1871.

Zucchini Surprise

½ cup chopped onion
1 cup Bisquick baking mix
½ cup Parmesan cheese
2 tablespoons parsley flakes
½ teaspoon salt
½ teaspoon oregano

½ teaspoon seasoned salt
½ cup vegetable oil
4 eggs, slightly beaten
Dash pepper and garlic
3 cups thinly sliced, unpeeled
 zucchini (2 medium-sized)

Mix together all ingredients except zucchini. Stir in zucchini. Place in greased 9x13-inch baking dish. Bake uncovered at 350° for 20-25 minutes or until golden brown. Makes 8-10 servings.

50 Years of Regal Recipes

Vegetables in Wisconsin Beer Batter

1⅓ cups flour
2 tablespoons Parmesan
 cheese
1 tablespoon parsley
1 teaspoon salt
Dash garlic
1 (12-ounce) can Wisconsin
 beer, at room temperature
 and flat

2 eggs, separated
Green peppers, cauliflower,
 onion, artichoke hearts,
 zucchini or broccoli,
 cut into bite-sized pieces
Oil for deep frying

In a large bowl, combine flour, cheese, parsley, salt, and garlic. Stir in beer and egg yolks. Beat egg whites until stiff and fold into beer mixture. Dip vegetable pieces into batter. Heat oil to 375° and fry a few pieces of batter-dipped vegetables at a time in oil until golden. Drain on paper toweling. Serve immediately.

License to Cook Wisconsin Style

Wisconsin is known as the beer capital of the US. The world's largest six-pack can be seen at G. Heileman Brewery at La Crosse.

Vegetable Tostadas

2 cups zucchini, thinly
  sliced (1 medium)
4 ounces fresh mushrooms,
  sliced
2 tablespoons chopped
  green pepper
1 cup onion, thinly sliced
  (1 medium large)
¼ cup chopped celery
Nonstick pan spray

4 flour tortillas
½ cup low-fat, low-sodium
  shredded Cheddar cheese
4 tablespoons fat-free sour
  cream
1 tomato, chopped
2 teaspoons hot pepper sauce
  or to taste

Combine vegetables, except tomatoes, in saucepan and simmer 10-12 minutes or microwave on HIGH for 6-8 minutes.

Spray small sauté pan with nonstick spray. Set on medium-high heat. Brown tortillas quickly on both sides and place on cookie sheet. Spoon vegetable mixture on each tortilla and top with cheese. Bake tortillas in 350° oven until cheese melts, about 3-5 minutes. To serve, top with sour cream, chopped tomatoes, and a few dashes of hot pepper sauce. Makes 4 servings.

Hint: You may substitute 4 ounces canned no-salt mushrooms undrained for fresh mushrooms.

Nutritional Analysis Per Serving: Total fat 3.175gm; Sat fat 0.487gm; Chol 0.0mg; Cal from fat 16%; Cal 172; Sod 298.6mg; Carb 31.04gm; Sugar 4.699gm; Prot 6.4767gm.

Spice of Life Cookbook

Eggplant Italienne

1 pound hamburger
1 cup onion, chopped
1 (21-ounce) jar Ragu
   Italian Sauce
1 large eggplant
Mild olive oil

1-2 cups small curd cottage
   cheese
½ pound Mozzarella cheese,
   cubed
Parmesan cheese

Brown meat and onion slightly. Add Ragu Sauce and simmer 10 minutes. Peel and slice eggplant. Put on an oiled cookie sheet and pour oil over so all pieces are well oiled. Brown under broiler, turning each piece. Place in 9x13-inch pan. Add cottage cheese, Mozzarella cheese, and sauce in layers with sauce on top. Bake 30-40 minutes, until bubbly. Serve with Parmesan cheese.

Cherry Berries on a Cloud and More

Acorn Squash and Apples Au Gratin

2 pounds acorn squash
¼ cup butter
½ cup onions, chopped
½ cup mushrooms, chopped
1 Golden Delicious apple
   (cored and sliced)
1 teaspoon garlic, minced

1 tablespoon flour
½ cup white wine
½ cup heavy cream
½ teaspoon salt (to taste)
½ teaspoon pepper (to taste)
4 ounces Swiss cheese (grated)
½ cup toasted bread crumbs

Clean and quarter squash. Boil in water until tender (about 30 minutes). Drain and set aside to cool. Remove peelings when sufficiently cooled to handle.

While squash is cooling, sauté (in butter) onions, mushrooms, apple, and garlic until onions are translucent. Whisk in flour until smooth, then slowly add wine and cream. Bring mixture to a boil. Simmer for about 10 minutes. Season with salt and pepper to taste.

Place peeled squash in small baking dish. Add sauce, top with cheese and bread crumbs. Bake in preheated oven at 350° for about 30 minutes (until cheese is bubbling and crumbs are golden brown.)

Recipe from Jacobi's of Hazelhurstt. Owner and Chef Allan Jacobi.

Wisconsin Cooks with Wisconsin Public Television

Eggplant Hater's Ratatouille

I concocted this when inundated with lots of fresh garden produce. Since I despise egg-plant, this is my own version of ratatouille. It's filthy cheap to make in summer when vegetables are plentiful. It's so good for you, you'd hardly believe it tastes so delicious.

5 tablespoons butter
1 medium zucchini,
** peeled and cut into**
** ½-inch strips**
1 medium green pepper,
** diced**
1 medium onion, cut into
** chunks**
2-3 large fresh tomatoes,
** cut in chunks**

8 ounces fresh mushrooms,
** sliced**
1 (8-ounce) can tomato paste
½ teaspoon garlic powder
1 teaspoon sugar
Pepper to taste
½ - ¾ pound grated
** Mozzarella cheese**

Melt butter in medium saucepan. Add zucchini, green pep-per, onion, tomatoes, and mushrooms. Cover and sauté until soft. Drain off excess liquid. Add ¾ can of tomato paste, garlic powder, sugar, and pepper. (If you like a little kick to it, add crushed hot peppers or Tabasco, to taste). Heat through and serve, covered with grated cheese.

Note: This can be served in one large or several small casseroles as a side dish to meat or fish. Can also be served over spaghetti or cooked spaghetti squash. Ground beef may be added to make a main dish.

Foxy Ladies

Tomato Dish

You'll want this recipe handy toward the end of summer, when fresh-picked tomatoes are available to add their special flavor to this dish.

⅓ cup butter or margarine
½ - 1 teaspoon salt
1 teaspoon sweet basil
¼ teaspoon pepper
½ cup diced celery
½ cup green pepper strips
¼ cup chopped onion

1 cup seasoned stuffing mix or any flavor seasoned croutons
4 tomatoes cut into 8 wedges each
2 teaspoons sugar

Melt butter or margarine. Add seasonings, celery, green pepper, and onion; sauté uncovered until vegetables are crispy tender (3-4 minutes). Add stuffing or croutons; toss. Layer tomatoes on and sprinkle sugar on top. Cover and cook 10 minutes. Serve immediately.

Marketplace Recipes Volume II

Tomato Cheese Pie

1 (7.5-ounce) tube buttermilk biscuits
2-3 large tomatoes, sliced
Sweet basil
Salt and pepper
1 small green pepper, sliced

1 large onion, sliced
1 cup mushrooms, sliced
¼ cup olive oil
1½ cups mayonnaise
1 cup grated Monterey Jack or Mozzarella cheese

Line a deep 10-inch pie dish with biscuits, pressing edges together to form a crust. Place half of tomatoes on biscuits. Season with salt, pepper, and basil. Sauté green pepper, onion, and mushrooms in oil. Drain. Place on top of tomatoes. Add remaining tomatoes. Season again. Combine mayonnaise and cheese and spread over top. Bake at 350° for 40-45 minutes.

All in Good Taste I

 Reader's Digest April 1997 issue cited 50 cities across the US as best places to raise a family. Sheboygan was No. 1, and Kenosha was No. 2. Way to go Wisconsin!

Sweet-Sour Red Cabbage

½ medium head red
  cabbage, shredded
¼ cup butter
½ medium onion, diced
1 tablespoon soy sauce

¼ cup vinegar
¼ cup sugar
1 raw sliced apple
¼ cup water
1 tablespoon flour

Place all ingredients, except flour, in a covered kettle and let simmer for at least an hour. Then stir and sift in the flour to thicken.

Family Fare

Sweet Sour Cabbage

1 (1-pound) can cut
  green beans
3 slices bacon, cut in
  1-inch pieces
½ cup white vinegar
¼ cup sugar

3 tablespoons chopped onion
¾ teaspoon salt
¼ teaspoon pepper
1 medium head cabbage,
  finely shredded

Drain beans; set aside. Fry bacon until crisp. Remove and drain on paper towel. Add to bacon drippings, vinegar, sugar, onion, salt, pepper, and cabbage. Cover and cook 15 minutes. Add beans and heat. Put into serving dish and garnish with bacon pieces.

Pelican Lake Women's Civic Club

German Style Green Beans

4 slices of bacon
2 tablespoons sugar
2 tablespoons cider vinegar

2 (9-ounce) boxes frozen
  green beans, cooked and
  drained

Cook bacon in skillet until crisp, 6-8 minutes. Remove bacon to paper toweling to drain. Pour off fat, reserving 2 tablespoons in skillet. Add sugar and vinegar to skillet. Heat through. Add beans, heat through. Transfer to serving dish. Crumble bacon over the top.

What's Cooking in St. Francis

Spinach Pie

This pie freezes well. It can be made ahead and reheated in the oven or in a microwave oven.

2 (10-ounce) packages
  frozen, chopped
  spinach
2 tablespoons butter
½ cup chopped onion
1 clove garlic, chopped fine
8 ounces (2 cups) grated
  Mozzarella cheese
3 tablespoons butter

3 tablespoons flour
1½ cups milk
1¼ teaspoons salt
¼ teaspoon pepper
Dash nutmeg
Dash dill weed
6 eggs, well beaten
1 (10-inch) or 2 (8-inch)
  pie crusts

TOPPING:
Grated Cheddar cheese
  (about ⅓ cup)

Slices of onion and tomato

Cook spinach as directed on package and press out water. Melt 2 tablespoons butter and sauté onion and garlic. Stir this into the drained spinach. Mix in the Mozzarella cheese.

    Melt 3 tablespoons butter and stir in 3 tablespoons flour. Add milk and cook, stirring constantly until thick. Add the salt and pepper, nutmeg, and dill weed. Stir this into the spinach mixture. Then fold in the beaten eggs. Pour into unbaked pie shells. Bake at 350° for 45-60 minutes (depending on the size of pie shells). During the last 10 minutes of baking, sprinkle grated cheese on top and place slices of onion and tomato decoratively on top of pie.

From Timm's Hill Bed and Breakfast.

Have Breakfast with Us II

Layered Spinach Supreme

1 cup Bisquick Baking Mix
¼ cup milk
2 eggs
¼ cup finely-chopped onion
1 (10-ounce) package frozen chopped spinach, thawed, drained, (or 10 ounces fresh chopped spinach, wilted with hot water)
½ cup grated Parmesan cheese
4 ounces Monterey Jack cheese, cut into ½-inch cubes
1 (12-ounce) carton creamed cottage cheese
½ teaspoon salt
2 cloves garlic, crushed
2 eggs

Heat oven to 375°. Grease baking dish (12x7½x2-inch). Mix baking mix, milk, 2 eggs, onion; beat vigorously for 20 strokes; spread into dish. Mix remaining ingredients; spoon evenly over batter in dish. Bake until set (about 30 minutes); let stand 5 minutes before cutting.

Marketplace Recipes Volume II

New Glarus Cheese and Onion Pie

1½ cups sliced onions
1 tablespoon butter
4 eggs
1 unbaked 9-inch pie shell
1½ cups half-and-half
½ teaspoon salt
¼ teaspoon nutmeg or to taste
⅛ teaspoon pepper
2 cups shredded Wisconsin Swiss or Baby Swiss cheese
1 tablespoon cornstarch

In a medium-sized skillet, sauté onions in butter until transparent, about 5 minutes; set aside. Beat eggs and brush pie shell with a small amount of the eggs. Add half-and-half, salt, nutmeg, and pepper to eggs. Toss cheese with cornstarch; cover bottom of pie shell with onion and cheese. Pour the egg mixture over the cheese and onions. Sprinkle with additional nutmeg if desired. Bake at 400° for 35-40 minutes or until set, browned and puffy. Cool slightly. Cut into wedges. Serves 6.

License to Cook Wisconsin Style

Broccoli Casserole

¼ cup oleo
¼ cup chopped onion
¼ cup chopped celery
½ (10¾-ounce) can cream
   of mushroom soup

⅔ cup uncooked rice
½ (8-ounce) jar Cheez Whiz
1 (10-ounce) package frozen
   chopped broccoli, thawed,
   drained, partially cooked

Preheat oven to 350°. In medium skillet, melt oleo. Add onions and celery and sauté until transparent. Remove from heat and set aside. In medium bowl mix soup, rice, and Cheez Whiz. Add onions and celery and gently add broccoli. Pour into well-greased 2-quart casserole and bake 35-40 minutes. Easy to double this recipe.

A Taste of Home

Sue's Gourmet Broccoli Bake

1 package frozen broccoli
   or fresh broccoli
¼ cup butter or margarine
¼ cup flour
1½ tablespoons chicken
   bouillon granules
½ teaspoon salt

2 cups milk
6 tablespoons butter or
   margarine
⅔ cup hot water
1 (6-ounce) package
   cornbread stuffing mix

Cook broccoli; drain. Place in bottom of buttered 2-quart casserole or cake pan. Melt ¼ cup butter in saucepan over low heat. Add flour, stirring until smooth. Cook one minute, stirring constantly. Stir in bouillon and salt; add milk gradually. Cook over medium heat, stirring constantly, until thickened. Meanwhile, melt 6 tablespoonfuls butter in hot water. Pour over stuffing mix and stir until moistened. Pour white sauce over broccoli and top with stuffing. Bake at 400° for 20-25 minutes. Yield: 8-10 servings.

St. John Evangelical Lutheran Church

Popular Saturday morning radio talk/quiz show, "Whad' Ya Know?" with Michael Feldman is based at station WHA in Madison. WHA is the oldest continually operating radio station in the world—since 1917.

Maple Glazed Carrots

6 medium carrots
3 tablespoons butter

3 tablespoons Wisconsin
 pure maple syrup
½ teaspoon ground ginger

Slice carrots and steam until tender firm. Melt butter. Add maple syrup and ginger to butter. Simmer carrots, uncovered, in this mixture until liquid is reduced and carrots are glazed with sauce.

Wisconsin Pure Maple Syrup Cookbook

Glazed Carrots

1 (14-ounce) package
 frozen baby carrots or
 2 cups fresh
¼ cup unsweetened apple
 juice or apple cider

¼ cup apple jelly
1½ teaspoons Dijon mustard

Place carrots and apple juice in medium nonstick skillet. Bring to a boil. Reduce heat; cover and simmer 7-9 minutes or until carrots are crisp-tender. Uncover; cook over medium heat until liquid evaporates. Stir in jelly and mustard; cook and stir over medium heat until jelly melts and carrots are glazed.
Serves 4.

Per Serving: Cal 85 (6.1% from fat); Fat 0.6g (Sat 0.1g); Chol 0mg; Fiber 2.5g; Sod 78.8mg. Diabetic Exchange: Not recommended.

Here's To Your Heart: Cooking Smart

Tangy Carrot Dish

1½ pounds carrots, peeled
¼ cup water reserved from
  cooking carrots
1 teaspoon onion and juice,
  grated

½ teaspoon yellow mustard
½ cup mayonnaise
¼ cup cheese, grated
½ teaspoon salt
¼ teaspoon pepper

TOPPING:
1 cup fresh bread crumbs
¼ cup butter, melted

½ teaspoon paprika

Slice carrots ½-inch thick. Cook in a small amount of water until crisp-done; drain. Reserve ¼-cup water for sauce. Combine water, onion and juice, mustard, mayonnaise, cheese, salt and pepper. Add carrots and spoon into buttered 2-quart casserole. Combine topping and sprinkle over carrot mixture. Bake at 350° for 20 minutes. Yield: 8 servings.

St. John Evangelical Lutheran Church

Yummy Yams

6-7 yams, cooked and
  chopped
½ cup liquid from
  cooked yams

3 eggs (beaten)
1 stick butter
½ cup brown sugar
½ cup white sugar

TOPPING:
1½ cups graham crackers
  (crushed)

½ stick butter, melted
½ cup pecans, chopped

In a large bowl, combine the first 6 ingredients and mix well. Pour into a greased baking dish. Combine the topping ingredients, mixing until well blended. Spread evenly over yam mixture. Bake at 350° for 45 minutes or until knife inserted comes out clean. Makes 8-10 servings.

Winning Recipes from Wisconsin with Love

Sweet Potato Casserole

6-8 sweet potatoes or yams
  (18 ounces) peeled,
  cooked and mashed
¼ cup margarine
1 teaspoon cinnamon

½ teaspoon nutmeg
2 apples, washed, cored and
  sliced
2 eggs
½ cup raisins

Mix all ingredients together and place in a greased ovenproof casscrole. Top with a little brown sugar. Bake at 350° for 40 minutes.

Cherry Berries on a Cloud and More

Twice-Baked Yams

2 pounds yams (about
  6 medium)
Vegetable oil
¼ cup sour cream
¼ cup milk
2 tablespoons packed
  brown sugar

2 tablespoons butter or
  margarine
⅛ teaspoon salt
2 tablespoons pecans, coarsely
  chopped

Rub yams with oil; prick with fork to allow steam to escape. Bake at 375° until tender, 35-45 minutes. Cut lengthwise; scoop out inside, leaving a thin shell. Mash yams until no lumps remain. Beat in sour cream and milk, then brown sugar, margarine, and salt until light and fluffy. Stir in pecans. Increase oven to 400°. Place shells in ungreased baking dish. Fill shells with mixture. Top each with pecan half. Bake, uncovered, until filling is golden, about 20 minutes.

Sunflowers & Samovars

Asparagus Stuffed Potatoes

4 medium baking potatoes
1-2 tablespoons milk
½ cup sour cream
1 teaspoon onion salt
⅛ teaspoon pepper
1 pound fresh asparagus,
cut into 1-inch pieces
and cooked

4 ounces shredded Cheddar
cheese
2 bacon strips, cooked and
crumbled

Bake potatoes at 400° for about one hour or until done. Cut a thin slice off the top of each potato and discard. Carefully scoop out pulp while leaving shell intact. In a mixing bowl, mash pulp with milk, sour cream, onion salt, and pepper until smooth. Fold in asparagus. Stuff shells; place in an ungreased shallow baking dish. Sprinkle with cheese and bacon. Return to oven for 20-25 minutes or until heated through.

Cooking with the Lioness Club

Scandinavian Salmon-Cheese-Potato

4 large potatoes
1 (7-ounce) can salmon,
drained
¼ cup chopped green
onion
1 egg
1 teaspoon dried dill weed

Little salt and pepper
6 tablespoons milk
2 cups Jarlsberg cheese,
shredded (any favorite
cheese will do)
1 tablespoon melted butter

Bake potatoes. Slice off top and carefully scoop out pulp. In bowl, mix potato, salmon, onion, eggs, dill, salt and pepper and milk. Stir in ¾ of cheese. Spoon mixture back into shells. Sprinkle with rest of cheese and brush with melted butter. Bake at 400° for 20 minutes.

Celebration of Grace

Zesty Pizza Potatoes

4 large potatoes
8 ounces shredded
  Mozzarella, Monterey Jack
  or Cheddar cheese
  (3½ cups)
4 green onions, sliced
½ teaspoon oregano

½ teaspoon basil
2 medium tomatoes, sliced or
  one pint stewed tomatoes
½ pound cooked Italian
  sausage or ground beef
Parmesan cheese

Bake potatoes at 400° until fork tender. In small bowl toss cheese, onions, oregano, and basil. Slice cooked potatoes lengthwise. Place cut sides up in baking dish. Sprinkle with half the cheese mixture. Top with tomatoes and meat, then remaining cheese mixture. Bake at 400° for 20 minutes or until golden brown and heated through. Sprinkle with Parmesan cheese if desired.

Wisconsin's Best

Lemon Potato Bites

2 tablespoons fresh lemon
  juice
1½ teaspoons fresh grated
  lemon peel
3 tablespoons fat-free
  Parmesan cheese

½ teaspoon sweet Hungarian
  paprika
3 large potatoes, cut in bite-
  sized pieces
Nonstick pan spray

Combine lemon juice, lemon peel, Parmesan cheese, and paprika in a medium-sized bowl. Add potatoes and toss to coat.

Spray roasting pan (for oven) or shallow glass baking dish (for microwave) with nonstick pan spray. Spread potatoes out in pan or baking dish. Bake in conventional oven at 400° for 30-35 minutes or until tender, stirring occasionally. Or, for microwave oven, cover dish with waxed paper and microwave on HIGH for about 12 minutes. If you do not have a rotating base, turn the dish half way through cooking. Let stand about 2-3 minutes before serving. Makes 4 servings.

Nutritional Analysis Per Serving: Total fat 0.508gm; Sat fat 0.094gm; Chol 5mg; Cal from fat 2%; Cal 242; Sod 61.22mg; Carb 54.23gm; Sugar 4.541gm; Prot 6.755gm.

Spice of Life Cookbook

Lithuanian Kugela

½ pound bacon, diced
1 small onion, diced
8 medium potatoes
1½ cups warm milk
1 teaspoon salt
½ teaspoon pepper
2 eggs, well beaten
¼ cup farina

Brown bacon lightly with onion. Cool. Grate 8 potatoes. Pour off most of potato juice, saving starch mixture that settles at bottom. Mix into grated potatoes the bacon, milk, reserved starch, salt, pepper, eggs, and farina. Pour into greased 8x8-inch pan. Bake at 350° for 1½ hours.

Serve with sour cream or just plain as a side dish. It is great the next day sliced and fried in butter.

Pelican Lake Women's Civic Club

Nonna Maisano's Fried Potatoes and Eggs

"This was a good Friday meal for the family."

4-5 potatoes, peeled and
  sliced
1 large onion, cut into
  slices (optional)
1 large green pepper, cut
  into slices (optional)
4-5 eggs, scrambled
Salt and pepper

In large cast-iron frying pan, add enough olive oil to cover bottom of pan. Fry potatoes until light brown. Add onions and peppers and cook, covered, for about 10 minutes. Add eggs and salt and pepper to taste. Brown on one side, then divide in half and flip to other side.

Grandmothers of Greenbush

Potatoes Romanoff

A great potato dish to serve with ham and baked beans. Can be prepared ahead and reheated. Flavor is even better the second day. Expect requests for second helpings!

7 cups cooked, diced
  potatoes
2 cups cottage cheese
1 teaspoon garlic salt
2 teaspoons salt

1 cup sour cream
2 tablespoons chopped onion
½ cup shredded cheese
Paprika

Combine all ingredients except cheese and paprika. Pour into a 9x13-inch pan and top with cheese and paprika. Bake at 350° for 45 minutes. Makes 6-8 servings.

Foxy Ladies

Potato Pancakes

Potatoes always were and still are one of my favorite foods. They were served at most dinners as we were growing up. I remember making potato pancakes by grating the potatoes on a hand grater, trying not to scratch my knuckles. It took a long time to grate enough for our whole family, but it was well worth it. I sure am glad that food processors and blenders were invented—they save time and fingers.

We were able to store potatoes and carrots all winter in special bins that Dad made in our cellar. They were large bins with ventilated bottoms covered with old rugs. By allowing ventilation under the vegetables, rotting and sprouting were prevented, which helped them stay fresh all winter.

3 cups peeled, grated
  potatoes
3 eggs

1 tablespoon minced onion
2 tablespoons flour
½ teaspoon salt

Blot potatoes on a clean dish towel or paper towel to remove excess moisture. Preheat griddle on medium heat. Beat eggs, onion, flour, and salt together. Add grated potatoes and stir until well blended. Fry ⅓-cup portions on a preheated greased griddle for about 2-3 minutes on each side or until golden brown. Serve with butter, applesauce, syrup, or fruit. Good for breakfast, lunch, or dinner. Serves 4.

Grandma's Home Kitchen

Colcannon

Who would believe that potatoes and cabbage combined with a few other well-chosen ingredients could seem so heavenly? This is Irish country food at its very simple best, from Executive Chef Tim Gurtner, 52 Stafford, Plymouth.

4 large potatoes, peeled
  and diced, about 4 cups
1 cup heavy whipping cream
½ teaspoon chopped garlic
1 teaspoon dried parsley
  flakes

1 teaspoon salt
½ teaspoon white pepper
1 cup chopped green cabbage
1 leek, white part only, diced

In an ovenproof medium saucepan over medium heat, place potatoes, cream, garlic, parsley, salt and pepper. Cook, stirring occasionally until mixture comes to a boil, about 5 minutes. Cover and bake in preheated 400° for 20 minutes.

While mixture bakes, blanch cabbage and leeks in boiling, salted water in a small saucepan just until tender, about one minute. Drain well, discarding liquid. Fold cabbage and leeks into potato mixture. Makes 6-8 servings.

Encore Wisconsin

Brewed Sauerkraut

3 strips bacon, diced
1 cup chopped onion
2 pounds sauerkraut,
  rinsed and drained
1 (12-ounce) can beer

2 tablespoons brown sugar,
  packed
½ teaspoon caraway seeds
Pepper to taste
1 cup coarsely shredded
  carrot

Fry bacon in 2-quart saucepan until crisp. Remove, drain, and set aside. Add onions to pan and sauté; stir in sauerkraut, beer, sugar, caraway seeds, and pepper. Bring to a boil, cover, and simmer for one hour. Add carrots and simmer uncovered for an additional 20 minutes, until carrots are tender. Spoon into serving bowl and garnish with bacon pieces. Serves 6.

Drink Your Beer & Eat It Too

Dandelions with Sour Cream

Dandelions often live only two years. Those gathered in spring are frequently old and about to flower, set seed, and die. Few people know it, but dandelions are at their very best in fall when their leaf rosettes are storing foodstuffs—often for the only winter they will know. They are worth trying in spring, but remember: autumn dandelions are sweetest.

Dandelions	**Hot, salted water**
1 tablespoon fat	**Sour cream or yogurt**
1 tablespoon flour	

Steam dandelions for 5 minutes over low heat. Add fat and flour and enough hot, salted water to make a thick sauce. Add sour cream or yogurt to taste. Stop cooking and eat!

The Wild Food Cookbook

Rhubarb Blueberry Jam

5 cups rhubarb, diced
1 cup water
5 cups sugar

1 cup blueberry pie filling
1 package raspberry Jell-O

Cook rhubarb in water over medium heat until tender. Add sugar and boil for 2 minutes. Stir in pie filling and cool for about 10 minutes. Add Jell-O and mix well. Pour into hot jars; process 15 minutes in boiling water or freeze. Yield: 12 servings.

RHUBARB-PINEAPPLE VARIATION:
5 cups rhubarb, diced
4 cups sugar
1 small can crushed pine-
  apple, including juice

2 small boxes raspberry or
  strawberry Jell-O

Boil rhubarb and sugar with pineapple and juice for 10 minutes. Remove from heat and add Jell-O. Stir well. Put in jars; cover with lids; let cool and freeze. Yield: 8 small jars.

Green Thumbs in the Kitchen

Beet Jelly

6 cups beet juice
2 boxes Sure-Jel
½ cup lemon juice

8 cups sugar
1 box raspberry Jell-O

Combine beet juice, Sure-Jel and lemon juice and bring to a boil. Add sugar and Jell-O and boil 6 minutes.

Favorite Recipes of the Wisconsin NFO

Mock Raspberry Jam

3 pounds green tomatoes
2 cups sugar

1 (3-ounce) package raspberry
  gelatin

Core tomatoes and cut into chunks. Process in blender until you have 2 cups. Boil 2 cups blended tomatoes with sugar for 15 minutes. Remove from heat and add powdered gelatin. Pour into clean containers. Refrigerate or freeze. Yield: 2 pints.

St. John Evangelical Lutheran Church

Refrigerator Pickles

7 cups thin-sliced cucumbers
1 cup thin-sliced onions
1 cup thin-sliced green
** pepper**
1 tablespoon salt

1 cup cider vinegar
2 cups sugar
1 teaspoon celery seed
1 teaspoon dry mustard

Mix cucumbers, onions, peppers, and salt together and let stand one hour. Drain. Boil vinegar, sugar, celery seed, and mustard. Let cool. Pour over pickles and keep in refrigerator. Will keep for two months. Ready to eat in 24 hours.

Cooking with the Lioness Club

Crisp Pickle Slices

4 quarts of sliced cucumbers
6 medium onions, sliced
3 cloves of garlic
1 green pepper, sliced
1 sweet red pepper, sliced
⅓ cup salt

3 cups white vinegar
5 cups sugar
1½ teaspoons turmeric
1½ teaspoons celery seed
2 tablespoons mustard seed

Slice cucumbers thin; add sliced onions, garlic, and peppers, cut in narrow strips. Add salt, cover with ice, let stand 3 hours. Drain. Combine remaining ingredients. Pour over cucumber mixture. Heat to boiling. Seal in hot sterilized jars.

Four Seasons at Hawks Inn

Wisconsin Apple Relish

**4½ cups tart, red apples,
finely chopped, unpeeled**
½ cup water
¼ cup lemon juice

½ cup raisins
1 package powdered pectin
5½ cups sugar
½ cup walnuts, chopped

Combine apples, water, lemon juice, and raisins in large pot. Add pectin and stir well. Place on high heat and bring to a boil, stirring constantly. Add sugar, stir and bring to a boil again. Cook at full boil for one minute, stirring constantly. Stir in nuts and remove from heat. Skim top. Spoon into jars with tightly fitting lids. Store in refrigerator. Makes 7½ pints.

Winning Recipes from Wisconsin with Love

The Wisconsin Herb Blend

**1 teaspoon dried rosemary,
crushed**
**2 teaspoons dried basil,
crushed**
**4 teaspoons dried onion
flakes**
**2 teaspoons dried lemon
balm, crushed**

**2 teaspoons dried parsley,
crushed**
**1 teaspoon dried tarragon,
crushed**
**2 teaspoons dried oregano,
crushed**
2 teaspoons dried garlic flakes

Mix thoroughly, put in airtight container and allow time to "mellow."

Note: Other variations are possible simply by adding combinations of favorite herbs and spices to this basic blend.

The Madison Herb Society Cookbook

Poultry

Snow blankets a typical Wisconsin dairy farm. Near Stevens Point.

Steve's Chicken Moscovy

1 stick butter
6 tablespoons farmers
 cheese
1½ teaspoons fresh dill,
 finely minced

6 whole, skinned, and boned
 chicken breasts
1 egg, beaten with ⅛
 teaspoon salt
¾ cup dry bread crumbs

Put 6 tablespoons butter, cheese, and dill in small saucepan. Gently heat and stir until mixture forms a soft paste. Pound breasts flat between sheets of waxed paper. Spread the cheese mixture on the breasts and roll up. Fasten with toothpicks or thread. Dip pieces into beaten egg, then into bread crumbs. Sauté in remaining butter until nicely browned on all sides. Bake at 300° for 30 minutes, uncovered. Remove to platter and serve with sauce.

WHITE DILL SAUCE:

6 tablespoons sour cream
2 heaping tablespoons fresh
 dill, finely minced
1½ cups chicken broth

3 tablespoons cornstarch,
 dissolved in a bit of
 cold water
Salt to taste

Heat sour cream, dill, and chicken broth until blended. Add cornstarch mixture. Stir and simmer until sauce is consistency of heavy cream.

Sunflowers & Samovars

Chicken Fettucini

Unusual but tasty!

1 cup picante sauce
¼ cup chunky peanut butter
2 tablespoons honey
2 tablespoons orange juice
1 teaspoon soy sauce
½ teaspoon ground ginger
4 chicken breasts, boned, skinned, cut into fondue size

2 tablespoons olive oil
6 ounces fettucini, cooked according to directions on package
¼ cup peanuts
¼ cup red bell pepper, chopped
Cilantro, chopped

Place first 6 ingredients in saucepan. Stir over low heat until blended. Cook chicken with olive oil in skillet (about 5 minutes). Add ¼ cup picante mix to chicken. Mix rest of picante mix with drained fettucini. Place fettucini mixture on large platter. Top with chicken; sprinkle with peanuts and chopped red bell pepper and chopped cilantro. Serves 4-6.

Cooks Extraordinaires

Chicken Monterrey

A dish that can be readied ahead and baked, while you do last-minute things.

4 boneless chicken breasts
1 (9-ounce) package Monterrey Jack cheese, sliced
1 can cream of chicken soup

¼ cup cooking sherry
½ package seasoned croutons, crushed
⅛ pound of butter or margarine

In a 9x13-inch baking pan or dish, layer the chicken breasts, sliced cheese, soup mixed with sherry, crushed croutons, and dabs of butter. Bake for 2 hours at 250°. Serves 4. Excellent with wild rice, tossed green salad, dessert, and coffee.

Foxy Ladies

Oven-Fried Chicken

1¼ cups seasoned croutons, crushed

¼ cup grated Parmesan cheese

2 tablespoons chopped fresh parsley

8 boneless skinless chicken breast halves

⅓ cup Dijon mustard

Heat oven to 450°. Line 15x10x1-inch baking pan with foil. In pie pan, combine croutons, Parmesan cheese, and parsley. Brush chicken pieces with mustard; roll in crouton mixture. Place chicken on foil-lined pan. Bake at 450° 15-20 minutes or until chicken is fork tender and juices run clear. Serves 8.

Per Serving: Cal 198 (27.6% from fat); Fat 6.1g (Sat 1.8g); Chol 75.9mg; Fiber 0.5g; Sod 450. Diabetic Exchange: 3 lean meat + 1 vegetable.

Here's To Your Heart: Cooking Smart

John's Chicken Divine

A family favorite.

2 boxes frozen broccoli, partially cooked

SAUCE:

2 cans cream of chicken soup

1 cup mayonnaise

8 ounces Cheddar cheese, shredded

8 chicken breasts, cooked and deboned

1 teaspoon lemon juice

Curry, to taste

Bread crumbs

Layer partially cooked broccoli spears in a 13x9-inch pan. Place chicken breasts on top (I split each breast in two). Mix sauce and pour over chicken. Sprinkle bread or cracker crumbs ton top. Bake at 325° for 35 minutes.

Peterson Pantry Plus Lore

Touch of Italy Chicken

4 chicken breasts, skinned
  and boned
Italian seasoning
Salt and pepper
½ (10-ounce) package
  fresh spinach, cooked
  and drained
Provolone cheese

4 teaspoons plus ½ cup (1
  stick) butter, divided
2 eggs
2½ cups bread crumbs
1 teaspoon Italian seasoning
1 teaspoon paprika

Wash chicken breasts; place between wax paper and pound thin. Sprinkle breasts with Italian seasoning, salt and pepper. Place ¼ of spinach down the center of each breast. Top with a finger of provolone cheese. Top with one teaspoon butter. Fold chicken like an envelope, encasing spinach, cheese and butter.

Beat eggs. Combine bread crumbs, Italian seasoning and paprika and mix well. Dip chicken in egg, then in bread crumbs, holding so envelopes don't unfold. Let dry in refrigerator for 15 minutes then re-dip in egg and crumbs. (You can bake at this time or hold them in the refrigerator for several hours.) When ready to bake, melt the stick of butter and roll the chicken in the butter, turning to coat. Place in a shallow baking dish and pour any remaining butter over the chicken. Bake at 375° for 25-30 minutes, turning once. Make a small cut in the chicken to check for doneness (no pink!) Makes 4 servings.

Apples, Brie & Chocolate

Chicken with 40 Cloves of Garlic

Grace Howaniec's reputation as the Sunday Cook really began with the publishing of this somewhat startling recipe.

1 (3½ - 4-pound) chicken, rinsed, cut in pieces, skinned
1 tablespoon unsalted butter
¼ cup plus 1 tablespoon olive oil (divided)
1 teaspoon salt
Freshly ground black pepper
40 cloves garlic, unpeeled, separated (about 3 bulbs)
½ cup dry white wine
1 teaspoon dried thyme leaves, crumbled
½ teaspoon dried leaf sage, crumbled
½ teaspoon dried leaf rosemary, crumbled
1 tablespoon fresh parsley, minced
4 small bay leaves
½ loaf French bread

Pat chicken pieces dry with paper towel. Heat butter and one tablespoon of the olive oil in large, cast-iron Dutch oven or ovenproof skillet. Brown chicken in batches (don't crowd) over medium-high heat about 5 minutes on all sides. Season with salt and pepper. Remove to plate lined with paper towels.

Pour off all accumulated fat from Dutch oven. Scatter garlic cloves over bottom of Dutch oven. Place chicken over garlic.

Pour wine and remaining ¼ cup olive oil over chicken; sprinkle with thyme, sage, rosemary, parsley, and bay leaves. Cover pan tightly with heavy aluminum foil; and then lid. Bake at 375° for 30 minutes. Carefully remove lid and foil; baste with oil-wine mixture. Replace foil and lid; bake 30 minutes more.

Meanwhile, slice bread into ¼-inch-thick slices. Toast on baking sheet in oven at 375° for 10-15 minutes, until crisp. Before serving, remove and discard bay leaves. Spoon chicken, sauce and several whole cloves of garlic onto each serving plate. Squeeze garlic directly out of skins onto toasted bread, discarding skins and eating garlic paste as you would a pâté. Makes 4-5 servings.

The Sunday Cook Collection

Sweet and Sour Chicken

¾ pound boneless cubed
  chicken
1 tablespoon oil
1 cup green and red pepper
  strips
1 tablespoon cornstarch
¼ cup light soy sauce

1 (8-ounce) can chunk
  pineapple in juice
3 tablespoons vinegar
3 tablespoons brown sugar
½ teaspoon ground ginger
½ teaspoon garlic powder
1½ cups Minute instant
  brown rice

Cook and stir chicken in hot oil in large skillet until well browned. Add peppers; cook and stir 1-2 minutes. Mix cornstarch and soy sauce. Add to pan with pineapple and juice, vinegar, sugar, ginger, and garlic powder. Bring to a full boil. Meanwhile, prepare rice as directed on package. Serve chicken over rice. Makes 4 servings.

Cooking with the Lioness Club

Baked Chicken In Cream

½ cup flour
½ teaspoon salt
½ teaspoon pepper
½ teaspoon paprika
½ teaspoon garlic salt

10 chicken thighs
¼ cup oil
1 chicken bouillon cube
  dissolved in 2 cups water
1 cup cream

Mix all dry ingredients. Wash chicken pieces in cold water and pat dry. Roll each piece in the flour mixture to coat all sides. Heat oil in heavy pan. Brown chicken on both sides. Remove chicken to a large, flat baking dish. Add remaining flour mixture to drippings in frying pan. Heat well and stir. Add the bouillon water, stirring until it comes to a boil. Add the cream and mix well. Pour this gravy over the browned chicken. Cover and bake one hour at 325°.

Family Fare

Creamed Chicken
with Cranberry Rollups

½ cup diced carrots
¼ cup diced celery
¼ cup diced white onion
Chicken broth
1½ cups cooked chicken, diced
½ cup water chestnuts

3 cups cream of chicken soup (or 1 can soup plus 1 soup can of milk)
½ cup fresh snow peas
½ cup sliced fresh mushrooms
⅛ teaspoon pepper

Sauté carrots, celery, and onion in small amount of chicken broth, water or white wine, until tender. Add chicken, and remaining ingredients. Pour into a 3-quart casserole dish.

TOPPING:
2 cups biscuit mix
½ cup milk

1 (8-ounce) can whole berry cranberry sauce (1 cup)

Mix baking mix and milk until soft dough forms; beat 30 seconds. Turn onto cloth-covered surface well floured with baking mix; knead 10 times. Roll dough into rectangle, 12x9-inches; spread with cranberry sauce. Roll up, beginning at 12-inch side. Cut into 1-inch slices. Arrange slices so swirls show onto hot chicken mixture. Bake at 425° for 20-25 minutes or until rollups are golden brown.

Four Seasons at Hawks Inn

Cranberry Chicken

4 chicken breast halves (or boneless, skinless breasts)
1½ cups whole berry cranberry sauce

1 cup chopped apples
½ cup raisins or prunes
¼ cup walnuts
1 tablespoon curry powder

Bake chicken for 30 minutes at 350°. While chicken is baking, mix together cranberry sauce, chopped apples, raisins, walnuts, and curry powder. Evenly distribute mixture on top of chicken. Return to oven for 30 minutes. Serve immediately.

Cherry Berries on a Cloud and More

Chicken Calvados

A sautéed chicken dish with an apple-flavored cream sauce.

1 (6-ounce) chicken breast, (boneless, skinless, whole or sliced)
Flour for dusting
2 ounces clarified butter
½ onion (cut in slices as for stir-fry)
6 mushrooms (sliced)
1 apple (sliced or diced)
Garlic (we use jar garlic in water or oil)
⅛ - ¼ teaspoon ground ginger
Salt or Lawry's to taste
2 ounces De Kuyper Apple Barrel Schnapps or Berentzen Apple Liquor
4 ounces heavy whipping cream

Dip chicken in flour and sauté in butter. Turn and add onion, mushrooms, and apple. After one minute, add a little garlic and ginger and seasoned salt. Continue to sauté. Add apple liquor and reduce. When most of liquor is reduced, add cream. Simmer until thick and bubbly.
Recipe by The Audubon Inn, Mayville. Executive Chef Steve Fox.

Wisconsin Cooks with Wisconsin Public Television

Chicken with Cranberry Sauce

1 chicken, cut-up
1 cup Russian dressing with honey
1 package dry onion soup mix
1 (16-ounce) can whole cranberry sauce

Mix the Russian dressing, dry onion soup and cranberry sauce. Pour over chicken and marinate 24 hours (do not drain). Bake at 300° for 2½ hours uncovered.

The Best Cranberry Recipes

 Spice Smell at Christmas: Simmer ½ orange rind and ½ lemon rind, cut up, 1 large cinnamon stick, ¼ cup whole cloves and 2 bay leaves for a wonderful waft throughout the house. From *Four Seasons at Hawks Inn.*

Lemony Chicken Kabobs

3 medium lemons
¼ cup olive oil
1 tablespoon sugar
1 tablespoon cider vinegar
  or wine
2 teaspoons salt

1 teaspoon cayenne pepper
1 garlic clove, minced
4 chicken breasts, boned
¾ pound zucchini, sliced into
  chunks
½ pound mushrooms

Mix the first 7 ingredients for marinade. Cut chicken into chunks. Clean mushrooms. Toss all into marinade. Cover and refrigerate for 2 hours or more. Thread on skewers and broil or grill about 15 minutes, brushing with Lemon Butter and turning regularly.

LEMON BUTTER:
¼ cup butter, melted
1 tablespoon lemon juice

1 tablespoon parsley
½ teaspoon salt

Sharing Our Best

Chicken and Dressing Casserole

2 boxes Stove Top Stuffing
1 chicken, cooked, deboned,
  cut up
1 can cream of mushroom
  soup

1 can cream of celery soup
1 can cream of chicken soup
Grated Cheddar cheese
Ritz cracker crumbs
1 stick butter, melted

Prepare stuffing as per directions on box; put in bottom of 9x13-inch cake pan. Over this, put a layer of chicken. Combine all soups and spread over chicken. Sprinkle with cheese. Over top, add a layer of Ritz cracker crumbs. Pour butter over all. Cover with foil and bake at 350° for 1 - 1½ hours. delicious.

Favorite Recipes of the Wisconsin NFO

Grilled Chicken Breast With Lemon Sauce and Angel Hair Pasta

I enjoyed Chef Tom D'Olivo's (Maria's Italian Cuisine, Oconomowoc) light and lovely entreé on my birthday this May on Maria's sunny outdoor patio. The flavors are perfect in this pretty dish—and it is simple to assemble and serve.

SAUCE:

4 tablespoons butter	½ cup Chablis wine
4 tablespoons flour	1 lemon, washed
3 cups chicken stock	

Make sauce by melting butter in medium saucepan. Whisk in flour until blended. Let cook for 2 minutes, stirring constantly. Gradually whisk in chicken stock and wine. Grate zest from lemon; set aside. Squeeze juice from lemon (you will need about 4 tablespoons juice) and whisk into sauce. Cook over medium-high heat, stirring constantly until thickened, about 3 minutes. Whisk in zest at end of cooking; set aside.

CHICKEN BREAST:

4 chicken breast halves (4 ounces each),
  skinned, ¼-inch thick,
  boned and pounded

Grill chicken breasts over hot coals or on high setting of gas grill, about 3 minutes per side or until juices run clear. Remove to warm serving plate.

PASTA:

4 tablespoons minced shallots, about 2 large	8 ounces angel hair pasta, cooked and drained
2 tablespoons butter	

Sauté shallots and butter together in small skillet until shallots are transparent, about 2 minutes. Mix into cooked pasta. Divide pasta and chicken breasts among four serving plates. Pour ¼ of sauce over each chicken breast and drizzle over pasta. Makes 4 servings.

Encore Wisconsin

Chicken Squares

1 (3-ounce) package cream cheese,softened
1 teaspoon melted margarine
1 tablespoon milk
1 teaspoon onion flakes
2 cups cooked and cubed chicken or ham
2 tubes refrigerated crescent rolls

Mix together cream cheese and next 4 ingredients; add to chicken. Put one tablespoon chicken mixture on each crescent square and press. Roll up and bake at 350° (about 18 minutes).

Look What's Cooking at C.A.M.D.E.N

Chicken Puff

1 package Pepperidge Farm puff pastry or phyllo pastry
1 package Uncle Ben's long grain and wild rice mix
2 egg whites
1 grated orange peel
1 jar mushrooms, drained (optional)
6 whole chicken breasts, skinned, boned, and halved
2 egg yolks
1 teaspoon water

Thaw pastry and roll into 12-inch circles. Cook rice according to package directions. Add egg whites, orange peel, and mushrooms. Place a large spoonful of rice mixture onto pastry circle. Top with chicken breast that has been salted and peppered (half of a whole breast works best). Pinch together pastry and turn over onto baking pan. Brush top with egg yolk and water mixture. Bake at 375° for one hour.

SAUCE:

1 jar currant jelly
1 tablespoon dry mustard
3 tablespoons Port wine

Combine ingredients and cook together. Serve hot in gravy boat with the puffs.

Celebration of Grace

Turkey on a Raft

1 head iceberg lettuce	1 pound turkey breast slices
1 cup fat-free whipped dressing	8 slices tomato (2 tomatoes)
¼ cup low-fat French dressing	¾ cup fat-free Cheddar cheese
	4 teaspoons fat-free reduced sodium Parmesan cheese

Slice lettuce crosswise in about 1-inch slices to create 4 lettuce rafts. Place on a cookie sheet.

Combine dressings and spread about 2 tablespoons on each lettuce raft. Layer each raft with first ¼-pound turkey slices and then 2 tomato slices. Stir Cheddar cheese into remainder of salad dressing mixture. Spread evenly over the top of each raft. Sprinkle each raft with one teaspoon of Parmesan cheese.

Place under the broiler about 4-5 inches away from the heat. Broil about 2-3 minutes until the cheese melts and the top starts to brown just a little. Makes 4 really refreshing servings.

Hint: You may want to cut a very small slice off the rounded ends of lettuce to stabilize your rafts. Use toothpicks to hold the rafts together so they don't fall apart as you serve them.

Nurtitional Analysis Per Serving: Total fat 2.292gm; Sat fat 0.329gm; Chol 99.96mg; Cal from fat 7%; Cal 309; Sod 723.5mg; Carb 24.33gm; Sugar 16.12gm; Prot 43.48gm.

Spice of Life Cookbook

Sour Cream Pheasants

2 pheasants
Flour
¼ teaspoon paprika
Butter and oil to brown
Salt and pepper

1 (8-ounce) carton sour
  cream
2 cups water (or more)
2 teaspoons celery salt
1 teaspoon garlic salt

Cut pheasants into pieces; roll in flour with paprika in it. In frying pan, brown several pieces at a time in butter and oil. Pour off excess oil after browning. Salt and pepper to taste. Mix last 4 ingredients together in blender and pour over the last few pieces of pheasant browning in pan (should be like a thin gravy). Bake all together in 350° oven for 2½ hours or until done. Be sure pheasant never dries out; watch that the gravy doesn't cook down or it might curdle on you. The gravy can also be put on baked potatoes.

Marketplace Recipes Volume I

Meats

The world-renowned Green Bay Packers play to a capacity crowd every time they hit the field.

Steak Bercy

SAUCE:

¾ cup butter, melted
2 tablespoons chopped
  green onions
½ cup dry red wine
2 tablespoons chopped
  parsley

1 tablespoon lemon juice
½ tablespoon beef base
3 cloves minced garlic
12 large mushroom caps

Combine all ingredients, including the mushroom caps, and simmer for 15 minutes.

ENTREÉ:

6 (8-ounce) fillet mignons   Salt and pepper to taste

GARNISH:

Mushroom caps

Grill steaks to desired liking, brushing several times with the sauce. Season to taste with salt and pepper. Pour one table-spoon sauce over each steak and serve immediately. Garnish with mushroom caps. Makes 6 servings.

Variation: Carpet-Bagger Bercy—Follow recipe for Steak Bercy, except prior to grilling, split steak to make a pocket, and fill steak with 4 ounces sautéed oysters.

Favorite Recipes from the Old Rittenhouse Inn

Braised Sirloin Tips

2 pounds beef, 1-inch
  cubes
1 (10½-ounce) can
  beef consommé
⅓ cup red Burgundy or
  red cranberry cocktail

2 tablespoons soy sauce
1 clove garlic, minced
¼ teaspoon onion powder
2 tablespoons cornstarch
¼ cup water
4 cups hot cooked rice

Brown meat all sides. Add consommé, wine, soy sauce, garlic, and onion powder. Heat to boiling. Reduce heat and simmer one hour. Blend cornstarch and water. Pour into meat. Cook one minute more. Serve over rice. Makes 8 servings.

St. Mark's Lutheran Church Cookbook

Tenderloin

1 beef tenderloin
4 tablespoons butter,
  softened
½ cup green onions, sliced
4 tablespoons soy sauce
2 teaspoons Dijon-style
  mustard
Dash fresh ground pepper
1 cup dry sherry

Spread tenderloin with 2 tablespoons butter. Put on rack in shallow pan. Bake, uncovered, at 400° for 20 minutes. Cook green onions in 2 tablespoons butter. Add soy sauce, mustard, pepper, and sherry. Heat just to boiling. Pour over tenderloin. Bake another 20-25 minutes for rare. Baste frequently. For sandwiches, chill; slice thin. Serve with condiments on hard rolls.

Picnics on the Square

Stuffed Tenderloin

4 cups herb stuffing mix
1 cup chopped mushrooms
¼ cup chopped onions
1 (11-ounce) can beef broth
1 whole beef tenderloin, slit
  lengthwise
4 strips bacon

Mix together the stuffing mix, mushrooms, onions, and broth. Stuff tenderloin and secure with toothpicks. Wrap with four strips of bacon. Bake at 350° for 1½ hours.

Dr. Martin Luther Church
100th Anniversary Cookbook

Italian Beef

1 (6-pound) round roast	½ teaspoon oregano
3 large onions	¼ teaspoon basil
1 tablespoon salt	½ teaspoon Italian seasoning
½ teaspoon onion salt	½ teaspoon salt
½ teaspoon garlic salt	1 teaspoon Accent

Place meat in roaster half filled with water, salt, and onions. Roast until tender. Let stand overnight in cold place. Slice very thin. Strain liquid and add remaining ingredients. Bring to boiling point. Place sliced beef and seasoned liquid in layers in large saucepan. Serve on French or Italian bread.

The Palmyra Heritage Cookbook

Sauerbraten

4 pounds chuck roast	2 teaspoons salt
1 cup water	½ teaspoon pepper
1 cup cider vinegar	12 peppercorns
2 medium onions, sliced	6 whole cloves
2 bay leaves	¼ cup brown sugar

GRAVY:

¼ cup brown sugar	6 gingersnaps
¼ cup raisins	

Place meat in earthenware or glass bowl. Combine the other ingredients and heat to boiling. Pour over the meat and allow to cool. Marinate 3-4 days in the refrigerator; turning meat twice daily. Do not pierce meat with a fork.

Drain meat and set marinade aside. Brown meat on all sides in hot fat in a heavy skillet. Add the marinade, cover pan and simmer slowly 3-4 hours or until tender. Remove meat from skillet and slice across the grain into scant ½-inch slices. Strain the liquid. Melt ¼ cup brown sugar in skillet; add liquid gradually and stir until sugar dissolves. Add ¼ cup of raisins and 6 crushed gingersnaps. Cook until smooth and thickened. If gravy is too thin, thicken with a flour and water paste. Return meat to gravy and heat. Makes 6 servings.

Create Share Enjoy!

Beef Stroganoff

1½ pounds stew meat
1 package dry onion
  soup mix
1 can cream of chicken
  soup

1 can cream of mushroom
  soup
1 (8-ounce) container sour
  cream
1 (8-ounce) can mushrooms,
  drained

Cut up stew meat. Put in casserole dish. Add soup mix and soups. Stir. Bake at 250° for 3½ hours, covered. Add sour cream and mushrooms. Stir and bake ½ hour more. Serve over noodles.

A Collection of Recipes

Football Stew

This is a great company dish, because the oven does the cooking while you visit with your guests, and there are no dirty dishes in the sink.

2 cups tomato juice
2 tablespoons sugar
3 tablespoons tapioca
2 teaspoons salt
1 pound beef stew meat

1 onion, diced
4 carrots, sliced
1 stalk celery, chopped
4 potatoes, cubed

Combine tomato juice, sugar, tapioca, and salt. Combine meat (do not brown) and vegetables. Top with tomato mixture, seal with aluminum foil and bake 4 hours at 250°. Serves 4.

Note: I usually double or triple the recipe and use a broiler pan or large cake pan. Serve with fruit salad and rolls.

Foxy Ladies

German Beef Stew

2 tablespoons flour
½ teaspoon celery salt
½ teaspoon ginger
¾ teaspoon salt
¼ teaspoon pepper
¼ teaspoon garlic powder
1½ pounds beef chuck,
   cut in 2-inch chunks
2 tablespoons salad oil

1½ cups sliced onion
1 (16-ounce) can tomatoes
¼ cup red wine vinegar
¼ cup dark molasses
½ cup water
5 carrots, peeled and cut into
   1-inch pieces
¼ cup dark raisins

Combine flour, celery salt, ginger, salt, pepper, and garlic powder. Coat beef on all sides with mixture. In large heavy pan or Dutch oven, heat oil, then add meat and brown on all sides, stirring frequently. Add onions and cook until lightly browned. Add tomatoes, vinegar, molasses, and ½ cup water. Cover and simmer 1½ hours, stirring occasionally. Add carrots and raisins; simmer one hour. Serve over hot cooked noodles.

St. Frederick Parish Centennial Recipe Collection

Irish Lamb Stew

3 pounds lamb shoulder,
   cut in 1½-inch cubes
2 tablespoons cooking oil
2 teaspoons salt
4 bouillon cubes, vegetable
¼ teaspoon pepper
4¼ cups hot water
4 potatoes, pared and cubed
   (5 cups)

4 medium onions, cut in
   ¼-inch slices
4 carrots, cut in 1½-inch
   sticks
1 (10-ounce) package frozen
   peas
¼ teaspoon dried thyme,
   crushed
¼ cup flour

In a heavy large saucepot, brown lamb in hot oil. Drain off excess fat. Season with salt and pepper; dissolve bouillon cubes in 4 cups hot water; pour over meat. Bring just to boiling. Cover, simmer 1½ hours or until meat is almost tender. Add potatoes, onions, carrots, peas and thyme. Cover; simmer 20-25 minutes longer. Combine ¼ cup water and flour. Stir into stew. Cook and stir until thickened and bubbly.

Four Seasons at Hawks Inn

Venison Stew

4 pounds venison stew meat (choice cut)
2 onions, thinly sliced
2 stalks celery, cut diagonally
12 carrots, chunked

1 teaspoon salt
⅛ cup sugar
¼ cup Minute Tapioca
1 cup V-8 juice
6-8 potatoes

Place meat in large roasting pan. Place onions, celery, and carrots on top of meat. Combine and pour salt, sugar, tapioca, and V-8 over vegetables and meat. Cover and seal tightly with foil. Bake at 250° for 5-6 hours. Add potatoes half way through cooking time. Serves 20.

A Taste of Christ Lutheran

Beef-Broccoli Strudel

1 pound ground beef
¼ cup dried bread crumbs
1 medium onion diced
½ cup sour cream
1 (10-ounce) package broccoli, thawed (leaves) and squeezed dry

4 ounces shredded Mozzarella cheese (more if desired)
1¼ teaspoons salt
¼ teaspoon pepper
½ pound phyllo dough
½ - 1 cup melted butter or margarine

Brown ground beef; add onions and cook until transparent. Add all remaining ingredients except phyllo and butter. Brush each sheet of phyllo with melted butter, layering sheets as you go. Starting at short end of phyllo, evenly spoon beef mixture to cover about half of the rectangle. From beef mixture side, roll phyllo jellyroll fashion. Place roll seam-side-down on cookie sheet. Brush with remaining butter. Bake 45 minutes at 350°. Cool 15 minutes for easier slicing. Serves 6.

Create Share Enjoy!

 Wisconsin is called the Badger State because lead miners in the 1820s lived in crude dugouts which reminded people of badger holes. Cornish miners built quaint stone cottages along Shake Rag Street, and that name comes from the custom of women shaking dishrags from the doorway, signaling the men in the mines across the valley that the noon meal was ready.

Spiedini

3 pounds beef tenderloin, sliced thin
3-4 cups bread crumbs, more if needed
Salt and pepper, to taste
Pinch of garlic powder
Grated Romano or Parmesan cheese

Chopped parsley
1 - 1½ pounds bacon
Olive oil or blended olive oil
2-3 large onions, cut into wedges

Slice tenderloin thin and pound. Pieces should be about 1½ x 3-inchs in size. Season bread crumbs with salt, pepper, garlic powder, cheese, and parsley to taste. You can also use already seasoned Italian bread crumbs. Set aside.

Lay bacon on baking sheet and cook almost until done, but not crispy. Cut into small pieces, about 4 to a slice. Dip each piece of tenderloin in oil and then in bread crumb mixture. Roll each piece, as a jellyroll. On a skewer, place one piece of onion, a piece of bacon, and then the rolled meat. Continue alternating onion, bacon, and meat until the skewer is full. Always try to top skewer with an onion piece. Drizzle a little oil on top of skewers before cooking. This helps to keep them moist. Bake in the oven at 325° until done. They should look nice and brown. Rotate the skewers as you cook them. Or they can be cooked outside on the grill.

Marquette University High School
Mother's Guild Cookbook

Corned Beef and Cabbage

3-4 pounds lean corned beef	2 tablespoons pickling spices
2 garlic buds, cut in half	3 potatoes, quartered
1 onion, chopped	6 small carrots, halved
2 bay leaves	4 sticks celery, cut in pieces
10 peppercorns	1 head cabbage, quartered

Put the corned beef in a big soup kettle and cover it with cold water. Add all of the other ingredients except the vegetables and bring water to a boil. Reduce the heat to a slow boil or simmer. Simmer for 3 hours per pound of corned beef. At this point, stop! Refrigerate overnight and remove all fat from the top.

When cooking the next day, bring to a slow boil and add potatoes, carrots, and celery. Cook for ½ hour or until vegetables are tender. During the last 15 minutes of cooking time, add the cabbage. Do not overcook the cabbage. Serve with buttered rye bread.

Blessed Be The Cook

Mock Chop Suey

1 pound ground beef	1 small can mushrooms
Water for simmering	(optional)
vegetables	1 can chow mein noodles
1½ cups chopped onions	Salt and pepper
1½ cups chopped celery	Soy sauce to taste
1 can cream of mushroom	
soup	

Preheat oven to 350°. Brown ground beef in a skillet; drain and remove to a casserole dish. Using the same skillet and a small amount of water, cook onions and celery. Mix all ingredients in the casserole, reserving ½ chow mein noodles. Bake 45 minutes; sprinkle remaining noodles on top; return to oven for 15 minutes. Yield: 4 servings.

Green Thumbs in the Kitchen

Sicilian Meat Roll

2 beaten eggs
½ cup tomato sauce
¾ cup bread crumbs
2 tablespoons parsley
½ teaspoon oregano,
  crushed
¼ teaspoon salt

¼ teaspoon pepper
1 clove garlic, minced
2 pounds ground chuck
4-6 slices thinly sliced
  boiled ham
1-2 cups shredded Mozzarella
  cheese

Spray a 9x13x2-inch pan with Pam. In large bowl combine the eggs and tomato sauce. Stir in bread crumbs, parsley, oregano, salt, pepper, and garlic. Add the ground chuck and mix well. On waxed paper pat meat into a 10x18-inch rectangle. Arrange ham slices on top of the ground chuck mixture, leaving a small margin around the edges. Reserving a handful of cheese, sprinkle the rest over the ham. Starting from the short end, carefully roll up meat, using paper to lift. Seal edges and ends. Place roll seam-side-down, in the baking dish. Bake at 350° about 1½ hours. (Center of the roll will be pink because of the ham). Sprinkle reserved cheese over top of meat roll and return to oven till cheese melts, about 2 minutes. Makes 8 servings.

Variation: Can be made with half ground chuck and half ground turkey. Garlic powder can be used if you don't have a garlic clove.

Create Share Enjoy!

Crunchy All Beef Meatloaf

1 pound ground beef,
  lean chuck
10 Ritz crackers, crushed or
  ¾ cup 40% bran flakes
1 egg
⅓ cup nonfat milk
¼ teaspoon soy sauce
¼ teaspoon Worcestershire
  sauce
½ cup water chestnuts,
  finely chopped
½ cup green pepper, finely
  chopped
Dash salt and pepper
Dash onion salt
Dash garlic salt
1½ cups tomato sauce,
  prepared

Place ground beef in a mixing bowl. Add crackers (to crush, place in plastic sandwich bag and crush with hands), slightly beaten egg, milk, and remaining ingredients, except tomato sauce. Mix well and place in baking dish, pour tomato sauce over top of loaf. Bake uncovered at 350° for 45-55 minutes. (Meatloaf is tasty without crunchy chestnuts and peppers for those who want a plain meatloaf.) Makes 6 servings. Calories per serving 206.

Luscious Low-Calorie Recipes

Cranberry Sauerkraut Meatballs

2 pounds ground beef
2 eggs
1 envelope regular onion
  soup mix
½ cup water
1 cup finely crushed cracker
  crumbs

Mix together and shape into meatballs. Brown in a skillet.

SAUCE:

1 (16-ounce) can sauerkraut,
  drained and snipped
1 (8-ounce) can cranberry
  sauce (whole or strained)
¾ cup chili sauce or catsup
2 cups water
⅓ cup brown sugar

Mix together and pour half of the sauce in a 9x13-inch baking dish. Arrange meatballs on sauce. Pour remaining sauce over meatballs. Cover with foil and bake for one hour at 325°. Remove foil. Bake another 30-40 minutes. Serve hot over noodles or rice.

The Best Cranberry Recipes

Swedish Meatballs
(Kottbullar)

2 tablespoons butter
¼ cup onion, finely
  chopped
½ - ⅔ cup fine dry
  bread crumbs
¾ cup light cream
¾ cup ground round steak

¼ pound ground veal
¼ pound ground lean pork
2 teaspoons salt
¼ teaspoon pepper
⅛ teaspoon cloves
⅓ cup butter
1¼ cups boiling water

Heat butter and sauté onion until soft and golden. Soak bread crumbs in cream. Combine onions and bread crumbs, meat, and seasonings; blend thoroughly, but lightly. Shape mixture with wet hands into meatballs. Heat butter and fry meatballs until brown on all sides, shaking pan continuously to prevent sticking. Add boiling water and simmer over lowest possible heat for 5 minutes.

Note: For smorgasbord, serve on toothpicks; for an entreé, make large meatballs and make cream gravy with juices.

Fifth Avenue Food Fare

Beth's Best Meatballs
In the whole world!

1½ pounds hamburger
1 can water chestnuts,
  diced
½ - 1 cup bread crumbs
2 eggs

2 tablespoons Worcestershire
  sauce
1 small onion
1 teaspoon salt and pepper

Mix all ingredients together and roll into meatballs. Fry in skillet on medium till brown all around.

SAUCE:
1 cup brown sugar
1 cup lemon juice
  concentrate
½ cup ketchup
½ cup barbeque sauce

1 cup water
4 tablespoons cornstarch
½ cup chopped green and red
  pepper

Mix in saucepan and simmer on low for 10 minutes; mix with meatballs.

Mt. Carmel's "Cooking with the Oldies"

Venison Meat Balls

This is one way small children will eat venison.

1½ pounds ground venison
2 cups grated raw potatoes
  (or run them through the
  meat grinder after
  venison)
1 tablespoon chopped onion
1½ cups soda cracker
  crumbs
1½ teaspoons salt

⅛ teaspoon pepper
1 egg
¼ cup milk
¼ cup butter
3 cups water, divided
½ package Lipton Beefy
  Onion Soup Mix
2-3 tablespoons flour

Combine venison, potatoes, onion, crackers, salt, pepper, egg, and milk; shape into 1½-inch balls. Brown balls slowly in butter in large skillet. Add ½ cup water and soup mix; cover. Simmer for 20 minutes or until done. Remove meatballs.

To make gravy, add ½ cup cold water to flour, combine well and add to pan with remaining water. Simmer until thick. Add meatballs. Heat.

Marketplace Recipes Volume I

Batter Fried Venison

**1 cup finely crushed
crackers
1 large onion**

**1 venison round steak, boned,
sliced, (¼ -⅜-inch thick)**

Run crackers through blender until finely crushed. Dice onion very fine and mix with the crackers. Using a large coated paper to work on and a meat tenderizing hammer, pound onion, and cracker mix into venison on both sides. Each piece of meat will expand almost double in size. Fry in hot oil or bacon drippings, turning once, for about 1½ minutes on each side. Serve hot as a main dish or cool for sandwiches.

What's Cook'n?

Beef or Venison Barbecue

**1 chuck roast or venison
(about 3 pounds)
½ cup chopped onion
1 tablespoon sugar
2 teaspoons dry mustard
2 teaspoons salt
½ teaspoon pepper**

**2 teaspoon paprika
⅓ cup vinegar
1 tablespoon Worcestershire
sauce
1 cup catsup
1 cup water**

Trim excess fat from roast. Place roast in crock pot or Dutch oven. Combine remaining ingredients in a small bowl and mix well. Pour over meat and cover. In Dutch oven simmer for 2½ hours or until very tender. In crock pot simmer for 5-6 hours or until very tender. Remove meat and using 2 small cooking forks, shred it. Return to sauce and check periodically to see that it doesn't burn. If sauce thickens too much, add a little more liquid. Recipe is best if made at least 24 hours before serving. Freezes well. If you prefer a sweeter sauce, add sugar. Yield: 12-15 servings on buns.

Cardinal Country Cooking

 Legend has it that, in 1885, Charles R. Nagreen invented the hamburger at Seymour's first fair when he flattened meatballs into patties and served them in between bread because they were more portable. The world's largest hamburger was grilled in Seymour at the Hamburger Hall of Fame in 1989. It weighed 5,520 pounds.

Awesome Sloppy Joes

Interestingly delicious!

1½ - 2 pounds ground beef
1 tablespoon oil
1 medium onion, chopped
¾ cup hot water
1 cup catsup
½ cup tomato juice
¼ teaspoon nutmeg
½ teaspoon ground cloves
1 teaspoon chili powder
1 teaspoon salt
½ teaspoon black pepper
1 (15-ounce) can (2 cups)
  pumpkin
8 hamburger buns

Brown the ground beef in a heavy skillet with the oil. Add chopped onion and cook for 5 minutes. Drain. In a large saucepan, cook the following: water, catsup, tomato juice, nutmeg, cloves, chili powder, salt, and pepper. Bring to a rolling boil. Add the meat, onions, and pumpkin. Simmer for 20 minutes. Serve on hamburger buns, or your favorite roll.

Cooking With Pride

Ground Beef Barbecue

2 pounds browned ground
  beef, drained
½ - 1 cup chopped onions
¾ cup catsup
½ cup water
2 tablespoons brown sugar
2 tablespoons lemon juice
¼ teaspoon dry mustard
1 teaspoon salt
1 teaspoon vinegar
1½ teaspoons Worcestershire
  sauce
½ teaspoon flavor enhancer
  (monosodium glutamate)
¼ cup chopped celery
  (optional)

Mix all ingredients. Cover and simmer 30 minutes to an hour. Add more catsup and water for thinner barbecue. Serve on buns.

A Taste of Home

Marinade for Almost Anything

1½ cups salad oil
¾ cup soy sauce
¼ cup Worcestershire
2 tablespoons dry mustard
2½ teaspoons salt
1 tablespoon pepper
½ cup red wine vinegar
1½ teaspoons parsley
2 cloves garlic, crushed
⅓ cup lemon juice

Combine ingredients. This is good for any grilled entrée, chicken, beef, pork, even fish. May marinate overnight, refrigerate. Makes 3¼ cups.

All in Good Taste II

Firecracker Barbecue Sauce

Every barbecue connoisseur has his or her own secret barbecue sauce. Interesting ingredients add kick to this chef's recipe that is sure to be a hit with your backyard barbecue crowd.

3 cups chili sauce
1 teaspoon ground black pepper
1 teaspoon ground ginger
1 teaspoon dry mustard
2 teaspoons granulated garlic
¼ cup liquid smoke

¼ cup apple cider vinegar
3 tablespoons packed brown sugar
1 teaspoon chili powder
1½ cups strong coffee
¼ cup Worcestershire sauce
1 teaspoon salt

In a large sauce pot, mix together chili sauce, pepper, ginger, mustard, garlic, liquid smoke, vinegar, brown sugar, chili powder, coffee, Worcestershire sauce, and salt. Simmer slowly for 30 minutes. Yields 4 cups.

Chef's Note: Use this sauce as a dipping sauce or brush on food being barbecued just before serving.

Masterpiece Recipes of The American Club

Farmhouse Barbecue Muffins

1 (10-ounce) tube refrigerated buttermilk biscuits
¾ pound ground beef
½ cup ketchup
3 tablespoons brown sugar

1 tablespoon cider vinegar
½ teaspoon chili powder
½ cup (2 ounces) Cheddar cheese, shredded

Separate dough into 10 biscuits, flatten into 5-inch circles. Press each into the bottom and up the sides of a greased muffin cup; set aside. In a skillet, brown ground beef; drain. In a small bowl, mix ketchup, brown sugar, vinegar, and chili powder; stir until smooth. Add to meat and mix well. Divide the meat mixture among biscuit-lined muffin cups, using about ¼ cup for each. Sprinkle with cheese. Bake at 375° for 18-20 minutes or until golden brown. Cool for 5 minutes before removing from tin and serving.

Fifth Avenue Food Fare

Mouth of Fire Rub

¼ cup chopped parsley
2 tablespoons coarse
    ground black pepper
2 tablespoons minced garlic
1 tablespoon paprika

2 bay leaves, finely crumbled
1 teaspoon cayenne pepper
1 teaspoon dry mustard
Pam spray
3 pounds London Broil

Combine first 7 ingredients. Spray surface of meat with cooking spray. Rub both sides of meat with spice mixture. Allow to set 30 minutes before grilling. Grill as usual. Makes about ½ cup (enough for 3 pounds of meat).

Good Cooking, Good Curling

Firehouse Dressing

1 pound hamburger
1 pound ground pork
4-6 stalks celery, diced

1 large onion, diced
1-2 cups water
1-2 bags onion and sage
    croutons

Cover and cook hamburger, pork, celery, and onion in large frying pan. Stir and break up meat. Add water. Pour croutons in large bowl. When celery is soft, pour and mix entire pan over croutons (if not moist enough, add water). Can be stuffed in turkey or other fowl or in roaster sprayed with non-stick spray. Bake at 350° for one hour with cover on.

This can be used for wild game or domestic birds. Great for stuffed pork chops or cornish hens. Can be frozen for future use.

The Crooked Lake Volunteer Fire Department Cookbook

Sloppy Pan Nachos

3 tablespoons oil, divided
2 large, chopped onions
1 chopped green pepper
1 teaspoon chili powder
2 pounds ground chuck
8 ounces unseasoned
  refried beans
1 teaspoon salt
¼ teaspoon black pepper
1 teaspoon oregano

½ teaspoon cumin
2 crushed cloves garlic
3 tablespoons medium hot
  picante salsa
1 (16-ounce) bag Tostito Chips
1½ cups grated Cheddar
  cheese
1½ cups grated Monterey Jack
  cheese

TOPPINGS:
Shredded lettuce
Chopped tomatoes
Chopped avocado
Chopped onion

Sliced olives
Sour Cream
Chunky-style salsa

Line 2 (15½x10½-inch) jellyroll pans with foil. Set aside. In large skillet, heat 2 tablespoons oil and sauté onions and green pepper until tender-crisp. Push to side of skillet. Add remaining one tablespoon oil and simmer chili powder one minute. Combine with vegetables and remove from pan. Brown meat in same skillet. Drain off fat. Add cooked vegetables, beans, and remaining seasonings including picante sauce. Simmer 5 minutes. Remove from heat. Into the prepared pans, layer Tostitos, overlapping. Top with meat filling. Cover with cheeses. Bake at 350° for 3-5 minutes or until cheese is melted. Serve with side dishes as appetizer, or for a light lunch or supper.

Note: Filling can be made in advance and frozen. This recipe is great for an informal party. Plan on lots of napkins and individual plates for people to build their own sloppy nachos. Serves 10-12.

All in Good Taste II

Interesting facts: The first ice cream sundae was concocted in Two Rivers in 1881; Wisconsin is a leading producer of ginseng; the Fox River is one of the few rivers in the nation that flows north; more than 800,000 deer roam Wisconsin's woods; Green Bay is know as the "Toilet Paper Capitol" of the world.

My Mother's Potato Pasty

3 cups flour
1 cup shortening
½ teaspoon salt
⅓ cup cold water

Mix as for pie crust. Roll thin and put on cookie sheet.

FILLING:
Sliced raw potatoes
Leftover roast beef
Gravy
1 medium onion, chopped
Salt and pepper
1 egg
¼ cup milk

Layer potatoes, beef, gravy, onion, salt and pepper over half of crust. Fold over crust and pinch together. Bake at 350° for 40 minutes. Beat egg and milk together. Cut a U on top of the crust and pour mixture over. Replace crust and bake 10 minutes more. Cut in squares and serve.

The Palmyra Heritage Cookbook

French Meat Pie

2 cups potatoes, put thru food grinder (can use frozen hash browns)
1 large onion, ground
4 pounds ground lean pork (shoulder pork)
½ teaspoon ground savory
½ teaspoon allspice
½ teaspoon sage
½ teaspoon cinnamon
Salt and pepper to taste
4 (9-inch) deep-dish pie crusts, with top crusts (use purchased frozen or homemade)

In enough water to cover, cook potato and onion until tender. Add meat and spices and simmer 30 minutes. Drain, put into pie crusts, and cover with top crusts. Bake at 400° for 20 minutes. If desired, freeze for later use; take right from freezer and bake again at 400° for 25-30 minutes or until hot and ready to serve. Makes about 4 pies.

Marketplace Recipes Volume I

Goose Blind Chili

The Goose Blind Chili recipe featured here won the best spice award at the Wisconsin State Chili Cook-Off in 1991.

2½ pounds ground beef
1 large onion, diced
1 green pepper, diced
4 stalks celery, sliced
1 tablespoon oil
2 teaspoons crushed garlic
1 tablespoon chili powder
1 teaspoon black pepper
1 teaspoon crushed red
  pepper flakes

1 teaspoon cumin
1 teaspoon seasoned salt
Pinch of basil
Pinch of thyme
1 (28-ounce) can tomato pureé
1 (28-ounce) can diced
  tomatoes
1 (28-ounce) can kidney beans
1 (16-ounce) can tomato juice

In large stockpot, brown ground beef; drain. In separate pan, sauté vegetables in oil and seasonings. When vegetables are tender and onion is translucent, blend in with beef. Add canned items and allow to simmer at least one hour.

Optional: For hotter chili with a Southwestern twist, add a few tablespoons of diced jalapeño peppers during the simmering process. Yields 12-15 servings.

Recipe from The Goose Blind, Green Lake, Wisconsin.

Our Best Cookbook 2

Pork Loin Roast
with Herbs and Glazed Apples

2 tablespoons balsamic
  vinegar
2 tablespoons dry sherry
1 tablespoon olive oil
1 tablespoon shoyu*
  or soy sauce
1 tablespoon cracked black
  peppercorns
2 (3-inch) sprigs fresh
  rosemary
2 (3-inch) sprigs fresh
  marjoram
2 (3-inch) sprigs fresh thyme
2 cloves garlic, minced

2 pork tenderloins (about
  ⅔-pounds each), trimmed
  of fat and membrane
2 tablespoons vegetable oil
  (preferably canola)
Salt, to taste
4 Gala, Golden Delicious or
  other cooking apples
2 tablespoons unsalted butter
  or margarine
1 (3-inch) sprig fresh sage
¼ cup bourbon
2 tablespoons honey

To marinate, combine vinegar, sherry, olive oil, shoyu* (a sweet soy sauce made from toasted wheat) or soy sauce, peppercorns, rosemary, marjoram, thyme, and garlic in a shallow glass baking dish. Add pork, turning to coat; cover with plastic wrap. Place in refrigerator for 1-4 hours, turning several times. Remove from refrigerator 20 minutes before cooking to bring to room temperature.

Preheat oven to 425°. Heat vegetable oil in a large skillet over medium heat. Remove tenderloins from marinade; place in skillet and brown pork on all sides, about 2 minutes per side. Place pork in a glass or cast-iron roasting pan; pour marinade over meat; add salt if desired. Place pan uncovered in oven and roast until internal temperature reaches 150°, about 20 minutes. Strain pan juices and reserve.

Core apples and slice into ¼-inch-thick rings. Melt butter in same skillet over medium-high heat. Add apples and sage; cook until apples begin to brown lightly, about 5 minutes, turning occasionally. Add bourbon and honey. Continue cooking until apples are almost translucent, another 10 minutes. Remove sage sprig. Place pork on a serving platter; surround with apple rings. Pour reserved sauce over meat. Cut pork into 1-inch-thick slices and serve immediately. Makes 6 servings.

Growing & Using Herbs

Ham Loaf

2 pounds ground ham
1 pound ground pork
2 eggs
1 green pepper, finely chopped

1 cup soda cracker crumbs
1 (8-ounce) can tomato sauce
¾ cup milk
1 teaspoon horseradish

Mix and shape into one large or 2 small loaves. Bake at 350°
for 1½ hours. The last ½ hour, pour sauce over ham loaf.

SAUCE:

¾ cup brown sugar
1½ tablespoons prepared mustard

¼ cup water
¼ cup vinegar

Boil for 10 minutes and pour over loaf, or microwave for 5
minute.

Peterson Pantry Plus Lore

Pork Tenderloin

2 (1-pound) pork tenderloins
8 strips bacon (or enough to cover)
½ cup soy sauce
1 tablespoon grated onion

1 clove garlic, grated
1 tablespoon vinegar
¼ teaspoon cayenne pepper
½ teaspoon sugar

Wrap tenderloin with bacon, using toothpicks to hold. Mix soy
sauce, onion, garlic, vinegar, pepper, and sugar in medium-sized
Pyrex dish. Add meat, spooning marinade over top. Cover dish
and refrigerate 3 hours, turning after 1½ hours. Remove cover
and bake at 300° for 2 hours, basting often. Remove toothpicks
before serving.

What's Cooking in St. Francis

Taliesin in Spring Green, was the home of Frank Lloyd Wright for nearly 50
years. A National Historic Landmark, the 600 acres of buildimgs and landscape is open for tours. Taliesin continues to serve as a working educational
facility and still houses an on-site architectural firm. Wright was born in
Richland Center in 1867.

Pineapple Chops

6 lean pork chops	⅓ cup honey
1 (20-ounce) can pineapple slices (in own juice)	2 tablespoons soy sauce
	¼ teaspoon ground ginger

Broil chops 5 inches from heat, 7-8 minutes. Turn chops and broil another 6 minutes. Meanwhile, drain pineapple; reserve 3 tablespoons juice. Combine juice with the honey, soy sauce, and ginger. Place 1 pineapple slice atop each pork chop and broil 6-7 minutes, basting frequently with honey-juice mixture. Spoon remaining juice over chops before serving.

Calories 313; Fat 9g.

Good Cooking, Good Curling

Pork Chops and Wild Rice

1 small package Uncle Ben's Wild Rice	1 teaspoon salt
6-8 pork chops, depending on size	¼ teaspoon garlic salt
	⅛ teaspoon pepper
1 medium onion, minced	2 tablespoons drippings from meat
1 cup celery, finely chopped	1 cup milk
1 cup green pepper, chopped	1 can mushroom soup
1 (8-ounce) package fresh mushrooms, chopped (optional)	

Make rice as directed on package. Fry pork chops on both sides until brown, season with salt and pepper as you fry. Mix vegetables, seasonings, rice, and meat drippings from pan (add a little water to frypan to get enough drippings). Put vegetable mixture in a buttered 9x13-inch cake pan. Arrange chops over vegetables. Pour milk and soup, mixed together over chops. Cover and bake in 350° oven for 1¼ hours.

Sacred Heart Centennial Cookbook

Pork Chops with Mandarin Oranges

6 pork chops
3 tablespoons brown sugar
½ teaspoon cloves
½ teaspoon cinnamon

1 teaspoon prepared mustard
¼ cup catsup
1 tablespoon vinegar
1 (12-ounce) can mandarin oranges

Brown pork chops. Mix together other ingredients, except oranges. Cook until tender. Remove excess fat. Add water, if needed. Watch carefully so sauce doesn't evaporate. Add mandarin oranges, including juice. Serve with rice or noodles.

Unbearably Good! Sharing Our Best

Oven Barbecued Pork Chops

6 pork chops
1 tablespoon Worcestershire sauce
2 tablespoons vinegar
2 teaspoons brown sugar

½ teaspoon pepper
½ teaspoon chili powder
½ teaspoon paprika
¾ cup ketchup
⅓ cup or more water

Heat oven to 325°. Put in baking dish. Bake uncovered for 1½ hours or until meat is tender.

Sparks from the Kitchen

Sugar Shack Cookout

2 tablespoons shortening
1 teaspoon soy sauce
1 teaspoon mustard
¾ cup maple syrup

1 tablespoon vinegar
1 teaspoon cornstarch
1 package hot dogs
1 package hamburger buns

Simmer first 6 ingredients in a saucepan for 8-10 minutes or until sauce is smooth and thick. Cut hot dogs halfway through in several places along one side only. Place on cookie sheet and grill, basting with sauce several times (as they cook, the hot dogs will form circle). Place rounded hot dogs on toasted hamburger buns and fill center with baked beans.

Wisconsin Pure Maple Syrup Cookbook

Cookies and Candies

Clowning around at Circus World Museum in Baraboo.

Wisconsin Whoppers

These are great high energy cookies for trips or after skiing, skating or other fun winter activities.

1¼ cups light brown
  sugar, packed
¾ cup granulated sugar
⅔ cup butter
1½ cups chunky peanut
  butter
3 eggs
6 cups rolled oats
  (not quick cooking)

2 teaspoons baking soda
1½ cups raisins or craisins
  (optional)
1 cup semi-sweet chocolate
  chips
4 ounces semi-sweet chocolate
  squares
½ teaspoon vanilla

With a mixer, cream sugars and butters about 3 minutes. Add eggs, one at a time. Beat one minute more. Add oats and baking soda. Mix in optional raisins and chips. Shred the chocolate squares with a knife and mix into cookie batter. Add vanilla. Drop by ¼ measuring cup (or any desired size) onto cookie sheets. Flatten cookies with bottom of a glass tumbler that is dipped frequently in water. Bake at 350° about 15 minutes.

A Collection of Recipes

Chocolate Chocolate-Chip Cookies

1 cup butter
¼ cup sugar
¾ cup brown sugar
1 teaspoon vanilla
2 eggs
1 (4½-ounce) package milk
  chocolate Jell-O instant
  pudding

2¼ cups flour
1 teaspoon baking soda
1 (12-ounce) package
  chocolate chips

Combine butter, sugars, vanilla, and beat until fluffy. Add eggs and pudding; beat well. Combine flour and baking soda and add to batter. Fold in chips. Drop by spoonfuls on cookie sheets. Bake at 375° for 8-10 minutes.

Centennial Cookbook

White Chocolate Chunk Cookies

The yield on this cookie recipe (4 dozen large cookies) might seem like a lot. But one taste may cause you to think the recipe just might be too small. We think this will become a family favorite at your house.

1 cup butter
1 cup packed brown sugar
1 cup granulated sugar
2 large eggs
1 teaspoon vanilla
2 tablespoons Irish Cream
 liquor
3 cups cake flour

1 teaspoon baking soda
½ teaspoon salt
1 cup chopped walnuts or
 macadamia nuts
1½ cups white chocolate
 chunks or white chocolate
 chips

In a medium bowl with electric mixer, cream the butter and sugars together until light and fluffy. Add eggs, vanilla, and Irish Cream liquor. Set aside. Sift flour, soda, and salt; add to butter mixture.

In a separate bowl, combine walnuts and white chocolate chunks, then add to mixture, just to blend. Drop by heaping tablespoon onto parchment paper covered cookie sheet, 2-inches apart and bake in a preheated 375° oven for approximately 11-13 minutes. Cool on wire rack. Yields 4 dozen large cookies.

The American Club

Cherry Winks
(The $5,000 Cooky)

Ruth Derousseau's prize-winning recipe, reprinted with permission from Pillsbury, was shown on the back of a 1951 Kellogg's Corn Flakes cereal box.

2¼ cups sifted Pillsbury's
  Best Enriched Flour*
1 teaspoon double-acting
  baking powder
½ teaspoon baking soda
½ teaspoon salt
¾ cup shortening
1 cup sugar

2 eggs
2 tablespoons milk
1 teaspoon vanilla
1 cup chopped pecans
1 cup chopped dates
½ cup chopped maraschino
  cherries
2½ cups Kellogg's Corn
  Flakes

Sift together flour, baking powder, soda, and salt. Combine shortening and sugar; cream well. Blend in eggs; add milk and vanilla. Blend in sifted dry ingredients; mix well. Add pecans, dates, and cherries. Mix well. Shape into balls using a level tablespoon of dough for each cooky. Crush corn flakes. Roll each ball of dough in corn flakes. Place on greased baking sheet. Top each cooky with ¼ maraschino cherry. Bake in moderate oven (375°) 10-12 minutes. Do not stack or store until cold. Makes about 5 dozen cookies.

Note: *If you use Pillsbury's Best Enriched Self-Rising Flour, omit baking powder and salt, decrease soda to ¼ teaspoon.

Green Thumbs in the Kitchen

Polka Dot Cookies

⅓ cup butter
¼ cup sugar
½ cup brown sugar
1 egg
1 teaspoon vanilla
1 teaspoon baking powder
¼ teaspoon soda

¼ teaspoon salt
2 cups flour
¼ cup milk
1 (6-ounce) package chocolate
    chips
½ cup cherries, chopped
½ cup nuts, chopped

Mix butter, sugar, and brown sugar. Add egg and vanilla. Mix in baking powder, soda, and salt. Add flour and milk. Add chips, cherries and nuts. Drop dough on baking sheet. Bake at 375° for 10-12 minutes.

Fifth Avenue Food Fare

Chocolate Drop Cookies

1 cup shortening
1 cup brown sugar
¾ cup white sugar
1 teaspoon vanilla
½ teaspoon maple flavoring
4 eggs

4 squares melted un-
    sweetened chocolate
3½ cups flour
1 teaspoon soda
½ teaspoon salt
¾ cup milk

Cream together shortening, brown sugar, white sugar, vanilla, and maple flavoring. Add eggs and chocolate. Mix flour, soda, and salt. Add dry ingredients alternately with milk to cream mixture. You may add nutmeats, if desired. Drop by teaspoonful onto cookie sheet and bake at 350° for 12-15 minutes.

Cardinal Country Cooking

Door County, the state's "thumb" extending into Lake Michigan, has more shoreline than any other county in the US—over 250 miles. Europeans came there in the seventeenth century. The Icelandic community of Washington Island, the Scandinavian community in and around Sister Bay, the Ephraim Moravians and the Belgians of southern Door bring a rich cultural heritage to this fascinating state.

Crunchy Chocolate Chip Cookies

½ cup butter
½ cup margarine
1 cup packed brown sugar
1 cup sugar
1 egg
1 tablespoon milk
2 teaspoons vanilla
3½ cups all-purpose flour

3 teaspoons baking soda
1 teaspoon salt
1 cup oil
1 cup quick cooking oatmeal
1 cup crushed cornflakes
1 (12-ounce) package
chocolate chips

Cream butter, margarine, and sugar. Add egg and mix well. Add milk and vanilla. Stir dry ingredients in to butter mixture, alternating with oil. Fold in oatmeal, corn flakes, and chocolate chips. Place on ungreased cookie sheet. Bake at 350° for 10-12 minutes.

Camp Hope Cookbook

Mom's Toasted Oatmeal Cookies

1 cup white sugar
½ cup brown sugar
2 eggs
2 teaspoons vanilla
½ cup Crisco (very impor-
    tant, do not substitute)
½ cup margarine
1 cup oatmeal, toasted in
    oven at 350° for 5 minutes

1 teaspoon baking soda
1 teaspoon salt
2 cups plus 4 tablespoons
    flour
½ cup chopped nuts
1 cup chocolate chips or
    raisins or craisins
    (dried cranberries)

Cream first 6 ingredients together. Stir in dry ingredients, nuts and chocolate chips. Drop by teaspoon on cookie sheet and flatten with a glass dipped in sugar. Bake at 350° for 8 minutes.

Cooking at Thimbleberry Inn

 At Lizard Mound County Park in West Bend, there are huge dirt mounds built by Indians hundreds of years ago that look like a lizard, a bird, and a wildcat.

Apricot Lilies
(A Butter Cookie)

¼ cup sugar
1 cup sweet, unsalted
butter, softened
1 (3-ounce) package
cream cheese, softened
1 teaspoon vanilla

2 cups all-purpose flour
¼ teaspoon salt
Approximately ½ cup apricot
jam (or another fruit jam)
Powdered sugar

Combine sugar, butter, cream cheese, and vanilla. Beat at medium speed until well mixed (about one minute). Reduce speed to low; add flour and salt. Continue beating until well mixed (about 1½ - 2 minutes). Divide dough into 4 parts. Wrap in plastic food wrap. Refrigerate until firm (at least 2 hours).

On lightly floured surface, roll out dough (¼ at a time) to ⅛-inch thickness. Keep remaining dough refrigerated. Cut with 2-inch round cookie cutter. Place on cookie sheets (½ inch apart). With thin spatula, fold dough over jam to form a lily shape. Gently press narrow end to seal. Jam will show on top of cone-shaped cookie. Heat oven to 375°. Bake 7-11 minutes or until edges are lightly browned. Cool completely. Sprinkle lightly with powdered sugar. Makes approximately 8 dozen cookies.

St. Mary's Family Cookbook

White Sugar Cookies

1 cup margarine or butter,
  softened
1½ cups powdered sugar
1 large egg
1¼ teaspoons vanilla

½ teaspoon almond extract
2½ cups flour
1 teaspoon baking soda
1 teaspoon cream of tartar

Cream butter and powdered sugar until light and fluffy. Add egg, vanilla, and almond extract. Blend in dry ingredients. Chill at least one hour. Roll ⅓ of the dough on floured pastry cloth or board. Cut in favorite shapes, sprinkle with granulated or colored sugar, and place on a lightly greased cookie sheet. Bake in 350° oven for 8-10 minutes. Roll dough thin for crisp cookies and bake for 6-7 minutes. Repeat with remaining dough.

Note: Here's a short-cut method: Using heaping teaspoonfuls of dough, make balls and place on greased cookie sheet. With the flat bottom of a glass dipped in sugar, flatten cookies. Quick and easy perfectly shaped sugar cookies! Makes 5½ - 6 dozen 2-inch cookies.

Every 1 A Winner! Blue Ribbon Recipes

Rosemary Shortbread Cookies

1 stick butter
¼ cup fine sugar
1½ cups white flour

2 tablespoons fresh, finely
  chopped rosemary

Cream butter and sugar, add flour and rosemary. Roll out dough, cut into 2-inch circles. Bake on ungreased sheet at 325° for about 15 minutes.

The Madison Herb Society Cookbook

Lemon-Zucchini Cookies

2 cups flour
1 teaspoon baking powder
½ teaspoon salt
¾ cup butter
¾ cup sugar
1 egg, beaten

Grated rind of 1 lemon
1 cup shredded zucchini
1 cup chopped walnuts or
   pecans
Lemon glaze

Combine flour, baking powder, and salt. Set aside. Cream butter and sugar. Beat in egg and lemon rind. Stir in flour mixture until smooth. Stir in zucchini mixture and nuts. Drop by rounded teaspoons on greased cookie sheets. Bake at 375° for 15-20 minutes. Drizzle with Lemon Glaze while still warm. Yield: 4 dozen.

LEMON GLAZE:
1 cup powdered sugar   1½ tablespoons lemon juice

Mix until smooth.

Picnics on the Square

Grandma Piper's Molasses/Date Cookies

1 cup sugar
1½ cups butter or
   margarine
1 cup molasses
4 eggs
½ cup hot water
   (not boiling); dissolve 2
   teaspoons soda in it

½ teaspoon salt
5 cups flour
1 teaspoon vanilla
2 teaspoons cinnamon
1½ cups nuts, chopped
1½ cups dates, chopped

Mix in order as shown and chill overnight in refrigerator. Roll out on floured board and cut into irregular shapes or triangles. Bake at 350° for approximately 10 minutes or until done.

Cooking at Thimbleberry Inn

Seeds and Spice Cookies

1 stick plus 2 tablespoons
  butter, softened
½ cup sugar
2 tablespoons black-
  strap molasses
2 egg yolks
2 teaspoons vanilla
1¾ cups all-purpose flour
1½ teaspoons ground coriander

¼ teaspoon cinnamon
⅛ teaspoon ginger
2 teaspoons anise seed
2 teaspoons fennel seed
1¼ teaspoons caraway seed
2 pinches salt
Powdered sugar

Cream butter, sugar, and molasses until light and fluffy. Add yolks and vanilla. Cream till light and fluffy, scraping sides of bowl often. Grind seeds with mortar and pestle or a coffee grinder until finely crushed. Mix together flour, coriander, cinnamon, ginger, seeds, and salt. Add to butter mixture. Mix till thoroughly blended, but don't overmix. Refrigerate cookie dough 3 hours. Measure about 2 teaspoons of dough per cookie. Form into balls, flatten bottoms. Place on cookie sheets. Bake 350° about 12 minutes, till "set" but not golden brown. Remove and cool. Roll in powdered sugar. Makes about 2½ dozen cookies.

The Madison Herb Society Cookbook

Pepparkakor

Swedish spice cookies have been a part of our Christmas tradition for years. It travels well, can be used to decorate tiny trees, and is the one cookie that when stored properly, seems to stay fresh forever. Add this classic to your cookie collection.

1 cup unsalted butter*
1½ cups sugar
1 tablespoon dark molasses*
1 large egg
3¼ cups flour
2 teaspoons baking soda
1 tablespoon ground
  cinnamon

1 tablespoon ginger
1 tablespoon ground cloves
1 tablespoon grated orange
  zest*
¼ cup freshly squeezed
  orange juice, strained*

In large mixing bowl with heavy-duty mixer, cream butter on medium-high speed until soft and light in color, about 2 minutes. Gradually beat in sugar until mixture is light and fluffy, about 3 minutes. Scrape down sides of bowl several times with rubber spatula. Add molasses and egg; beat until well combined.

In separate large mixing bowl, whisk together flour, soda, and spices until blended. Add gradually to butter mixture, beating to combine. Mix in orange zest and juice; blend well, about one minute.

On a floured board or surface, roll out one-fourth of dough (that has been dusted with flour) to 1⁄16-inch thickness. Using heart-shaped cookie cutter, cut dough into hearts; transfer with metal spatula to greased cookie sheets, placing one inch apart. Repeat process with three remaining portions of dough. Remaining dough scraps can be worked back into dough portions for additional cuttings.

Bake at 350° until brown, 10-12 minutes; watch closely. Remove cookies to wire rack to cool thoroughly. Cover and store. Makes about 100 cookies in 3x2¼-inch heart shapes.

Note: *Don't use margarine. The small amount of molasses is correct. One medium orange should yield enough zest and juice for this recipe.

The Sunday Cook Collection

Butterscotch Cheesecake Bars

1 (6-ounce) package
  butterscotch chips
⅓ cup butter or margarine
2 cups graham cracker
  crumbs
1 cup chopped nuts

1 (8-ounce) package cream
  cheese
1 (14-ounce) can sweetened
  condensed milk
I teaspoon vanilla
1 egg

Preheat oven to 350°. Melt butterscotch chips and butter. Stir in crumbs and nuts. Press half of mixture firmly into bottom of 13x9-inch pan. In large mixing bowl, beat cheese until fluffy. Beat in condensed milk, vanilla, and egg. Mix well. Pour into prepared pan. Top with remaining crumb mixture. Bake 25-30 minutes, or until toothpick inserted in center comes out clean. Cool. Chill. Refrigerate leftovers.

Look What's Cookin' at Wal-Mart

Easy Cheesy·Lemon Bars

No question about it, these superior Lemon Bars will be the first to disappear when served at any gathering.

1 (18-ounce) package lemon
  cake mix
½ cup butter or margarine,
  melted
1 egg
1 (7.2-ounce) package
  powdered white frosting
  mix

2 teaspoons lemon extract
1 (8-ounce) package cream
  cheese, softened
1 cup powdered sugar
1 tablespoon butter or
  margarine
2-3 tablespoons milk

Combine cake mix, butter or margarine, and egg; mix well. Press into 9x13-inch pan. With electric mixer, blend frosting mix, lemon extract and softened cream cheese. Beat well. Pour over bottom layer. Bake at 350° for 30-40 minutes. Cool. To prepare frosting, combine powdered sugar, butter or margarine, and milk. Beat well; spread or drizzle on bars.

Marketplace Recipes Volume II

Raspberry Bars

½ cup butter or margarine, room temperature
1 cup packed brown sugar
1½ cups all-purpose flour
½ teaspoon salt
½ teaspoon baking soda

1½ cups quick-cooking oatmeal
¼ cup water
1 teaspoon lemon juice
⅔ cup raspberry jam

Preheat oven to 350°. Cream butter and sugar until fluffy. Stir together flour, salt, and soda; stir into creamed mixture. Add oats and water and mix until crumbly. Firmly pat half the mixture into a greased 9x13-inch pan. Stir lemon juice into jam and spread gently over mixture in pan. Sprinkle with remaining crumb mixture. Bake at 350° for 25 minutes. Cool and cut into bars. Makes 40 bars.

Cherry Berries on a Cloud and More

Cheesy Rhubarb Bars

CRUST:
1 cup flour
½ cup butter

5 tablespoons sugar

Mix together and press into 9x13-inch pan.

FILLING:
2 eggs, slightly beaten
⅛ teaspoon salt
1½ cups sugar
¼ cup flour

1 (8-ounce) package cream cheese
2 cups rhubarb, peeled and finely cut

Bake at 350° for 10 minutes. Mix together and pour over crust.

TOPPING:
¼ cup butter
½ cup flour

2½ tablespoons powdered sugar

Mix and crumble on top of filling. Bake at 350° for 40-45 minutes or until set.

A Taste of Home

Audrey's Cheese Bars

2 (8-ounce) cans crescent
  rolls
1 cup sugar
2 (8-ounce) packages cream
  cheese, softened

1 egg, separated
1 teaspoon vanilla
½ cup sugar
½ cup nuts
½ teaspoon cinnamon

Put one package of crescent rolls on bottom of 9x13-inch pan. Mix 1 cup sugar, cream cheese, egg yolk, and vanilla; spread on top of crescent rolls. Put other package of rolls on top and spread beaten egg white on top. Sprinkle with ½ cup sugar, nuts, and cinnamon. Bake at 350° for 30 minutes.

Favorite Recipes of Pommern Cooks

Mixed Nut Bars

1½ cups flour
½ cup butter
¾ cup brown sugar
1 (6-ounce) package
  butterscotch chips

⅓ cup light corn syrup
2 tablespoons butter
1 can mixed salted nuts

Mix flour, ½ cup butter, and sugar together. Pat into 9x13-inch pan. Bake 10 minutes at 350° and cool. Heat over low heat the butterscotch chips, corn syrup, and 2 tablespoons butter. Cover bottom of the crust with nuts. Pour melted mixture over nuts. Bake for 10 minutes.

What's on the Agenda?

Cherry Nut Bars

2 cups flour
2 cups quick cooking oats
1½ cups sugar
½ cup pecans or walnuts, chopped
1 teaspoon baking soda
1 cup butter, melted (may use margarine)
1 (21-ounce) can cherry pie filling
1 cup miniature marshmallows

Combine flour, oats, sugar, nuts, soda, and butter. Mix at low speed until crumbly consistency. Set aside 1½ cups for topping. Press remaining into a 9x13-inch pan. Bake at 350° for 12-15 minutes or until lightly browned at edges. Carefully spread pie filling over crust; sprinkle with marshmallows and remaining crumb mixture. Bake for 25-30 minutes more or until lightly browned. Cool. Yield: 4 dozen small bars.

St. John Evangelical Lutheran Church

Bun Bars

2 cups peanut butter
2 ounces baking chocolate
1 (12-ounce) package milk chocolate chips
1 (12-ounce) butterscotch chips
1 (16-ounce) can Spanish peanuts

Melt peanut butter, chocolate, and chips in double boiler or microwave. Spread ½ of mixture in well buttered 10x15-inch jelly roll pan. Chill. Add peanuts to remaining mixture and set aside.

FILLING:

¼ cup regular vanilla pudding mix
½ cup evaporated milk
½ teaspoon vanilla
1 cup melted butter
2 pounds powdered sugar

Combine pudding mix and milk. Cook until very thick and well blended. In medium-size mixing bowl, beat pudding mixture, vanilla, and butter with powdered sugar. Spread on chilled chocolate layer. Refrigerate until firm. Spread chocolate peanut mixture on top and store in refrigerator. Cut into small one inch squares to serve. Freezes well. Yield: 4 dozen.

All in Good Taste II

Peanut Squares

CRUST:

1½ cups flour
⅔ packed brown sugar
½ teaspoon baking powder
½ teaspoon salt
¼ teaspoon baking soda

½ cup oleo
1 teaspoon vanilla
2 egg yolks
3 cups mini-marshmallows

Heat oven to 350°. Combine all crust ingredients except marshmallows. Press firmly in bottom of ungreased 9x13-inch pan. Bake at 350° for 12-15 minutes or until light golden brown; remove from oven. Immediately sprinkle with marshmallows. Return to oven for 1-2 minutes or until marshmallows just begin to puff. Cool while preparing topping.

TOPPING:

⅔ cup corn syrup
½ cup oleo
2 teaspoons vanilla
1 (12-ounce) package peanut
  butter chips (2 cups)

2 cups crisp rice cereal
2 cups salted peanuts

In large saucepan, heat corn syrup, oleo, vanilla, and peanut butter chips until chips are melted and mixture is smooth; stir constantly. Remove from heat, stir in cereal and peanuts. Immediately spoon warm topping over marshmallows; spread to cover. Refrigerate until firm. Cut into bars.

Centennial Cookbook

Goofy Bars

"These are my absolute favorite bars," says 3rd grader, Ian Laessig.

2 eggs
1 white or yellow cake mix
1 cup brown sugar

1 cup miniature marsh-
  mallows
1 cup chocolate chips

Put eggs in a measuring cup and mix well; add enough water to make ⅔ cup. Mix well with cake mix and brown sugar and place in a greased 9x13-inch cake pan. Sprinkle with marshmallows and chocolate chips. Bake in a 350° oven for 25-30 minutes. Cool before cutting into bars.

A Collection of Recipes

Macadamia Nut Bars

1 cup butter or margarine
¾ cup brown sugar
¾ cup white sugar
1 teapsoon vanilla
½ teaspoon salt
1 teaspoon soda

2 eggs
2¼ cups flour
1 small jar macadamia nuts,
  chopped
12 ounces white chocolate
  chips

TOPPING:
12 ounces white chocolate chips, melted

Cream butter or margarine with white and brown sugar. Add vanilla, salt, soda, and eggs. Mix well. Add flour and mix again. Stir in nuts and white chocolate chips. Pour into greased 15½x10½-inch baking pan. Bake at 375° for 25 minutes. Cool. Spread with melted topping.

Celebrating 150 Years of Faith and Food

Tumbledowns

½ cup sugar
½ cup brown sugar, firmly
  packed
½ cup shortening or butter
½ cup peanut butter
2 tablespoons milk
1 teaspoon vanilla
1 egg

1 (6-ounce) package chocolate
  chips
1 (6-ounce) package Heath
  bits
1½ cups miniature
  marshmallows
1¾ cups flour
1 teaspoon baking soda
½ teaspoon salt

In a large bowl, combine sugar, brown sugar, shortening, peanut butter, milk, vanilla, and egg. Blend at medium speed until smooth. Stir in flour, soda, and salt. Mix well. Add the chocolate chips, Heath bits, and marshmallows and mix.

Using a teaspoon, drop 2 inches apart on ungreased cookie sheet. Bake at 375° for 8-12 minutes until light golden brown. Let cool slightly before removing from pan. Makes 36 cookies.

Winning Recipes from Wisconsin with Love

Chocolate Mint Bars

CAKE:

½ cup butter, softened
½ cup sugar
4 eggs

1 cup flour, sifted
1 pinch salt
1 can Hershey chocolate syrup

Cream butter and sugar. Add eggs, one at a time. Fold in flour and salt. Stir in chocolate syrup. Bake 20-25 minutes in 9x13-inch pan, 350°. Cool.

FILLING:

½ cup butter, softened
2 cups powdered sugar

3 tablespoons creme de
   menthe syrup
   (found in ice cream section)

Cream butter, powdered sugar, and creme de menthe and spread on top of cooled bars.

FROSTING:

1 (6-ounce package semi-
   sweet chocolate chips

6 tablespoons butter

Melt chocolate chips and butter. Spread or pour while warm on top of filling.

Cooking with Grace

Caramel Bars

1 package caramels
1 can evaporated milk
1 box German cake mix
¾ cup melted butter

1 cup chopped nuts
1 (6-ounce) package chocolate
   chips

Melt caramels and ⅓ cup evaporated milk over low heat. Mix cake mix, melted butter, ⅓ cup evaporated milk, and nuts together. In a greased 9x13-inch pan, put ½ the dough. Press with fingers to fit the pan. Bake 6 minutes at 350°. Sprinkle the chocolate chips on top of the dough, spoon on melted caramel mix and cover with remaining dough (will be lumpy—will even out while baking). Bake 18 minutes at 350°. Cool in refrigerator.

What's Cooking in St. Francis

Rosie's Brownies

2 cups sugar
2 cups flour
1 teaspoon baking soda
½ cup oil
4 tablespoons cocoa

1 cup water
2 eggs
½ cup sour cream
1 teaspoon vanilla

Heat oven to 350°. Mix sugar, flour, and baking soda together in a bowl. Bring oil, cocoa, and water just to a boil; pour over flour mixture.

Beat eggs and gradually add to sour cream and vanilla. Add to above. Put in jellyroll pan in and bake 20 minutes.

FROSTING:
½ cup margarine
⅓ cup milk
4 tablespoons cocoa

1 teaspoon vanilla
¾ pound powdered sugar
Nuts, optional on top

Boil margarine, milk, and cocoa one minute; add vanilla and powdered sugar. Sprinkle nuts on top, if desired.

Sparks from the Kitchen

Buster Bars

BARS:

1 package Oreo cookies
⅓ cup melted butter

½ gallon vanilla ice cream
2 cups peanuts

Crush Oreos. Mix with butter. Put in 13x9-inch pan. Spread ice cream over crust. Put peanuts over ice cream, then the Fudge Sauce. Freeze until firm.

FUDGE SAUCE:

1 can Eagle Brand
  Condensed Milk

2 cups chocolate chips

Microwave until melted. Cool slightly and put on Buster Bars.

Country Cupboard

Date Rum Balls

¼ cup butter or margarine
1 (8-ounce) package
  chopped, pitted dates
½ cup firmly packed brown
  sugar
1 egg

2 cups Rice Krispies cereal
½ cup coconut
½ cup chopped nuts
½ teaspoon rum
Powdered sugar to roll ball in

Cook together over medium heat, margarine, dates, and brown sugar. Remove from heat and stir in the egg. Continue cooking until mixture comes to a full boil. Stir constantly. Stir in dry ingredients and rum. Cool until mixture can be handled and shaped into 1-inch balls. Roll balls into powdered sugar.

Mt. Carmel's "Cooking with the Oldies"

Reese's Peanut Butter Cups

½ cup shortening
½ cup sugar
½ cup brown sugar
½ cup peanut butter
1 egg

1 teaspoon vanilla
½ teapoon salt
¾ teaspoon baking soda
1¼ cups flour
Peanut butter cups

Cream together shortening, sugars, and peanut butter. Beat in egg and vanilla; add dry ingredients. Shape into 1-inch balls and put in mini-muffin tin. Bake 8-10 minutes at 325°. Remove from oven; press the peanut butter cup in the center. Let cool before removing. Makes approximately 4 dozen.

Sacred Heart Centennial Cookbook

Honey Coconut Bites
(Candy)

½ cup butter
2 tablespoons milk
1 cup flour
¾ cup honey

½ teaspoon salt
1 cup grated coconut
1 teaspoon vanilla
2 cups crushed crisp rice cereal

Combine all ingredients except vanilla and cereal in a saucepan. Cook over medium heat, stirring constantly until dough leaves the sides of the pan and forms a ball. Remove from heat and cool. Add vanilla and cereal. Shape into 1-inch balls. May be rolled in additional coconut. Chill thoroughly. Makes about 42 pieces.

Every 1 A Winner! Blue Ribbon Recipes

Honey Pecan Rolls
(Candy)

2 teaspoons flour
½ teaspoon salt
¼ cup evaporated milk
4 teaspoons butter, melted

1 cup honey
½ teaspoon vanilla
1 cup chopped pecans
1 cup mini-marshmallows

Combine flour, salt, and milk in saucepan. Mix in butter and honey. Cook over high heat, stirring constantly, to firm ball stage, 258° on candy thermometer. Remove from heat and quickly stir in vanilla. Place layer of pecans in the bottom of a buttered 9x9-inch pan. Cover pecans with ¼-inch hot caramel mixture. Cover with marshmallows. Cover marshmallows with remaining caramel mixture. Cut into strips 1 inch wide and 2 inches long and shape into rolls. Wrap each roll in waxed paper. Chill. Makes about 24 pieces.

Every 1 A Winner! Blue Ribbon Recipes

Emigrants from Glarus, Switzerland located in the Little Sugar River Valley in the heart of Green County in 1845. New Glarus is now truly "Little Switzerland" with the architecture in the Swiss Emmenthal style. Each year there is a Heidi Festival which features a play, alphorn playing, yodeling, folk dancing and flag throwing.

Craisin-Pistachio Clusters

Dried cranberries (craisins) are a relative newcomer to the dried fruit scene. I love their bright red color and their pleasantly tart flavor. They pair perfectly with white chocolate and natural shelled pistachios in this so-simple Christmas candy. You can experiment with varying amounts of craisins and pistachios.

1 pound white confectionary coating (also called white chocolate)*
1 cup craisins (4 ounces)

1 cup natural (non-dyed) pistachios, shelled (8 ounces, unshelled)

Bring one cup water in bottom pan of double boiler to boil over high heat; remove from heat. Cut confectionary coating into ½-inch pieces and drop in top half of double boiler, then place over hot water in bottom pan. Stir constantly until coating is melted and mixture is smooth. Stir in craisins and pistachios.

Drop fruit mixture from tablespoons onto wax paper or parchment paper-lined trays. Refrigerate until firm, about one hour. Package in paper candy liners in covered container. Makes 36 clusters.

Note: *White confectionary coating is sold in bulk in supermarket produce departments.

The Sunday Cook Collection

Goof Balls

1 package caramels
1 can sweetened condensed milk

½ stick butter
Marshmallows
Rice Krispies

Melt caramels, milk, and butter in microwave. Dip large marshmallows in mixture. Then roll in Rice Kirspies.

St. Charles Parish Cookbook

Honey Almond Caramel Corn

Don't save this one for the holidays—try it now. But watch out, it's a little addictive.

Oil
10 cups popped popcorn
¼ cup dried coconut
   (optional)
1 cup brown sugar
½ cup honey
2 tablespoons butter
1 tablespoon cider vinegar
½ teaspoon salt
1 cup toasted whole
   almonds, coarsely chopped*
½ teaspoon baking soda

Oil a very large bowl and a baking sheet. Place popcorn in bowl; sprinkle coconut over it (optional). Pour ½ cup water in a heavy, medium saucepan. Add brown sugar, honey, butter, vinegar, and salt. Bring to a boil over medium-high heat and cook until mixture reaches 250° on a candy thermometer. Stir in nuts and continue to cook until mixture reaches 265°. Turn off heat; stir in baking soda (mixture will turn opaque and creamy). Immediately pour over popcorn and stir to coat all the kernels.

Spread caramel corn on baking sheet. Cool completely. Break into serving pieces. Store airtight. (A clean-up hint: very hot or boiling water will melt away any sticky mess.) Makes 2½ quarts.

*To toast nuts, bake at 350° in a single layer 10-15 minutes, tossing once or twice.

Fresh Market Wisconsin

Puppy Chow

1 (12-ounce) bag chocolate
   chips
1 stick margarine
1 cup creamy peanut butter
1 (12.3-ounce) box Crispix
   cereal
3 cups powdered sugar

Melt chips, margarine, and peanut butter in microwave for 1½ minutes. Remove. Mix with cereal until cereal is well coated. Put 3 cups of powdered sugar in large brown grocery bag. Add mixture and shake until coated.

Wisconsin's Best

Caramels

1 cup butter
1 pound brown sugar
(2¼ cups)
Dash of salt

1 cup light corn syrup
1 (14-ounce) can sweetened
condensed milk
1 teaspoon vanilla

Melt butter. Add brown sugar and salt. Stir until thoroughly combined. Blend in corn syrup. Gradually add milk, stirring constantly. Cook and stir over medium heat till mixture reaches firm ball stage. Remove from heat and stir in vanilla. Pour into buttered 9x11-inch pan; cool completely. Cut into bite-size squares. Wrap individually in wax paper squares.

Centennial Cookbook

Old Fashioned Peanut Brittle

2 cups sugar
1 cup water
1 cup light syrup
¼ teaspoon salt

1 tablespoon butter
1 cup peanuts
1 teaspoon baking soda

Mix sugar, water, and syrup in large saucepan. Cook over moderate heat until a small amount forms a soft ball in cold water. Then add salt, butter, and peanuts and continue cooking, stirring until candy becomes a golden brown. Add baking soda. Stir up and pour on large sheet of waxed paper. Break into pieces. Cool.

What's Cooking in St. Francis

Butter Toffee

1 cup sugar
½ teaspoon salt
¼ cup water

½ cup butter
½ cup walnuts (optional)
1 cup chocolate chips

Combine first 4 ingredients and cook to 285° (hard crack) stirring constantly. Add ½ cup chopped walnuts, if desired. Pour onto well-greased cookie sheet. Sprinkle one cup chocolate chips over immediately. Allow a few minutes to melt and spread, using back of teaspoon. Cool and break.

A Collection of Recipes

Heath Candy

1 cup pecans, crushed
¾ cup brown sugar

½ cup butter
½ cup semi-sweet chocolate pieces

Sprinkle pecans onto the bottom of a greased 9-inch pan. Combine sugar and butter in a saucepan and bring to a boil, stirring for 7 minutes. Remove from heat and spread over nuts. Sprinkle chocolate pieces on top. Cover pan so heat will melt chocolate pieces, then spread them over the top. Cut into squares and refrigerate to set.

Favorite Recipes of the Wisconsin NFO

Creamy Maple Fudge

3 cups brown sugar
⅓ cup Wisconsin pure
  maple syrup
⅓ cup milk

2 tablespoons butter
Salt
½ teaspoon vanilla
½ cup chopped nuts

Combine all ingredients except vanilla and nuts. Stir gently over low heat until dissolved. Do not stir, but boil to soft-ball stage. Cool. Beat until thick and creamy. Add flavoring and nuts. Pour into greased pan, and cut before mixture cools and hardens.

Wisconsin Pure Maple Syrup Cookbook

Dad's Favorite Fudge

4 pounds powdered sugar
1 cup cocoa
1 tablespoon vanilla

1 pound butter
1 pound Velveeta cheese

Place into a large bowl the powdered sugar, cocoa, and vanilla. Melt over low heat, the butter and Velveeta cheese, stirring constantly. Add to dry ingredients and mix thoroughly. Pour into 2 buttered, 9x13-inch pans, or one extra-large cake pan. Chill. Makes two large pans.

Look What's Cookin' at Wal-Mart

Fudge

½ stick butter
1 cup white sugar
1 cup brown sugar
¼ cup white syrup

½ cup evaporated milk
¼ teaspoon salt
1 teaspoon vanilla
½ cup butternuts

Melt butter in heavy pan. Remove from heat and add sugars, syrup, and evaporated milk. Bring to a full boil, stirring constantly for 2½ - 3 minutes. Test for soft ball in cold water. Remove from heat and add salt and vanilla. Stir until somewhat cooled, then add butternuts or your choice. Stir until it holds its shape. Drop by spoonfuls on wax paper. Makes about 30 pieces.

Variation: Chocolate Fudge: When the above reaches the soft ball stage, add one packet of Choco-Bake and blend well. Continue as above. In this, I use black walnuts.

St. Mary's Family Cookbook

Fantasy Fudge

3 cups sugar
¾ cup margarine
1 (5⅓ -ounce) can evaporated milk
1 (12-ounce) package semi-sweet chocolate pieces

1 (7-ounce) jar Kraft Marshmallow Creme
1 cup chopped nuts
1 teaspoon vanilla

Combine sugar, margarine, and milk in heavy 2½-quart saucepan; bring to a full rolling boil, stirring constantly. Continue boiling 5 minutes over medium heat, stirring constantly to prevent scorching. Remove from heat, stir in chocolate pieces until melted. Add marshmallow creme, nuts, and vanilla; beat until well blended. Pour into greased 13x9-inch pan. Cool at room temperature, cut into squares. Makes 3 pounds.

The Octagon House Cookbook

 The Republican Party was founded at the Little White Schoolhouse in Ripon in 1854. Ripon is also home to the equine giants, Larson's Famous Clydesdales.

Cakes

On national and state registers of historic places, Holy Hill is a national shrine of Mary run by the Discalced Carmelite of Friars located in Hubertus thirty miles north of Milwaukee.

Easy Brandy Alexander Cheesecakes

CAKES:

½ cup softened butter
2 (8-ounce) packages cream
  cheese
2 eggs
¾ cup sugar
¼ cup flour

2 teaspoons creme de cocoa or
  Kahlua
2 teaspoons brandy
1 cup whipping cream
15 chocolate sandwich
  cookies (Oreos)

Cream butter and cream cheese. Beat in eggs. Add sugar, flour, creme de cocoa, brandy, and whipping cream. Beat until well mixed. Line cupcake tins with 30 paper liners. Twist cookies apart and place half in each of the liners. Fill with batter until liners are almost full. Bake at 350° for 25-30 minutes or until lightly browned; cool.

TOPPING:

1 cup whipping cream
¼ - ½ teaspoon instant
  coffee powder
1 teaspoon brandy
1 teaspoon creme de cocoa or
  Kahlua

2 teaspoons sugar
Freshly grated nutmeg, for
  garnish

Combine all topping ingredients. Stir and store in refrigerator for 10 minutes or longer. Remove from refrigerator and beat until soft peaks form. Frost the cheesecakes with this mixture and sprinkle with nutmeg. Store in refrigerator.

Cardinal Country Cooking

Grandma's Cheesecake

CRUST:

2½ cups graham cracker crumbs

½ cup margarine
¼ cup sugar

Melt butter and mix in graham cracker crumbs and sugar. Press in a 9x13-inch pan bottom and sides.

FILLING:

2 (8-ounce) packages cream cheese
3 eggs

1¼ cups sugar, divided
1 teaspoon vanilla
16 ounces sour cream

Mix together the cream cheese, eggs, ¾ cup sugar, and vanilla. Beat by mixer for 1 or 2 minutes on high until smooth. Pour in crust; bake at 350° for 30-35 minutes. Cool 10 minutes. Mix together sour cream and ½ cup sugar; pour on top and bake for an additional 10 minutes.

What's Cooking in St. Francis

Delightful Cheesecake

CRUST:

2½ cups graham cracker crumbs

2 tablespoons powdered sugar
½ cup butter, melted

Mix ingredients together. Save ⅓ of this mixture for topping. Press remainder in bottom and sides of 9x13-inch pan.

FILLING:

1 (3-ounce) package lemon Jell-O
1 cup hot water
1 (8-ounce) package cream cheese

½ cup sugar
1 teaspoon vanilla
1 pint whipping cream

Dissolve Jell-O in hot water in large mixer bowl. Cool until consistency of egg whites. Add cream cheese, sugar, vanilla, and whipping cream. Whip or beat all together until smooth and fluffy. Pour into crumb crust and top with crumbs. Chill.

Sharing Our Best

Lowfat Cheesecake

1 (8-ounce) package light
  cream cheese, softened
1 (8-ounce) carton light
  Cool Whip

1 cup powdered sugar
Graham cracker crust
1 (21-ounce) can cherry pie
  filling

Beat well cream cheese, Cool Whip, and powdered sugar. Fold into graham cracker crust. Refrigerate about 2 hours. Pour cherry pie filling over top before serving.

Note: No-fat cream cheese can be used, but it doesn't seem to set up as well.

Taste and See

Chocolate Chip Cheesecake

1½ cups graham cracker
  crumbs
⅓ cup Hershey's cocoa
⅓ cup sugar
⅓ cup melted butter or
  margarine
3 (8-ounce) packages cream
  cheese

1 (14-ounce) can sweetened
  condensed milk
3 eggs
2 teaspoon vanilla
1 cup Hershey's semi-sweet
  mini-chips, divided
1 teaspoon flour

Preheat oven to 300°. In bowl combine graham cracker crumbs, cocoa, sugar, and butter; press evenly into bottom of 9-inch springform pan. In large mixer bowl beat cream cheese until fluffy. Gradually add condensed milk, beating until smooth. Add eggs and vanilla. Mix well.

In small bowl toss ½ cup mini chips with flour to coat; stir into cheese mixture. Pour into pan and sprinkle remaining ½ cup chips evenly over top. Bake at 300° for one hour. Turn off oven, allow to cool in oven for one hour. Remove from oven and cool to room temperature. Refrigerate before serving.

Celebrating 150 Years of Faith and Food

Brownie Swirl Cheesecake

1 (8-ounce) package
  brownie mix
2 (8-ounce) packages cream
  cheese
½ cup sugar
1 teaspoon vanilla

2 eggs
1 cup milk chocolate chips,
  melted
Whipped cream
Cherries for garnish

Grease bottom of 9-inch springform pan. Prepare basic brownie mix as directed on package; pour batter evenly into springform pan. Bake at 350° for 15 minutes. Combine cream cheese, sugar, and vanilla, mixing at medium speed on electric mixer until well blended. Add eggs one at a time, mixing well after each addition. Pour over brownie mix layer. Spoon melted chocolate over cream cheese mixture; cut through batter with knife several times for marble effect. Bake at 350° for 35 minutes. Loosen cake from rim of pan; cool before removing rim of pan. Garnish with whipped cream and cherries.

A Collection of Recipes

Lemon Refrigerator Cake

1 tablespoon unflavored
  gelatin
¼ cup cold water
6 slightly beaten egg yolks
1½ cups sugar, divided
¾ cup lemon juice

1½ teaspoons lemon rind
6 egg whites
1 large angel food cake
1 cup heavy whipping cream,
  whipped

Soften gelatin in the cold water. Combine yolks, ¾ cup sugar, lemon juice, and lemon rind, and cook over hot (not boiling) water, stirring constantly until mixture coats a metal spoon. Remove from heat and add softened gelatin. Stir until dissolved. Beat egg whites until stiff and gradually add remaining sugar, beating constantly. Fold into custard. Tear cake into small pieces and arrange a layer in large oiled angel food pan. Pour part of the custard over cake. Alternate layers until all is used. Chill until firm. Unmold and frost with whipped cream. Serves 12-14.

Family Fare

Poppy Seed Torte

Poppy Seed Torte has been a tradition in our family for years. Whenever there's a party, we make this torte.

CRUST:

1½ packages graham crackers, crushed (about 30 squares)

½ cup butter, melted
¼ cup sugar

In small bowl, mix ingredients with fork. Reserve ¼ cup; pat remainder into bottom and up sides of 9x13x2-inch glass pan.

FILLING:

½ cup sugar
3 tablespoons cornstarch
¼ cup poppy seeds
3 cups whole milk

4 egg yolks, lightly beaten
¼ cup butter
1 teaspoon vanilla

In heavy 2-quart saucepan, mix together sugar, cornstarch, and poppy seeds. Stir in milk. Cook over medium heat, until boiling and slightly thickened, stirring constantly. Spoon some of the hot pudding into egg yolks and mix well. Stir yolk mixture into pudding and continue cooking until thick and bubbly; stirring constantly. Remove from heat and stir in butter and vanilla; stir until butter melts. Cool to room temperature. Spoon into crust.

MERINGUE TOPPING:

4 egg whites, room temperature

1 (7-ounce) jar marshmallow cream

Preheat oven to 325°. In large bowl, beat egg whites until frothy. Add jar of marshmallow cream. Beat until stiff peaks form. Carefully spoon meringue onto filling, spreading evenly to cover filling to edge of glas pan. Sprinkle reserved crumbs on top. Bake for 30 minutes until meringue is nicely browned. Cool on rack to room temperature. Refrigerate until serving. Makes 18 servings.

50 Years of Regal Recipes

Rhubarb Torte

1 cup sugar
3 tablespoons cornstarch
4 cups sliced rhubarb
½ cup water
Few drops red food coloring
1 recipe Graham Cracker
  Crust

½ cup whipping cream
1½ cups tiny marshmallows
1 (3½-ounce) package instant
  vanilla pudding mix

Combine sugar and cornstarch; stir in rhubarb and water. Cook and stir till thickened. Reduce heat; cook 2-3 minutes. Add food coloring. Spread on cooled Graham Cracker Crust. Cool.

Whip cream; fold in marshmallows. Spoon on rhubarb mixture. Prepare pudding according to package directions; spread over all. Sprinkle with reserved crumbs. Chill. Makes 9 servings.

GRAHAM CRACKER CRUST:
4 tablespoons melted butter
  or margarine, reserve 2
  tablespoons

1 cup graham cracker crumbs
2 tablespoons sugar

Combine all ingredients, reserve 2 tablespoons crumb mixture. Pat remainder in 9x9-inch pan. Bake at 350° for 10 minutes. Cool.

The Octagon House Cookbook

Peach Torte

2 cups flour
¾ cup butter
10 tablespoons powdered
  sugar (approximately
  ⅔ cup)
2 beaten eggs
1½ cups sugar

¾ teaspoon baking soda
¼ teaspoon salt
½ teaspoon vanilla
¼ cup flour
4 cups fresh sliced peaches
¾ cup chopped nuts
  (optional)

Blend flour, butter, and powdered sugar together with pastry blender. Pat into a greased 9x13-inch baking pan. Bake 18-20 minutes at 350°. Cream together eggs and sugar; add and blend baking soda, salt, vanilla, and flour. Stir in sliced peaches and nuts if desired. Pour over crust and bake 40-45 minutes in 350° oven. Serve with whipped cream or ice cream.

A Taste of Christ Lutheran

Peach Coffee Cake

1 (18-ounce) package yellow cake mix
3 eggs
½ teaspoon lemon extract

1 (21-ounce) can peach pie filling
½ cup pecans or walnuts

Combine cake mix, eggs, lemon extract, and peach pie filling, and beat at medium speed for 2 minutes. Add nuts. Pour batter into greased 9x13-inch pan.

TOPPING:
½ cup sugar
½ cup flour
½ teaspoon nutmeg

½ teaspoon cinnamon
½ stick margarine
½ cup pecans and walnuts

Mix topping ingredients until crumbly and sprinkle on batter. Bake at 375° for 30-35 minutes.

Cooking with the Lioness Club

Kimberly's Strawberry Coffee Cake

Every cook has one of those "whip-it-up-in-a-jiffy" company cakes. It looks like you really fussed, and they'll never believe how easy it was!

1 cup flour
½ cup sugar
2 teaspoons baking powder
½ teaspoon salt
½ cup milk

1 egg
1 teaspoon vanilla extract
2 tablespoons butter, melted
1½ cups fresh strawberries, sliced

STREUSEL:
½ cup flour
½ cup sugar

¼ cup butter, softened

In large bowl, mix flour, sugar, baking powder, and salt. Add milk, egg, vanilla, and butter. Stir until well blended. Pour into greased and floured 8-inch springform pan. Top with berries. Make streusel by combining flour, sugar, and butter; sprinkle over berries. Bake at 375° for 30 minutes, or until golden brown and toothpick inserted in cake comes out clean. Slice into 8 wedges and serve. Serves 8.

Variations: Add sliced plums and nutmeg, sugar and streusel . . . the list goes on. Top the warm cake with frozen yogurt, ice cream, or whipped cream for a terrific dessert.

Have Breakfast with Us . . . Again

Laura Ingalls Wilder's Gingerbread with Chocolate Frosting

1 cup brown sugar
½ cup shortening
½ cup molasses
2 teaspoons baking soda
1 cup boiling water
3 cups flour

1 teaspoon each: ginger, cinnamon, allspice, and nutmeg
¼ teaspoon cloves
½ teaspoon salt
2 eggs

Blend brown sugar and shortening; mix molasses well with this. Mix baking soda with boiling water (be sure cup is full of water after foam runs off into cake batter). Mix all well. Blend flour with spices and salt. Sift all into the mixture and mix well. Add lastly, 2 well-beaten eggs. The mixture should be quite thin. Pour into a greased 9x13-inch baking pan. Bake in a moderate oven (350°) for 30 minutes. Cool and frost with Boiled Chocolate Frosting.

BOILED CHOCOLATE FROSTING:

2 cups sugar
2 heaping tablespoons
  cocoa

⅔ cup milk
½ cup butter
2 teaspoons vanilla

Mix sugar and cocoa together; add milk, a little at a time, then the butter. Boil for 6 minutes. Remove from heat and add vanilla and let cool. Beat until creamy.

Note: May add one teaspoon table syrup when adding vanilla, to prevent sugaring.

Trinity Lutheran Church of Norden Anniversary Cookbook

Royal Almond Cake
(Mazurka)

½ pound butter
½ pound flour (2 cups)
½ pound almonds, ground
1 pound sugar
5 eggs

In a medium mixing bowl, beat ingredients at medium speed for 5-10 minutes, until batter has a velvet sheen. Do not overbeat! Spread into greased jellyroll pan. Bake at 325° for 45 minutes until lightly browned. Cut into desired shapes. Simple and good.

Sunflowers & Samovars

Pig Lickin' Good Cake

1 (18- or 19-ounce) package
  yellow cake mix
4 eggs, beaten
½ cup oil
1 cup mandarin orange
  sections and juice

FROSTING:
1 (12-ounce) container Cool
  Whip
1 (3.4-ounce) package
  instant vanilla pudding
1 cup crushed pineapple,
  drained

Mix together cake mix, eggs, oil, orange segments, and juice. Spoon into greased 9x13-inch pan; bake according to package directions. Cool. Mix frosting ingredients together; spread over cooled cake. Refrigerate. Makes 12-18 servings.

50 Years of Regal Recipes

Nutmeg Cake

2 cups flour
2 cups brown sugar
½ cup shortening
1 egg
1 teaspoon nutmeg
1 cup sour cream
1 teaspoon soda
½ cup chopped nuts

With hands, blend flour, sugar, and shortening into crumbs. Put ½ into cake pan; stir into remaining crumbs the rest of ingredients, except nuts. Pour over crumbs in a 9-inch pan, cover with nuts and bake at 350° for 35-40 minutes.

Look What's Cooking at C.A.M.D.E.N

Classic Cranberry Cake with Sauce Topping

¾ cup butter, softened
1 cup sugar
2 eggs
1 cup sour cream
1¾ cups flour

¼ teaspoon baking soda
1½ teaspoons baking powder
2 cups fresh cranberries, halved
1 teaspoon vanilla

Cream butter and sugar; add eggs and sour cream. Reserve 2 tablespoons flour. Mix together the remaining flour, soda, and baking powder. Sprinkle the reserved flour over the halved cranberries and stir them into the batter with spoon. Add vanilla. Pour the batter into greased and floured 9x13-inch pan. Bake 30 minutes at 350°.

SAUCE TOPPING:

1½ cups granulated sugar
1 cup whipping cream

2 tablespoons butter
1 teaspoon vanilla

Mix sugar, cream, and butter in medium saucepan; boil 2 minutes, stirring constantly. Remove from heat. Add vanilla. Serve warm sauce over cake. Sauce may be reheated as used.

Blessed Be The Cook

Beet Cake

½ cup cocoa
1½ cups cooking oil
1 teaspoon vanilla
1¾ cups flour
1½ cups sugar
1½ teaspoons baking soda

1 teaspoon salt
¾ cup egg substitute* for low cholesterol or 3 eggs
1¼ cups cooked, mashed beets
¼ cup chopped nuts

Mix cocoa, cooking oil, and vanilla in mixing bowl. In another bowl, mix flour, sugar, baking soda, and salt. Mix together; add to cocoa mixture. Blend in eggs and beets. With electric mixer, beat at medium speed 2 minutes. Stir in nuts. Pour into a 9x13-inch baking pan. Bake at 350° for 23-30 minutes. Frost if desired. It's a delicious devil's food cake, and no cholesterol*.

St. Frederick Parish Centennial Recipe Collection

14-Carat Cake

2 cups sifted flour
2 teaspoons baking powder
1½ teaspoons baking soda
1½ teaspoons salt
2 teaspoons ground
   cinnamon
2 cups sugar
1½ cups salad oil
4 eggs

2 cups finely shredded, pared
   carrots
1 (8½-ounce) can crushed
   pineapple, drained
½ cup chopped walnuts
1 (3½-ounce) can flaked
   coconut
Cream Cheese Frosting

Sift together flour, baking powder, baking soda, salt, and cinnamon in mixing bowl. Add sugar, oil, and eggs. Beat at medium speed of electric mixer one minute. Stir in carrots, pineapple, walnuts, and coconut. Turn into 3 greased and floured 9-inch round cake pans. Bake in 350° oven for 40 minutes, or until cake tests done. Cool in pans on racks 10 minutes. Remove from pans; cool on racks.

CREAM CHEESE FROSTING:

½ cup butter or regular
   margarine
1 (8-ounce) package cream
   cheese, softened

1 teaspoon vanilla
1 (1-pound) box
   confectioners' sugar

Cream together butter, cream cheese, and vanilla in a bowl at medium speed of electric mixer. Gradually add confectioners' sugar, beating well until smooth and creamy. If mixture is too thick to spread, add a little milk. Fill layers and frost top and sides of cake.

Country Heart Cooking

Coconut Almond Carrot Ring

1½ cups flour
1½ teaspoons baking
  powder
½ teaspoon salt
1 teaspoon cinnamon
1 cup sugar

1 cup oil
2 eggs
1 cup grated carrots
1½ cups chopped almonds
½ cup raisins
⅔ cup coconut

Mix flour, baking powder, salt, and cinnamon. Beat sugar and oil at medium speed until well mixed. Stir in flour mixture. Add eggs and beat well. Stir in carrots, nuts, raisins, and coconut. Pour into greased and floured Bundt pan. Bake at 350° for 45 minutes. Frost with cream cheese frosting.

Celebrating 150 Years of Faith and Food

Praline-Topped Oatmeal Cake

1½ cups boiling water
1 cup quick-cooking rolled
  oats
1½ cups sifted flour
1 teaspoon baking soda
½ teaspoon salt
1 teaspoon cinnamon
½ cup butter or margarine

1 cup brown sugar, firmly
  packed
1 cup sugar
2 eggs
1 teaspoon vanilla
¾ cup chopped walnuts
Praline Topping

Pour boiling water over oats and let stand 20 minutes. Mix and sift flour, soda, salt, and cinnamon. Cream butter. Add sugars gradually and cream until light and fluffy. Add unbeaten eggs, one at a time, beating well after each addition. Add vanilla and oatmeal mixture and blend well. Add flour mixture gradually. Fold in nuts. Mix only enough to keep the batter smooth. Pour batter into greased 9x9-inch pan and bake 30-40 minutes at 350°. Spread Praline Topping carefully over hot cake and return to oven. "Broil" topping just long enough to make it brown and bubbly. Watch carefully.

PRALINE TOPPING:

½ cup brown sugar
2 tablespoons flour
¼ cup melted butter
2 tablespoons water

½ cup finely chopped walnuts
¾ cup shredded or flaked
  coconut

Combine all ingredients and spread on hot cake.

Foxy Ladies

Kahlua Fudge O.D. Cake

This cake is surprisingly easy, but very, very good.

5 ounces unsweetened
  chocolate
2 cups flour
1 teaspoon baking soda
¼ teaspoon salt
¼ cup instant espresso
  powder

½ cup Kahlua
2 sticks unsalted butter
2 cups sugar
1 teaspoon vanilla
3 large eggs
Additional liqueur
Powdered sugar

Melt chocolate and set aside to slightly cool. Sift flour, baking soda, and salt. Set aside. In a large glass measuring cup, dissolve espresso in small amount of boiling water. Add cold water to make 1½ cups. Add Kahlua. Set aside.

In large food processor or bowl, cream butter. Mix sugar and vanilla until creamy. Add eggs one at a time, mixing well after each addition. Add chocolate and beat well. Add coffee mixture and blend. Add dry ingredients and mix only to combine. Batter will be thin.

Pour into well-buttered Bundt pan. Rotate pan or knock bottom to be sure batter is spread evenly. Bake in preheated 325° oven for 50-60 minutes. Remove from oven and let cool 15 minutes. Remove from pan and let cool completely. After removing from pan, sprinkle warm cake with additional ½ cup coffee liqueur (or less if preferred). Before serving, sprinkle top with powdered sugar sifted through a strainer. Enjoy!

Picnics on the Square

Chocolate Cake Ritz
with Hot Chocolate Sauce

1 egg	¾ cup flour
½ cup refined sugar	½ teaspoon baking powder
¼ cup granulated sugar	¼ cup cocoa
substitute	½ teaspoon instant coffee
¼ cup margarine, melted	⅓ cup hot water
1 teaspoon vanilla	6 Ritz crackers, crumbled

Beat egg; gradually add sugar, margarine, and vanilla, mix well. Sift together flour and baking powder. Add half the flour mixture to the egg mixturre. Add cocoa. Mix hot water with instant coffee and add. Stir in remaining flour mixture. Crush crackers in a plastic bag until small crumbles and add to mixture. Bake at 350° in a 9x13-inch well-greased cake pan for 20 minutes. Serve with Maxine's Hot Chocolate Sauce. Serves 8. Calories per serving 144.

MAXINE'S HOT CHOCOLATE SAUCE:

1 tablespoon cocoa	1 tablespoon water
1 tablespoon nonfat milk	Few drops liquid sugar
powder	substitute, to taste
½ cup water	½ teaspoon vanilla
½ teaspoon cornstarch	

Mix cocoa, powdered milk, and water together and cook over medium heat, stirring constantly. Mix cornstarch and water together to make paste and slowly add some of the hot mixture to the paste; gradually add remaining mixture. Cook 5 minutes over low heat stirring frequently. Add vanilla and sugar substitute. Serve over cake or with ice cream. Serves 8. Calories pcr scrving 7.

Luscious Low-Calorie Recipes

The Green Bay Packers have been NFL champions 12 times and captured the first two Super Bowl titles and another one in 1997. The team name came from the local meat-packing industry.

Pumpkin Pie Cake

1 large can pumpkin
1 can condensed milk
3 eggs
1 cup sugar
1 teaspoon nutmeg
½ teaspoon cloves

½ teaspoon ginger
½ teaspoon salt
2 teaspoons cinnamon
1 yellow cake mix
1 cup nuts
2 sticks margarine

Mix together like making a pumpkin pie, the pumpkin, milk, eggs, sugar, nutmeg, cloves, ginger, salt, and cinnamon. Pour into a 9x13-inch pan. Sprinkle cake mix over pie mixture and press well. Sprinkle nuts on top and melt margarine and pour over top. Bake at 350° for 50 minutes.

A Taste of Christ Lutheran

Chips of Chocolate
Peanut Butter Cake

2¼ cups flour
2 cups brown sugar
1 cup peanut butter
½ cup margarine
1 teaspoon baking powder
½ teaspoon baking soda

1 cup milk
1 teaspoon vanilla
3 eggs
1 cup semi-sweet chocolate
   chips

In large bowl, blend first 4 ingredients at low speed until crumbly. Reserve one cup. Add remaining ingredients (except chocolate chips) to crumb mixture. Blend at low speed, then beat 3 minutes. Pour 2½ cups batter into greased Bundt pan. Sprinkle with chips and reserved crumb mixture. Spread remaining batter over this. Bake for 55-65 minutes at 350°. Cool completely.

GLAZE:

½ cup chocolate chips
1 tablespoon margarine

2 tablespoons milk
½ cup powdered sugar

Combine first 3 ingredients in saucepan and heat on low until melted. Beat in sugar. Drizzle on cake.

Country Cupboard

Chocolate Eclair Cake

1 cup water
½ cup margarine
1 cup flour
4 eggs
1 large package instant
  vanilla pudding

2½ cups milk
1 (8-ounce) package cream
  cheese, softened
Cool Whip
Hershey's chocolate syrup

Boil water and margarine; remove from heat. Stir in flour and eggs (one at a time), beating well in between. Spread in a greased jellyroll pan. Bake at 400° until brown, about 30 minutes. Prepare pudding with milk; whip in cream cheese. Spread over cooled puffed layer. Top with Cool Whip. Drizzle Hershey's syrup over top.

Camp Hope Cookbook

Caramel Apple Cake

The Best!

3 eggs
2 cups sugar
1½ cups vegetable oil
2 teaspoons vanilla extract
3 cups flour

1 teaspoon salt
1 teaspoon baking soda
3 cups chopped, peeled apples
1 cup chopped pecans

In mixing bowl, beat eggs until foamy; gradually add sugar. Blend in oil and vanilla. Combine flour, salt, and baking soda; add to egg mixture. Stir in apples and pecans. Pour into a greased 10-inch tube pan. Bake at 350° for 1 hour 15 minutes. Cool in pan 10 minutes. Remove to serving plate.

TOPPING:
½ cup butter
¼ cup milk

1 cup packed brown sugar
Pinch salt

Combine all ingredients in saucepan; boil 3 minutes, stirring constantly. Slowly pour over warm cake. (Some topping will run down sides onto serving plate. Keep spooning back onto cake a few more times.)

Cooking with Grace

Chocolate Chiffon Cake

CAKE:

½ cup cocoa
1 cup boiling water
1¾ cups cake flour
1¾ cups sugar
1½ teaspoons baking soda

¾ teaspoon salt
½ cup vegetable oil
8 eggs, separated
2½ teaspoons vanilla
½ teaspoon cream of tartar

Stir cocoa in boiling water until smooth. Cool 20 minutes. Mix flour, sugar, baking soda, and salt in bowl. Make a well in center and add in order: oil, egg yolks, cocoa mixture, and vanilla. Beat with spoon until smooth. Beat egg whites and cream of tartar in large bowl until stiff peaks form. Gradually pour egg yolk mixture over egg whites and mix, gently folding with rubber scraper just until blended. Pour batter into ungreased tube pan and bake in 325° oven for 60-65 minutes. Cool, remove from pan, and frost with Chocolate Glaze.

CHOCOLATE GLAZE:

⅓ cup margarine
2 cups powdered sugar
2 ounces unsweetened
  chocolate, melted and cooled

2-4 tablespoons hot water

Melt margarine; add powdered sugar and chocolate. Add water a little at a time until glaze is smooth and easy to spread. Makes 12-16 servings.

Every 1 A Winner! Blue Ribbon Recipes

Apple Sponge

Apples
1 cup brown sugar
3 well beaten eggs
Rind of 1 lemon, grated

1 teaspoon baking powder
4 tablespoons water
1 cup sugar
1 cup flour

Cut several apples into small pieces. Place them into a buttered baking dish to ¼-full. Put brown sugar over the apples. Make a sponge of remaining ingredients. Pour over the apples and bake 45 minutes in moderate oven (about 350°).

Flavors of Washington County

Wisconsin Apple Cake

1¾ cups flour	6-8 apples
1 teaspoon baking powder	¼ cup oleo
2 tablespoons sugar	1 cup sugar
⅔ cup oleo	3 tablespoons flour
1 egg	½ teaspoon cinnamon

Sift first 3 ingredients into a bowl. Cut in ⅔ cup oleo until mixture resembles corn meal. Beat egg; add to flour mixture, mixing lightly. Press dough into a 9x13-inch pan with the fingers, bringing up the sides about 1-inch.

Core and peel apples. Cut into slices. Arrange close together in rows on the pastry dough. Cut the ¼ cup oleo into the remaining sugar, flour, and cinnamon until crumbly. Sprinkle the apples with sugar topping. Bake in 375° oven for about 45 minutes. Serve warm or cold, plain or with ice cream.

Celebration of Grace

Bavarian Apple Torte

¾ cup margarine	2 eggs
½ cup sugar	¾ teaspoon vanilla
½ teaspoon vanilla	2 cups apples, finely diced
1½ cups flour	½ cup sugar
2 (8-ounce) packages cream cheese, softened	1 teaspoon cinnamon
½ cup almonds, chopped	
½ cup sugar	

Mix together first 4 ingredients. Press into a well-greased cheese cake pan or deep pie plate. Beat the cream cheese and sugar well. Add eggs and vanilla. Beat well. Pour over crust. Mix together apples, sugar, and cinnamon. Spoon over cheese mixture. Sprinkle on nuts. Bake at 350° for 50-60 minutes.

St. John Evangelical Lutheran Church

According to Native American legend, a giant serpent created the dells of the Wisconsin River. Geologist say it's the result of thousands of years of glacial waters eroding the Cambrian sandstone.

Blitz Torte

¾ cup sugar
¾ cup butter
6 egg yolks, beaten
½ cup milk

1½ cups flour, sifted with
   1½ teaspoons baking
   powder
1 teaspoon vanilla

Cream sugar and butter. Add beaten egg yolks. Add flour mixture and milk alternately to the first mixture. Add vanilla. Put in 2 (9-inch) layer pans.

Beat 6 egg whites until stiff. Add 1½ cups sugar and beat. Put egg whites over top of batter in pans. Sprinkle with ⅓ cup nuts. Bake 20 minutes at 350°, then 20 minutes at 375°.

Our Favorite Recipes

German Baked Cheese Torte

CRUST:

20 graham crackers
½ cup granulated sugar

½ teaspoon cinnamon
¼ cup shortening

Place crackers in plastic bag (preferably Ziploc). Close bag, removing any air inside. Using a rolling pin, roll over crackers until they become fine crumbs. Remove crumbs from bag and place in bowl. Add sugar, cinnamon, and shortening to crumbs and mix thoroughly. Butter a torte or springform pan and line with crumb mixture, reserving one cup for topping.

FILLING:

2 pounds cottage cheese
1 cup sugar
2 tablespoons flour
4 eggs, beaten

1 can sweetened condensed
   milk
1 teaspoon vanilla

Put cottage cheese through ricer or food mill. Add sugar and flour; mix well. Add eggs, sweetened condensed milk, and vanilla; mix well. Pour into crust. Sprinkle top with remaining crumbs. Bake about one hour and 15 minutes at 375° until set, but not hard.

Old World Swiss Family Recipes

Pies and Desserts

Larson's Famous Clydesdales proudly shows off its newest member a five-day-old baby Clydesdale. Ripon.

Cherry-Berries on a Cloud

6 egg whites   **¼ teaspoon salt**
½ teaspoon cream of tartar   **1¾ cups sugar**

Heat oven to 275°. Grease a 9x13x2-inch pan. Beat egg whites, cream of tartar and salt until frothy. Gradually beat in sugar. Beat until stiff and glossy, about 15 minutes. Spread in pan. Bake 60 minutes. Turn oven off and leave meringue in oven until cool, about 12 hours or overnight.

FILLING:
2 (3-ounce) packages cream   **1 teaspoon vanilla**
   cheese, softened   **2 cups whipped cream**
1 cup sugar   **2 cups miniature**
                                 marshmallows

Mix cream cheese with sugar (add gradually) and vanilla. Gently fold in whipped cream and marshmallows. Spread over meringue and refrigerate 12 hours or overnight. Cut into serving pieces and top with Topping.

TOPPING:
1 can cherry pie filling   **2 cups sliced, fresh**
1 teaspoon lemon juice   **strawberries or 1 package**
                                 frozen strawberries, thawed

Stir the can of cherry pie filling with juice into the sliced strawberries. Serves 12-16.

Cherry Berries on a Cloud and More

Cherry Fluff

1 can cherry pie filling
1 large can crushed
  pineapple
1 can sweetened condensed
  milk

1 (9-ounce) Cool Whip
½ cup nuts, chopped
  (optional)

Mix all ingredients and refrigerate overnight.

Taste and See

Cherry Breeze

⅓ cup butter
  cup corn flake crumbs
½ cup lemon juice
1 (8-ounce) package cream
  cheese, softened

1 (14-ounce) can sweetened
  condensed milk
1 teaspoon vanilla
1 can cherry pie filling

Melt butter. Stir in corn flake crumbs. Pat into 8x8-inch pan.
Chill. In a bowl, mix lemon juice, cream cheese, sweetened
condensed milk and vanilla. Pour over corn flake mixture. Chill.
Top with cherry pie filling. Keep refrigerated until served.

Camp Hope Cookbook

Baked Apples

Apples
Cinnamon and sugar or
  brown sugar
Cinnamon candies

Raisins (added to cinnamon
  mixture)
Mini-marshmallows

Core apples and fill with any of the mixtures. Place on foil.
Gather foil up over the top and twist together. Bake over coals,
turning occasionally.

What's Cook'n?

 Wisconsin's state tree is the sugar maple. Wisconsin ranks fourth in the nation's production of maple syrup.

Lace-Crusted Apples

5 tart cooking apples
3 tablespoons raisins
1 tablespoon lemon juice
Water
1½ teaspoons grated lemon
   peel
1 tablespoon lemon juice

½ teaspoon cinnamon
1½ cups brown sugar, firmly
   packed
½ cup finely chopped walnuts
½ cup melted butter
Vanilla ice cream

Peel and core apples. Cut into ⅓-inch thick lengthwise slices. Place in saucepan with raisins, lemon juice, and water to cover halfway. Cover; bring to a boil. Simmer until tender, about 5 minutes. Drain well. Turn into a 10-inch oven glassware pie plate. Sprinkle with lemon peel, lemon juice, and cinnamon. Combine brown sugar, walnuts, and melted butter; sprinkle over fruits. Broil about 6 inches from heat until sugar is melted and golden brown. Cool slightly. Tap crust to break and top with ice cream. Makes 6 servings.

Country Heart Cooking

Apple Mahldoschen
(Apple Custard Dessert)

SINGLE PIE CRUST:
1 cup flour
½ teaspoon salt

⅓ cup shortening
3 tablespoons water

Roll pie crust into 12x15-inch rectangle.

3 large apples, peeled
½ cup sugar
1 teaspoon cinnamon
1 tablespoon flour

1 egg
¼ cup milk
½ teaspoon vanilla
Pinch of salt

Shred apples over pie crust to 1-inch of edge. Sprinkle sugar, cinnamon, and flour over apples. Roll up, starting with long side, to finished edge underneath. Cut into 1-inch slices and place in rows into a 9x9-inch pan. Bake at 350° for 45 minutes or until top crust is lightly brown. Beat egg, and add milk, vanilla, and a pinch of salt. Pour over apple dessert and bake for another 15 minutes.

St. Frederick Parish Centennial Recipe Collection

Cranberry Apple Pie

1 cup sugar	5 apples, peeled, cored,
4 tablespoons cornstarch	chopped
1 teaspoon cinnamon	1 (12-ounce) bag of
½ teaspoon nutmeg	cranberries
1 teaspoon orange peel,	1 (9-inch) pie shell
finely grated	(bottom crust only)

Combine dry ingredients and seasoning. Toss with prepared apples and cranberries. Pour into unbaked pie shell and bake without streusel topping for 30 minutes at 350°.

TOPPING:

1 cup flour	1 teaspoon cinnamon
⅓ cup brown sugar	⅓ cup butter
⅓ cup sugar	

Combine dry ingredients. Cut butter into dry ingredients until mixture is coarse and crumb-like. Sprinkle topping over partially baked pie. Bake completely assembled pie at 350° for another 30 minutes or until crumb topping appears golden brown.

The White Gull Inn, Door County

Cranberry Apple Pie

2½ cups cranberries,	3 tablespoons tapioca
chopped	Dash of cinnamon
1½ cups apples, chopped	Pastry for 2-crust 9-inch pie
1½ cups sugar	

Combine first 5 ingredients and let stand while rolling pastry. Bake at 375° for 50-60 minutes.

The Best Cranberry Recipes

 Wisconsin produces nearly one-third of the nation's crop of cranberries, and leads the nation in the production of cranberry juice. Harvest in late September attracts tens of thousands to "Cranberry Country."

Dairy State Apple Pie

CRUST:

1 cup all-purpose flour
5 tablespoons butter or
  margarine
½ cup shredded Cheddar
  cheese

½ teaspoon salt
3-4 tablespoons milk

In a bowl, stir flour, butter, cheese, and salt until crumbly. Sprinkle with milk, one tablespoon at a time, stirring until pastry holds together. Form into a ball. Roll out on a lightly-floured board. Transfer to a 9-inch pie pan; trim and flute edges.

FILLING:

1 (3-ounce) package cream
  cheese, softened
1 egg

½ cup sugar
5 cups sliced, peeled
  baking apples

In a mixing bowl, beat cream cheese, egg, and sugar until smooth. Stir in apples; pour into crust.

TOPPING:

¼ cup all-purpose flour
¼ cup sugar
¼ teaspoon ground
  cinnamon

2 tablespoons butter or
  margarine
¼ cup chopped walnuts or
  hickory nuts
Vanilla ice cream

In another bowl, mix flour, sugar, and cinnamon. Cut in butter until crumbly. Stir in nuts. Sprinkle over apples. Bake at 350° for 15 minutes. Reduce heat to 300°. Bake for 30 minutes, or until apples are tender. Yield: 8 servings.

What's on the Agenda?

Apple Slices

3 cups slifted flour	1 cup sugar
1 teaspoon salt	1 teaspoon cinnamon
1 cup shortening	1 egg white, beaten stiff
7 tablespoons milk	1 cup sifted powdered sugar
1 egg yolk, beaten	3 tablespoons water
1 cup crushed cornflakes	1 teaspoon vanilla
8 large apples, cut up	

Sift together flour and salt. Cut in shortening until crumbly. Combine milk and egg yolk. Stir into crumb mixture until evenly moistened. Divide dough almost in half. Roll out large half; place on 10½x15½-inch pan. Press dough up on side of pan; sprinkle with crushed cornflakes. Arrange apple slices over cornflakes. Combine sugar and cinnamon; sprinkle over apples. Roll out other half of dough to fit top. Make vents in top. Moisten edges of dough with water; seal. Spread egg white over crust. Bake at 375° for one hour or until golden. Combine powdered sugar, water, and vanilla for glaze. Drizzle over bars while warm. Cut into squares for serving.

Sharing Our Best

Apple Sour Cream Pie

This is the best thing I make!

PIE:

2 tablespoons flour	1 cup (½ pint) sour cream
¾ cup sugar	6 medium apples, peeled,
¾ teaspoon cinnamon	pared and sliced
⅛ teaspoon salt	1 (9-inch) graham cracker
1 egg	crust
½ teaspoon vanilla	

TOPPING:

⅓ cup sugar	¾ teaspoon cinnamon
⅓ cup flour	¼ cup butter, creamed

Preheat oven to 400°. Combine all pie ingredients except apples and crust. Add the apples and pour mixture into crust. Bake for 15 minutes, reduce heat to 350° and bake for 30 minutes. Combine Topping ingredients and crumble over pie. Bake at 400° for 10 minutes. Serve warm or cold.

Good Cooking, Good Curling

Apple-Pear-Cranberry Crisp

6 large apples
3 large pears
1 cup raw cranberries
1 cup oatmeal

1 cup brown sugar
⅔ cup flour
⅔ cup margarine, softened

Pare and slice apples and pears. In a 7½x11-inch baking dish, layer apples, then pears. Sprinkle cranberries over all. Combine oatmeal, brown sugar, flour, and margarine. Sprinkle over fruit. Bake at 350° for 40-45 minutes. Top with Cool Whip to serve.

Sacred Heart Centennial Cookbook

Chocolate Mousse Pie

At The Norske Nook, Osseo, owner Jerry Bechard and his staff enjoy trying new things, especially creating new pie varieties. This recipe is one of their creations that is now a favorite of customers, too.

5 cups heavy Wisconsin
    whipping cream
1½ teaspoons vanilla
2 cups powdered sugar
¾ cup dry chocolate
    pudding mix

3 tablespoons cocoa
3½ cups whipped topping,
    divided
1 (10-inch) crust, baked
1 tablespoon shaved semi-
    sweet chocolate

Mix cream and vanilla together in a large electric mixing bowl. Beat one minute. Add powdered sugar and beat another minute. Add the pudding mix and cocoa; beat until firm. Fold in 1½ cups whipped topping and pour into crust. Chill until very firm. Top with remaining whipped topping and garnish with shaved chocolate. Yields 8 servings.

Our Best Cookbook 2

Hawks Inn provided some of the last pleasurable lodging and dining travelers enjoyed as they headed westward during the gold-rush days. It was built at Delafield (between Milwaukee and Madison) two years before Wisconsin became a state. In 1847 the Milwaukee Sentinel declared it "The Best Kept Hotel in the Territory."

Classic German Chocolate Pie

1 (9-inch) pie crust

FILLING:

4 ounces (1 bar) sweet
  cooking chocolate,
  chopped
⅓ cup butter, softened
  (no margarine please)

¾ cup sugar
2 tablespoons flour
3 eggs, separated
1 teaspoon vanilla extract

Preheat oven to 375°. In a large saucepan over low heat, melt chocolate and butter, stirring until smooth. Remove from heat. Add sugar, flour, egg yolks, and vanilla; stir until well blended. In small bowl, beat egg whites until stiff peaks form. Fold into chocolate mixture. Pour into pie crust-lined pan. Bake 24-30 minutes or until filling is set. Remove from oven; cool while preparing topping.

TOPPING:

½ cup sweetened condensed
  milk (not evaporated)
1 egg

1 cup flaked coconut
½ cup chopped pecans
1 teaspoon vanilla extract

In small bowl, combine all topping ingredients; blend well. Drop by teaspoonfuls over baked filling; spread very carefully. Broil 6-8 inches from heat for 2-3 minutes or until coconut begins to brown. Watch carefully; do not burn crust. Cool on wire rack 30 minutes. Refrigerate for 2-3 hours before serving.

Cooking with Pride

Caribbean Chocolate Bananas

A charming way to treat a banana, this tantalizing tropical fruit provides excellent snack satisfaction for all ages. The chocolate sauce may be drizzled warm over angel food cake or dessert crêpes filled with ice cream. Pour it into plastic ice cube trays, bury a whole roasted almond or hazelnut in each compartment and freeze. Dip fresh strawberries or shortbread cookies in the sauce for enhanced flavor fulfillment.

**4 ripe bananas
8 popsicle sticks
1 cup butter (2 sticks)
1 (15-ounce) can coconut
   cream**

**1 (28-ounce) bag semi-
   sweet chocolate chips
½ cup toasted chopped nuts,
   Macadamias, almonds,
   peanuts (optional)**

Peel bananas and cut in half horizontally. Insert a popsicle stick into each half, place in sealed storage container and freeze. Melt butter in a medium saucepan over low heat. Add coconut cream, chocolate chips; stir continuously until chocolate is melted. Remove from heat and cool 10 minutes.

Pour chocolate mixture into a small bowl and dip frozen bananas one at a time. Roll dipped bananas in nuts and serve immediately or freeze until ready to use. Yield: 8 chocolate-coated bananas.

Vegetarian International Cuisine

Italian Tortoni

**2 egg whites
¼ teaspoon salt
4 tablespoons sugar
2 cups whipping cream
½ cup sugar
2 teaspoons vanilla**

**¼ teaspoon almond extract
½ cup blanched, toasted
   almonds, finely chopped
   or ¼ cup almonds plus
   ¼ cup macaroon crumbs**

Beat egg whites and salt. Beat 4 tablespoons sugar in gradually. Set aside. Whip cream, add ½ cup sugar, vanilla, and almond extract. Fold in egg white mixture and almonds or almond/macaroon mixture. Put into individual custard-cup-size serving dishes and freeze. Let sit out of freezer about 15 minutes before serving. Makes 8 rich, elegant servings.

*Marquette University High School
Mother's Guild Cookbook*

Sour Cream-Raisin Pie

1 unbaked pie crust
3 slightly-beaten eggs
1¼ cups sugar
1 teaspoon cinnamon
1 tablespoon cornstarch

½ teaspoon salt
¼ teaspoon cloves
1½ cups sour cream
1½ cups raisins, ground

Prepare 1 (9-inch) pie crust. Do not prick crust. Combine eggs, sugar, cinnamon, cornstarch, salt, and cloves in mixing bowl. Mix well. Stir in sour cream and the ground raisins. Pour into the prepared pie shell. Bake at 450° for 10 minutes, then at 325° for 20-25 minutes until knife put in center of pie comes out clean. Makes 1 (9-inch) pie.

Note: If you don't have sour cream, add 1⅓ tablespoons vinegar to milk to sour.

Sacred Heart Centennial Cookbook

Maple Pecan Pie

1 pie shell, unbaked
¼ cup butter
⅔ cup firmly packed brown
  sugar
⅛ teaspoon salt

¾ cup maple syrup
3 eggs, beaten until light
1 cup broken pecans
1 teaspoon vanilla

Cream butter, brown sugar, and salt. Stir in other ingredients. Turn into lined pie pan. Bake for 10 minutes at 450° and then turn heat down to 350°. Bake for 30-35 minutes longer. Serve with whipped cream.

Wisconsin Pure Maple Syrup Cookbook

Ethel's Upside Down Rhubarb Dessert

4 cups rhubarb, cut fine
1 small package strawberry
   Jell-O
1 cup sugar

3 cups miniature
   marshmallows
1 yellow cake mix

Spread rhubarb on bottom of a 9x13-inch greased pan. Sprinkle dry strawberry Jell-O on top. Sprinkle sugar over Jell-O. Spread marshmallows on top. Mix cake mix according to package directions; pour over marshmallows. Bake according to cake mix directions. Cut and turn rhubarb up. Serve with Lucky Whip. Enjoy!

Peterson Pantry Plus Lore

Danish Puff Pastry

1 cup flour
½ cup margarine

2 tablespoons water

Blend flour, margarine, and water. Roll into a ball. Divide in half. Spread the 2 halves on a large cookie sheet to 4x12 inches each.

TOPPING:
1 cup water
½ cup margarine
1 teaspoon almond extract

1 cup flour
3 eggs

Boil water and margarine. Remove from heat and add almond extract and flour. Mix until in a ball. Add eggs and beat in by hand, one at a time. Spread evenly on crust to edges. Bake at 350° for one hour or less until golden.

ICING:
1½ cups confectioners'
   sugar
2 tablespoons margarine

1 teaspoon vanilla
1-2 teaspoons warm water

Cream ingredients together and spread on pastry. Top with chopped nuts.

Cooking with the Lioness Club

Mom's Pie Crust

Flaky pie crust was very important in our home kitchen. As important as the ingredients was the handling of the dough. "Don't overwork the dough—it will get tough" were the instructions I heard often.

2 cups flour
1 teaspoon salt

¾ cup shortening, or
⅔ cup lard
¼ cup cold water

Measure flour into a medium mixing bowl and add salt. Add shortening. With a pastry cutter, cut shortening into flour until pea-size pieces are formed. Add cold water and mix with a fork. If dough is still very dry and won't squeeze together, add more water, a tablespoon at a time.

Divide dough in half. Form half of dough into a ball with your hands, working it just until it stays together. Let it rest and do the same with the other half. Place one ball on a well-floured board and roll out, turning dough and flouring board several times.

For single crust pies, put the crust into two 9-or10-inch pie plates and press edges into a nice edge. For double crust pies, put one crust on the bottom and add filling. Put other crust on top, making holes in top for steam to escape. For baked single crust, preheat oven to 375° and poke crust with fork about 10 times. Bake for 12-15 minutes or until just golden brown.

Grandma's Home Kitchen

Coconut Impossible Pie

4 eggs
¼ cup soft butter
½ cup flour
⅛ teaspoon salt
1 teaspoon vanilla

¼ cup sugar
½ teaspoon baking powder
2 cups milk
1 cup flaked coconut
Nutmeg

Combine above ingredients in blender; blend 2 minutes. Pour into well-greased 10-inch pie plate and bake at 350° for one hour.

Favorite Recipes of the Wisconsin NFO

Easy Peach Dessert

1 large can peaches or
 1-quart home-canned
 with juice
1 box Betty Crocker Butter
 Brickle dry cake mix

Coconut and nuts, optional
½ cup melted butter

Pour peaches in a 9x13-inch pan. Sprinkle dry cake mix over top. Pour melted butter over this. (May sprinkle coconut and nuts on top of batter before pouring butter on.) Bake 30-40 minutes at 350°. Serve with whipped cream or ice cream.

Cooking in West Denmark

Pumpkin Ice Cream Squares

1½ cups graham cracker
 crumbs
¼ cup sugar
¼ cup melted butter
1 (16-ounce) can solid
 pack pumpkin
½ cup brown sugar

½ teaspoon salt
1 teaspoon cinnamon
¼ teaspoon ginger
⅛ teaspoon cloves
1 quart vanilla ice cream,
 softened
Whipped cream and pecans,
 optional

Mix crumbs with sugar and butter. Press into bottom of 9-inch square pan. Combine pumpkin with sugar, salt, and spices. Fold in ice cream. Pour into crumb-lined pan. Cover; freeze until firm. Cut into squares about 20 minutes before serving. Top with whipped cream and pecans. Makes 9 (3-inch) squares.

Unbearably Good! Sharing Our Best

Wisconsin Cheese Pie
With Apple Cider Marmalade

12 ounces cottage cheese (or ricotta)
16 ounces softened cream cheese
1½ cups sugar
1 teaspoon vanilla

1 lemon, seeds removed, quartered
4 eggs, slightly beaten
1 unbaked 9-inch pie shell
Whipped cream for garnish
Fresh strawberries for garnish

Preheat oven to 350°. Combine all pie ingredients except eggs. Blend in food processor until smooth. Fold in eggs. Pour into pie shell. Bake at 350° for 30 minutes. Cool completely before serving. Garnish, and serve slices in plate with Apple Cider Marmalade.

APPLE CIDER MARMALADE:

5 cups firm apples, cored and slivered (unpeeled)
1 cup apple cider
½ cup orange juice concentrate

½ cup grated orange rind
½ cup grated lemon rind
1 (1¾-ounce) package pectin
7 cups sugar

Place apples, cider, orange juice concentrate, rinds, and pectin in a large saucepan or jelly kettle. Bring the mixture to a rolling boil. Add sugar and stir until completely dissolved. Bring to a rolling boil again. Boil 65 seconds, stirring constantly. Remove the mixture from heat. Cool for 3 minutes. Skim off any foam with a slotted spoon. Ladle into sterilized jars, seal and process in a water bath according to manufacturer's instructions. Yields 7 cups.

Note: Many varieties of firm apples will work, but we prefer Cortlands.

Recipe from Old Rittenhouse Inn, Bayfield. Innkeepers Mary and Jerry Phillips.

Wisconsin Cooks with Wisconsin Public Television

 The world-famous House on the Rock in Spring Green may well be Wisconsin's most well known attraction. Designed by Alex Jordan, the house features "The Infinity Room" that projects 218 feet out over the scenic Wyoming Valley. With 3264 windows, there is indeed no other room like it in the world. This architectural wonder also houses the world's largest carousel.

Cheese Torte

1 envelope plain gelatine	12 ounces cream cheese
¼ cup cold water	1 cup sugar
¾ cup hot water	2 teaspoons vanilla
Juice of ½ lemon or 1 teaspoon ReaLemon juice	1 pint whipping cream, whipped
	Graham cracker crust

Dissolve gelatine in cold water, then add hot water and lemon juice. Cream cheese and add sugar and vanilla. Add cooled gelatine. Fold in whipped cream. Pour in graham cracker crust. Makes enough for a 9x9-inch pan. For a 9x13-inch pan, make 1½ recipes.

Centennial Cookbook

Himmels Futter

Heavenly food!

2 cups sugar	1 tablespoon baking soda
4 oranges, chopped	1 cup sugar
4 apples, chopped	2 tablespoons flour
1 pound nuts, chopped	8 bananas, sliced
8 ounces dates, chopped	2 cups cream, whipped
1 egg, beaten	

Pour sugar over apples and oranges and let sit overnight. Combine nuts, dates, egg, baking soda, 1 cup sugar, and flour. Put in 9x13-inch pan, bake for ½ hour at 350°. Cool. Break into pieces in large bowl. Cover with apple-orange mixture; slice bananas over top, cover with whipped cream. Can be a dessert or a salad.

Wisconsin's Best

Schaum Torte

6 egg whites, beaten stiff
2 cups sugar

1 tablespoon vinegar
1 teaspoon baking powder

Add sugar gradually to egg whites and beat for several minutes. Add vinegar and baking powder. Put ½ the mixture into a spring-form pan and add the other ½ on top in as many table-spoons as you wish to cut the torte. Bake one hour in a 275° oven. When done, lift off the top and fill with whipped cream, into which has been folded pineapple, diced fine and thoroughly drained. Put top back on and cut into pieces.

Flavors of Washington County

Snickers Bar Mousse Dessert

Healthy dessert.

1 large box instant
  sugar-free chocolate
  pudding
2 cups skim milk
2 cups lite Cool Whip,
  thawed

2 tablespoons chunky
  peanut butter
Graham crackers, crushed
  (enough to cover the bottom
  of a 9x13-inch pan)

Mix together pudding mix and skim milk until blended. Fold in lite Cool Whip and peanut butter. Line bottom of a 9x13-inch pan with crushed graham crackers. Pour pudding mixture over crackers and chill until set. Makes 12-15 servings.

Cooks Extraordinaires

Lemon Pineapple Icebox Pie

1 can Eagle Brand
  Condensed Milk
1 (6-ounce) can crushed
  pineapple, drained

1 (13½-ounce) Cool Whip
½ cup pecans, chopped
½ cup lemon juice
1 graham cracker crust

Mix Eagle Brand, pineapple, and Cool Whip. Fold in chopped nuts. Mix lemon juice in last and stir until mixture becomes stiff. Pour into graham cracker crust and chill.

Country Cupboard

Baked Lemon Pudding

This baked pudding is very easy to make and can be served warm or cold. Be sure to use fresh lemon juice for best flavor. While pudding is baking, it separates into a thin bottom layer of lemon sauce with a fluffy cake-like layer on top.

¾ cup sugar, divided
5 tablespoons flour
¼ teaspoon baking powder
⅛ teaspoon salt
2 eggs, separated

3 tablespoons fresh lemon
  juice
Grated rind of 1 lemon
1½ tablespoons butter, melted
1 cup milk

Preheat oven to 375°. Combine ½ cup sugar with flour, baking powder, and salt. Beat egg yolks until light; add lemon juice, rind, butter, and milk. Beat well with a spoon. Stir in dry ingredients until smooth. Beat egg whites until foamy; gradually beat in remaining ¼ cup sugar until stiff but not dry. Fold into flour mixture.

Transfer mixture to 1-quart baking dish. Put baking dish in a larger pan filled with warm water. Bake at 375° for 40-45 minutes until top is firm and nicely browned. Makes 6 servings.

50 Years of Regal Recipes

Chocolate Refrigerator Dessert

2 (4-ounce) cakes German
  sweet chocolate, melted
3 tablespoons sugar
3 tablespoons water
3 egg yolks
½ teaspoon vanilla

Few grains salt
3 egg whites, beaten until stiff
1 cup cream, whipped
1 large or 2 small loaf angel
  food cakes
Salted almonds, if desired

Add sugar and water to melted chocolate. Cook, stirring constantly, until smooth. Remove from heat. Stir in egg yolks, vanilla, and salt. Cool. Fold in beaten egg whites and cream. Tear angel food cake into bite-size pieces. Put into 9x13-inch pan alternately with chocolate mixture. Sprinkle with almonds, if desired. Refrigerate for 24 hours.

St. Charles Parish Cookbook

Grandma's Bread Pudding

We did a large amount of baking at our home in the country where we grew up. Although we went through a lot of food because there were so many of us, there were often leftover bread and coffee cakes that would get a bit stale. The bread was dried for bread crumbs, which I still do today. The coffee cakes were often cut in cubes and put into a custard for bread pudding. Bread pudding served with cream or fruit was an ideal dessert or a complement to Sunday afternoon coffee time.

3 eggs
⅓ cup sugar
¼ teaspoon salt
3 cups scalded milk

1 teaspoon vanilla

**1 teaspoon cinnamon (½
    teaspoon if using coffee cake)**
**3 cups cubed bread or coffee
    cake**

Preheat oven to 350°. Beat eggs, sugar, and salt lightly in a medium mixing bowl. Beat in milk, then vanilla and cinnamon. Place bread or coffee cake in a 8x10-inch glass baking dish. Pour egg mixture over bread and let stand for about 15 minutes. Sprinkle top with a small amount of additional cinnamon.

Place baking dish in a cake pan filled with 1 inch warm water. Bake in preheated oven 50 minutes or until table knife inserted close to middle comes out clean. Remove from oven and take out of the pan of water. Cool baking dish on a rack. May be served warm or cooled. Good served with whipped topping, fruit, or vanilla sauce. For variety, you can add flavored coffeecake (like apricot), or your favorite flavor. Serves 8.

Grandma's Home Kitchen

Pumpkin Pie Dessert Squares

CRUST:

1 (18.5-ounce) package
  yellow cake mix (save
  1 cup for topping)

½ cup butter, melted
1 egg, beaten

Mix cake mix, butter, and egg. Press into 13x9-inch baking pan.

FILLING:

1 can pumpkin pie filling
2 eggs, beaten

⅔ cup milk

Mix and pour over crust.

TOPPING:

1 cup cake mix
¼ cup sugar

1 teaspoon cinnamon
¼ cup butter

Combine cake mix, sugar, cinnamon, and butter; mix lightly and sprinkle over filling. Bake at 350° until knife comes out clean (45-50 minutes). Cool, cut into squares and serve with whipped cream.

Thank Heaven for Home Made Cooks

Lynn's No Stir Chocolate Sauce

½ cup butter
2¼ cups powdered sugar
⅓ cup evaporated milk

3 ounce chopped unsweetened
  chocolate

Place butter and powdered sugar in top of a double boiler. Add chocolate and milk. Place over simmering water and cover. Cook 30 minutes. Do not stir. Remove from heat and beat with wire whip until smooth.

Microwave: Assemble in same manner using a Pyrex bowl. Cover with plastic wrap. Cook on roast 5 or 6 minutes (or full power 4 or 5 minutes). Beat until smooth. Yield: 2 cups.

All in Good Taste I

Mud Pie

½ gallon butter pecan ice cream
¾ cup margarine, divided
1 (14-ounce) can condensed milk
1 (16-ounce) can Hershey's syrup
¼ cup chopped pecans
1 teaspoon vanilla
26 Oreo cookies
1 large carton whipped topping
Chopped pecans for top

Take ice cream out to soften. Bring ½ cup margarine, condensed milk, syrup, and pecans to a boil. Simmer a few minutes. Add vanilla and set aside to cool. Crush Oreo cookies; add ¼ cup melted margarine. Press into a 9x13x2-inch pan. Place in the freezer for 30 minutes. Arrange softened butter pecan ice cream over crust. Place in freezer for 30 minutes.

Pour cooled fudge sauce over ice cream layer and place in freezer for 30 minutes. Spread one large carton Cool Whip (or 1 pint whipping cream, whipped with one tablespoon sugar and ½ teaspoon vanilla) on top; sprinkle with chopped pecans. Place in the freezer for 24 hours before serving.

Note: Whipped cream layer could be added just before serving.

Country Heart Cooking

Fruited Ice

Many people have requested this fruit recipe.

1 (20-ounce) can crushed pineapple
1 (16-ounce) can apricot halves, drained and chopped
1 (16-ounce) package frozen strawberries
1 cup sugar
1 cup water
2 bananas

Boil sugar and water and add to fruit mixture. Slice in bananas and fill foil cups and freeze. Makes about 30 foil cups.

Thank Heaven for Home Made Cooks

Fantastic Frozen Strawberries

Bright red, slightly thickened and more like fresh berries.

4 quarts strawberries
3 cups sugar

1 package Sure-Jell
1 cup water

Put cleaned berries in large bowl and add sugar. Mix carefully. Mix Sure-Jell and water. Boil one minute. Pour over berries and mix carefully. Let stand 10 minutes and put in freezer containers. Remember these are frozen berries, not freezer jam.

Celebrating 150 Years of Faith and Food

Fruit Soup

1 cup dried apricots
1 cup dried prunes
1 cup raisins
½ cup dates
1-2 small slices lemon
2 cups canned peaches or
  pears, cut up

½ teaspoon cinnamon
1 (4.75-ounce) package
  strawberry or currant-
  raspberry Danish dessert
  (similar to a pudding and
  pie filling)

Soak dried fruit for several hours in water that is twice the volume of the fruit. An hour before supper, add lemon and cook, boiling slowly and stirring occasionally. Add canned fruit and cinnamon. Pour Danish dessert into fruit soup, stirring constantly until it thickens and is a clear, red color. If soup is too thick, add more water (should be somewhere between soup and stew consistency). Makes 8-10 servings.

Note: Any combination of fruit on hand may be used, or all dried, or all canned. If Danish dessert is not available, thicken with cornstarch or tapioca. Serve plain or with cottage cheese, yogurt, whipped cream, or vanilla ice cream.

Seasons of a Farm Family

 Wisconsin has nearly 15,000 lakes! Practically all the natural lakes have resulted from glaciers. Lake Winnebago is the state's largest inland lake. It is 137,708 acres.

Ice Cream in a Can

1 cup cream	2 eggs
1 cup milk	½ cup sugar

Beat together. Put mixture in small coffee can with lid. Place in large coffee can. Put ice and ¾ cup canning salt between cans. Put lid on and roll on floor for 15 minutes. A delicious treat and activity for kids!

St. Charles Parish Cookbook

Cherry Soup

Some people say they come to Pommerntag just for this wonderful fruit soup!

4 cups water	3 cups fresh pitted sour
1¾ cups sugar	cherries

Boil water with sugar, add cherries and cook to soften. Check sweetness and add more sugar if necessary. Bring to a good boil.

DUMPLING MIXTURE:

1 egg, beaten	¾ cup milk
½ teaspoon baking powder	Pinch of salt
4 tablespoons flour, heaping	

Mix together. It will look like cake batter. Continue cooking while dribbling (pour in slowly) the cherry mixture. Remove from heat. Eat warm or cold.

Favorite Recipes of Pommern Cooks

Crystallized Violets

When I was a freshman, one evening my date handed me the first voilet of spring. I looked at it, told him its Latin name, and then I ate it. It was our last date.

Voilets grow in the woods, in meadows, and on high, dry ledges. It is a reflection on some of us that they often grow in ravines among old tin cans, bleach bottles, and rotting tires. I prefer to gather my voilets far from rubbish and dumps.

Violets   **Granulated sugar**
Egg white

Preheat oven to 250°. Beat 1 or 2 egg whites until stiff. Dip each violet in the beaten egg white, then roll each flower in granulated sugar. Put them on waxed paper in a 250° oven until they are dry (about 10-15 minutes).

The Wild Food Cookbook

The La Crosse, the Black and the Mississippi Rivers converge in the La Crosse area. Indian legend has it that where three bodies of water meet, there will be no big winds. In recorded history there is no record of a tornado touching down in Riverside Park where these rivers meet.

CATALOG *of*
CONTRIBUTING COOKBOOKS

Ninety-five cookbooks from all regions of Wisconsin have contributed recipes to this collection. The contributing cookbooks range from large Junior League editions to modest church cookbooks from small communities. Each cookbook has contributed a sampling of their most popular recipes, capturing the flavor of the state. The BEST OF THE BEST STATE COOKBOOK SERIES' goal is to *Preserve America's Food Heritage*. Since many of the contributing cookbooks have gone out of print, the BEST OF THE BEST COOKBOOKS serve to preserve a sampling of those wonderful family recipes that might have otherwise been lost.

A-PEELING APPLE RECIPES
Friends of Retzer Nature Center
Waukesha, WI

ALL IN GOOD TASTE I & II
Service League of Fond du Lac
Fond du Lac, WI

APPLES, BRIE & CHOCOLATE
by Nell Stehr
Amherst Press • Amherst, WI

THE BEST CRANBERRY RECIPES
From the Eagle River Cranberry Fest
Eagle River, WI

BLESSED BE THE COOK
St. Anne's Altar Society
Camp Douglas, WI

CAMP HOPE COOKBOOK
Camp Hope • Stevens Point, WI

CARDINAL COUNTRY COOKBOOK
School District of Brodhead Playground
Committee • Brodhead, WI

CELEBRATING 150 YEARS OF FAITH
AND FOOD
Christ Lutheran Church Women
DeForest, WI

CELEBRATION OF GRACE
ANNIVERSARY COOKBOOK
Our Savior's Lutheran Church
Oconomowoc, WI

CENTENNIAL COOKBOOK
Second Presbyterian Church • Racine, WI

CHERRY BERRIES ON A CLOUD AND
MORE...
Trinity Pilgrim United Methodist Women
Brookfield, WI

A COLLECTION OF RECIPES
St. Joseph's Home and School Assn.
Stratford, WI

COOKING AT THIMBLEBERRY INN
by Sharon Locey • Bayfield, WI

COOKING IN WEST DENMARK
West Denmark Lutheran Church
Luck, WI

COOKING WITH GRACE
St. Bernard Parish • Wauwatosa, WI

COOKING WITH PRIDE
Pridefest Celebration Committee
Milwaukee, WI

COOKING WITH THE LIONESS CLUB
OF BROWN DEER
Brown Deer Lioness • Brown Deer, WI

COOKS EXTRAORDINAIRES
Service League of Green Bay, Inc.
Green Bay, WI

COUNTRY CUPBOARD
by Lois Krueger • Washington Island, WI

COUNTRY HEART COOKING
by Lois A. Johnson • Plainfield, WI

CREATE, SHARE, ENJOY!
St. Joseph's Christian Women's Society
Brookfield, WI

CROOKED LAKE VOLUNTEER FIRE
DEPARTMENT COOKBOOK
Ladies Auxiliary • Crivitz, WI

DR. MARTIN LUTHER CHURCH
100TH ANNIVERSARY COOKBOOK
Dr. Martin Luther Church
Oconomowoc, WI

DRINK YOUR BEER & EAT IT TOO!
Amherst Press • Amherst, WI

ENCORE WISCONSIN
Amherst Press • Amherst, WI

EVERY 1 A WINNER!
by Sue-Ann K. Dondlinger • Richfield, WI

FAMILY FARE: A DEVOTIONAL
COOKBOOK
Arleth Erickson • Grantsburg, WI

FAVORITE RECIPES FROM THE OLD
RITTENHOUSE INN
Amherst Press • Amherst, WI

FAVORITE RECIPES OF POMMERN
COOKS
Pommerscher Verein Freistadt
Germantown, WI

FAVORITE RECIPES OF THE WISCONSIN
NFO
Sauk City, WI

FIFTH AVENUE FOOD FARE
Fifth Avenue United Methodist Church
West Bend, WI

50 YEARS OF REGAL RECIPES
Amherst Press • Amherst, WI

FLAVORS OF WASHINGTON COUNTY
Washington County Historical Society, Inc.
West Bend, WI

FOUR SEASONS AT HAWKS INN
Hawks Inn Historical Society, Inc.
Delafield, WI

FOXY LADIES
by Ellen Kort • Appleton, WI

FRESH MARKET WISCONSIN
Amherst Press • Amherst, WI

GOOD COOKING, GOOD CURLING
Alpine Curling Club • Monroe, WI

GRANDMA'S HOME KITCHEN
Amherst Press • Amherst, WI

GRANDMOTHERS OF GREENBUSH
Amherst Press • Amherst, WI

GREEN THUMBS IN THE KITCHEN
Green Thumb, Inc. Wisconsin Program
Neillsville, WI

GROWING & USING HERBS
Amherst Press • Amherst, WI

HAVE BREAKFAST WITH US...AGAIN
Amherst Press • Amherst, WI

HAVE BREAKFAST WITH US II
Wisconsin Bed and Breakfast Homes and
Historic Inns Assn. • Sheboygan, WI

HERE'S TO YOUR HEART:
COOKING SMART
The Heart Care Center • Waukesha, WI

LICENSE TO COOK WISCONSIN STYLE
Penfield Press • Iowa City, IA

LOOK WHAT'S COOKING AT C.A.M.D.E.N.
C.A.M.D.E.N. Foundation Inc.
Milton, WI

LOOK WHAT'S COOKIN' AT WAL-MART
Children's Miracle Network
Black River Falls, WI

LUSCIOUS: LOW CALORIE RECIPES
WITH POUNDATION CONVERSATION
BY MAXINE
by Maxine Toler Vaneven
Kaukauna, WI

THE MADISON HERB SOCIETY
COOKBOOK
The Madison Herb Society • Madison, WI

MARKETPLACE RECIPES 1981-1987
AND 1988-1991
Action Advertising Inc. • Fond du Lac, WI

MARQUETTE UNIVERSITY HIGH
SCHOOL MOTHER'S GUILD
COOKBOOK
Marquette University High School
Milwaukee, WI

MASTERPIECE RECIPES
OF THE AMERICAN CLUB
Amherst Press • Amherst, WI

MT. CARMEL'S "COOKIN' WITH THE
OLDIES"
Mount Carmel Medical and Rehabilitation
Center • Burlington, WI

THE OCTAGON HOUSE COOKBOOK
The Watertown Historical Society
Watertown, WI

OLD WORLD SWISS FAMILY RECIPES
Monroe Swiss Singers of Monroe, WI
Monroe, WI

OUR BEST COOKBOOK 2
A SECOND SERVING
Amherst Press • Amherst, WI

OUR FAVORITE RECIPES
St. John's Guild • West Bend, WI

THE OVENS OF BRITTANY COOKBOOK
Amherst Press • Amherst, WI

THE PALMYRA HERITAGE COOKBOOK
Palmyra Historical Society
Palmyra, WI

PELICAN LAKE WOMEN'S CIVIC CLUB
Pelican Lake, WI

PETERSON PANTRY PLUS LORE
Marjorie Peterson Read • Madison, WI

PICNICS ON THE SQUARE
Wisconsin Chamber Orchestra
Madison, WI

SACRED HEART CENTENNIAL
COOKBOOK
Sacred Heart Altar Society • Mondovi, WI

SEASONED WITH LOVE
Trinity United Church of Christ
Brookfield, WI

SEASONS OF A FARM FAMILY
Amherst Press• Amherst, WI

SHARING OUR BEST
St. Joseph's Parish • Stevens Point, WI

SPARKS FROM THE KITCHEN
Syd and Florence Herman
Manitowoc, WI

SPICE OF LIFE COOKBOOK
by Treva Davis • Dousman, WI

ST. CHARLES PARISH COOKBOOK
St. Charles Parish • Cassville, WI

ST. FREDERICK PARISH CENTENNIAL
RECIPE COLLECTION
St. Frederick Parish • Cudahy, WI

ST. JOHN EVANGELICAL LUTHERAN
CHURCH
St. John Ladies Aid • Stratford, WI

ST. MARK'S LUTHERAN CHURCH
COOKBOOK
Sarah Circle, St. Mark's • Manawa, WI

ST. MARY'S FAMILY COOKBOOK
St. Mary's Council of Catholic Women
Bloomington, WI

THE SUNDAY COOK COLLECTION
Amherst Press • Amherst, WI

SUNFLOWERS AND SAMOVARS
RECIPE COLLECTION
St. Nicholas Orthodox Church
Kenosha, WI

TASTE & SEE
St. Philip Neri Catholic Church
Milwaukee, WI

A TASTE OF CHRIST LUTHERAN
Mabel E. Jackson/Celebration Committee
Sharon, WI

A TASTE OF HOME
South Wood County YMCA Women's
Auxiliary • Port Edwards, WI

THANK HEAVEN FOR HOME MADE
COOKS
First Congregational U.C.C.
Oconomowoc, WI

TRINITY LUTHERAN CHURCH OF
NORDEN ANNIVERSARY COOKBOOK
Norden Youth League • Mondovi, WI

UNBEARABLY GOOD! SHARING OUR
BEST
Waushara County Homemakers (HCE)
Wautoma, WI

VEGETARIAN INTERNATIONAL
CUISINE
From the Chefs of The Cheese Factory
Restaurant • Wisconsin Dells, WI

WHAT'S COOK'N?
Manitou Girl Scout Council
Sheboygan, WI

WHAT'S COOKING IN ST. FRANCIS
St. Francis High School Booster Club
St. Francis, WI

WHAT'S ON THE AGENDA?
The Woman's Club of DePere • DePere, WI

THE WHITE GULL INN, DOOR
COUNTY
Amherst Press • Amherst, WI

THE WILD FOOD COOKBOOK
Amherst Press • Amherst, WI

WINNING RECIPES FROM
WISCONSIN...WITH LOVE
by The Cooks of Wisconsin
The Branches/Strawberry Point, Inc.
Prior Lake, MN

WISCONSIN COOKS WITH
WISCONSIN PUBLIC TELEVISION
Friends of WHA-TV, Inc. • Madison, WI

WISCONSIN PURE MAPLE SYRUP
COOKBOOK
Wisconsin Maple Syrup Producers
Holcombe, WI

WISCONSIN'S BEST
Women's Auxiliary WAPHCC
Waukesha, WI

INDEX

Collect the Series!
Best of the Best State Cookbook Series

Cookbook collectors love this Series! The forty-two cookbooks, covering all fifty states (see next page for listing), contain over 15,000 of the most popular local and regional recipes collected from approximately 3,000 of the leading cookbooks from these states. The Series not only captures the flavor of America, but saves a lot of shelf space.

To assist individuals who wish to collect the Series, we are offering a **Collect the Series Discount Coupon Booklet.** With the Booklet you get:

Collect the Series!
BEST OF THE BEST STATE COOKBOOK SERIES
With this Special *Collect the Series* Discount Coupon Booklet

OVER 3 MILLION STATE COOKBOOKS SOLD!   *continued inside . . .*

Call **1-800-343-1583** to order a free, no-obligation Discount Coupon Booklet.

- 25% discount off the list price ($16.95 minus 25% = $12.70 per copy)
- With a single order of five copies, you receive a sixth copy free. A single order of ten cookbooks, gets two free copies, etc.
- Only $4.00 shipping cost for any number of books ordered (within contiguous United States).

Recipe Hall of Fame Cookbook Collection
is also included in the
Collect the Series Discount Coupon Booklet.

304 pages • $19.95   304 pages • $19.95   304 pages • $19.95   240 pages • $16.95

The four cookbooks in this collection consist of over 1,200 of the most exceptional recipes collected from the entire
BEST OF THE BEST STATE COOKBOOK SERIES.
**The Hall of Fame Collection can be bought
as a four-cookbook set for $40.00.**
This is a 48% discount off the total individual cost of $76.80.

QUAIL RIDGE PRESS
P. O. Box 123 • Brandon, MS 39043 • 1-800-343-1583
E-mail: info@quailridge.com • www.quailridge.com

BEST OF THE BEST STATE COOKBOOK SERIES

ALABAMA	HAWAII	MINNESOTA	OREGON
ALASKA	IDAHO	MISSISSIPPI	PENNSYLVANIA
ARIZONA	ILLINOIS	MISSOURI	SO. CAROLINA
ARKANSAS	INDIANA	NEVADA	TENNESSEE
BIG SKY *Includes Montana, Wyoming*	IOWA	NEW ENGLAND *Includes Rhode Island,*	TEXAS
CALIFORNIA	KENTUCKY	*Connecticut, Massachusetts,* *Vermont, New Hampshire,*	TEXAS II
COLORADO	LOUISIANA	*and Maine*	UTAH
FLORIDA	LOUISIANA II	NEW MEXICO	VIRGINIA
GEORGIA	MICHIGAN	NEW YORK	VIRGINIA II
GREAT PLAINS	MID-ATLANTIC	NO. CAROLINA	WASHINGTON
Includes North Dakota,	*Includes Maryland,*	OHIO	WEST VIRGINIA
South Dakota, Nebraska, *and Kansas*	*Delaware, New Jersey, and* *Washington, D.C.*	OKLAHOMA	WISCONSIN

All BEST OF THE BEST COOKBOOKS are 6x9 inches, are comb-bound, contain over 300 recipes, and total 288–352 pages. Each contains illustrations, photographs, an index and a list of contributing cookbooks, a special feature which cookbook collectors enjoy. Scattered throughout the cookbooks are short quips that provide interesting information about each state, including historical facts and major attractions along with amusing trivia. Retail price per copy $16.95.

To order by credit card, call toll-free **1-800-343-1583**,
visit **www.quailridge.com**, or use the Order Form below.

Order Form

Send check, money order, or credit card info to:
QUAIL RIDGE PRESS • P. O. Box 123 • Brandon, MS 39043

Name _____

Address _____

City_____

State/Zip _____

Phone # _____

Email Address _____

❏ Check enclosed

Charge to: ❏ Visa ❏ MC ❏ AmEx ❏ Disc

Card # _____

Expiration Date _____

Signature _____

Qty.	Title of Book (State) or HOF set	Total

Subtotal	_____
Mississippi residents add 7% sales tax	_____
Postage ($4.00 any number of books)	+ $4.00
TOTAL	_____